(Con

In these ̣ the role of th of Chiang sy ...., ̤ue true circumstances of the China-Tibet episode and the China-India border dispute, as well as the clouded crystal balls which saw Russia and China lying down together like lambs. And he explodes the wishful thinking about the Chinese starving or revolting, along with our all too glib supposition that the Communist regime will one day "pass away."

Mr. Greene's new book is written with tremendous vigor, conviction, and a slashing wit. It is bound to provoke controversy, but it is unique and important reading for all Americans.

Felix Greene, a former senior official of England's BBC, retains his British passport, but has lived in America for many years and is well-known throughout the country as a lecturer on current affairs. He has made three visits to China. Those in 1957 and 1960 resulted in his previous and widely acclaimed book, *Awakened China.* A CURTAIN OF IGNORANCE contains a "Postscript from Peking" which Mr. Greene added during his third visit, which took place in the Fall of 1963. Mr. Greene and his wife live in Palo Alto, California.

A CURTAIN OF
IGNORANCE

A
CURTAIN
OF
IGNORANCE

How the American Public Has Been

Misinformed about China

FELIX GREENE

Doubleday & Company, Inc., Garden City, N.Y.

Grateful acknowledgment is made for permission to include the following copyrighted material:

BOOKS

Excerpts from *Senator Joe McCarthy* by Richard Rovere. Copyright © 1959 by Richard H. Rovere. Used by permission of Harcourt, Brace & World, Inc.

Excerpt from *China Shakes the World* by Jack Belden. Copyright 1949 by Jack Belden. Reprinted with the permission of Harper & Row, Publishers, Incorporated.

Excerpts from *Two Kinds of Time* by Graham Peck. Copyright 1950 by Graham Peck. Reprinted by permission of Houghton Mifflin Company.

Excerpts from *Scratches on Our Minds* by Harold R. Isaacs. Copyright © 1958 by the Massachusetts Institute of Technology. Reprinted by permission of The John Day Company, Inc.

Excerpts from *The Prospects for Communist China* by W. W. Rostow, et al. Copyright 1954 by the Massachusetts Institute of Technology. Reprinted by permission of The M. I. T. Press.

Excerpt from *The Political Economy of Growth* by Paul Baran. Copyright © 1957 by Monthly Review, Inc. Reprinted by permission of the Monthly Review Press.

Excerpts from *The Other Side of the River*, by Edgar Snow. Copyright © 1962 by Edgar Snow. Reprinted by permission of Random House, Inc.

Excerpts from *Thunder Out of China* by Theodore H. White and Annalee Jacoby. Copyright 1946 by William Sloane Associates, Inc. Reprinted by permission of William Sloane Associates.

Excerpts from *Communist China and Asia* by A. Doak Barnett. Copyright © 1960 by the Council on Foreign Relations. Reprinted by permission.

MAGAZINES

Excerpt from *Business Week* (November 20, 1948). Reprinted by permission.

Excerpt from an article in *China Trade and Economic Newsletter*. Reprinted by permission of Mrs. Joan Robinson and *China Trade and Economic Newsletter*, 15 Hanover Square, London W.1.

Excerpt from *Eastern Horizon* (September 1960). Reprinted by permission of Sir Herbert Read and *Eastern Horizon*.

Excerpt from "China's Economic Growth" by Professor Charles Bettleheim, *The Economic Weekly*, Bombay, November 22, 1958. Reprinted by permission.

Excerpts from articles by Colina MacDougall, Professor Etienne, and the Shanghai correspondent for *Far Eastern Economic Review*. Reprinted by permission of Far Eastern Economic Review, Ltd.

Excerpts from his article in September 8, 1949 issue of *The New Republic*, used by permission of Walter Lippmann.

Excerpt from an article by Professor Urban Whitaker (October 7, 1961). Reprinted by permission of *The Nation*.

ACKNOWLEDGMENT

I wish to express my gratitude to the Louis M. Rabinowitz Foundation of New York for a grant that made possible the considerable research that was involved in the preparation of this book.

FELIX GREENE
Palo Alto, California
September 1963

CONTENTS

Part III. CHINA WANTS WAR

Part IV. SOME MINOR MYTHS

Part V. HOW IT WORKS

AUTHOR'S NOTE

Whenever I am asked what nationality I am, I find myself hesitating because nothing I can say would be really true.

I was born and educated in England—formally educated, that is. My education about the modern world we live in began after I left Cambridge and came to this country where for nearly two years (it was during the Depression) I drove trucks, picked fruit, and for a few painful months I tried to become interested in the advertising business. I then went back to England where I ran for Parliament (and was soundly trounced) and joined the B.B.C. I did not live in America again until I returned to New York to head the B.B.C. office there, which I did for five years.

Since those far-off days I have lived most of the time in the U.S., but finding all kinds of good reasons for returning to Britain at least once a year. Technically, I am still British. I traveled to China on both my visits on a British passport and could not have gone on an American. When I add it all up I find, however, that I have now lived almost half my life in America; my wife is American, my home is here, my child goes to school here. I am tied to America (as I am to Britain) by countless affectionate associations of friendship and work. So what am I?

This rather rambling personal note is necessary to explain what might otherwise appear puzzling—why, though formally British, I have written this book as if I were an American. I wrote it this way because the book is about America and because I feel so much a member of the family that I cannot bring myself to write about this country as if I were merely a visitor looking in.

The truth is that I can never think of myself as exclusively either American or British. I am both. If in a more enlightened period a dual Anglo-American citizenship is evolved for those in my predicament, I will be first in line to claim *that* passport—for that is what I really am.

FOREWORD

This book proposes to challenge the accuracy of some of the reports about Communist China conveyed to the American people by the press, the experts, and by public officials.

Most people in the United States—certainly the majority under thirty—if they have relied on our press for their information about China, can have come to only one conclusion: that China's backwardness, her shortage of food, and what is thought of as the prevailing misery of her people, are due to the Communists; that during the civil war in China evil men threw out the good men; and that though the good men were defeated and are now in exile, it is America's moral obligation to support them against the ruthless and aggressive tyrants who have reduced the Chinese masses to unspeakable indignities and suffering.

Having been twice to China in recent years, I believe this is not a true picture.[1] It is not the picture accepted by others in the Western world who have had a far closer and more continuous contact with Communist China than we have had. It is a concept that I believe the best intelligence in our own country knows is not true. And yet this picture governs our actions. In many significant ways we are basing national policies on a concept of China that is unreal.

[1] Since this was written, I returned to China for a third visit. See "Postscript from Peking."

To say that those who control our press, the specialists and the politicians have misinformed the public in regard to events in China, is a very grave charge. In this book I propose to give what I believe to be evidence in support of this charge. It does not imply that these men have combined in any conscious conspiracy. It does not imply that they are disloyal or unpatriotic. But it does imply in an area where great passions are aroused, those responsible for providing reasonably authentic information have failed in their duty. On an issue which involves our future security, our lives, our commerce, our national honor, the American people have been misled.

This is not a new phenomenon in our history.

In 1920 Mr. Walter Lippmann and Mr. Charles Merz submitted the news that readers of the New York *Times* were receiving about events in Russia to a very detailed scrutiny. (They chose the New York *Times* as being one of the best newspapers in the United States.) Their conclusion was that as far as professional journalism was concerned the reporting of the Russian Revolution was "nothing short of a disaster." They thought that on the essential questions the net effect of the reporting was "almost always misleading, and misleading news is worse than none at all. . . ."[2]

This book will examine the reporting and interpretation of events in China over a much longer period. The conclusions reached are precisely the same.

Mr. William Lederer has called this country "A Nation of Sheep." I reject this title as a slander. I know of no other country with as high a proportion of intelligent and concerned citizens as the United States. The American people are basically generous, genuinely wanting to find their way through the hazards that beset them in the world in as decent a way as possible. The people of America have responded to world events in a perfectly rational

[2] "A Test of the News," a supplement to the *New Republic*, August 4, 1920.

and predictable way *given the information with which they have been provided.* Certainly in regard to China we are not a nation of sheep, but a nation that has been profoundly misinformed.

The circumstance which impelled me to write this book can easily be described. I am one of the very few American-based correspondents who have been to China during the past fourteen years. I am the only one who has been there twice. (Since this was written I have been for the third time.) I went to China first in 1957. As a correspondent I had kept myself—or I thought I had—reasonably well informed of developments throughout the world. I first went to China carrying with me all the assumptions that any careful reader of the American press would have carried. I went expecting to find a country of vast squalor and disease; I prepared myself to see a people embittered and resentful, living under the rigid coercions of a police state. I expected to see fear as I had seen it in Russia and in Hitler's Germany. This was the country I expected, but it was not the country I found. The discrepancy between what I had been led to expect and what I saw was bewildering and shocking.

I went to China again for a much longer visit in 1960. Between these two visits great changes were taking place in China. Knowing I was returning, I read carefully every account I could find of the commune development and the "great leap forward." I read Mr. Joseph C. Harsch's graphic accounts of the communes (written for *The Christian Science Monitor*)—"the greatest mass sacrifice of human heritage, human comfort and human effort in all time." I read about the barracks into which the peasants were being herded. I read about the children being torn from their mothers' arms. I read Mr. R. H. Shackford's articles written for the Scripps-Howard newspapers entitled "Chain Gang Empire"—the "first serious effort in history to put a whole nation on what amounts to a prison chain gang." In *Life* I saw artists' drawings of burning villages and weeping mothers. After my experience of 1957 I read these accounts with caution and skepticism, but I was nevertheless influenced by them.

I returned to China in 1960 with anxiety as to the new devel-

opments which I would find there. And again I experienced the
same bewilderment and shock at finding a country so greatly in
contrast to what I expected. I traveled widely through China,
thousands of miles. I saw no barracks, and found no Westerner
who had; I could see no evidence that children had been torn
from their mothers' arms; and I learned that the foreign embassies
in Peking had no belief in these stories either. I found that in all
significant respects, the accounts of the commune development
appearing in the American press had been misleading. During the
five months I lived in China, American newspapers were sent to
me. It was a curiously disturbing experience to read reports, even
in some of our most responsible press, that seemed to bear so
little relationship to the country I was in and the people I was
moving among.

In the fourteen years since the Chinese Communists assumed
power, countless myths about events in China have been implanted in the public's mind. This book has required a long and
meticulous examination of news reports, editorials, analyses, commentaries, magazine articles, and books. Literally thousands of
items have been read and classified. And yet I cannot claim that
this is an exhaustive book. It is only a beginning. The sheer volume
of material prevents thorough analysis in a single volume. So here
I have dealt with only a handful of instances and examples.

I do not claim that my findings are completely free of error,
though the checking has been careful. Some readers may consider
that I have overstated my conclusion; others with more information
may think that I could have presented my case more effectively.
Whatever its failings, I hope that this book will succeed in establishing at least a prima facie case that reporting and expertise
on China in this country has been on a deplorably low level.

I wish to make one thing clear. *It is not the purpose of this
book to examine the defects or virtues of the present system in
China.* That examination I have made in another book.[3] It may

---

[3] *Awakened China: The Country Americans Don't Know* (New York:
Doubleday, 1961); published in paperback edition under the title, *China,
the Country Americans Are Not Allowed to Know* (New York: Ballantine
Books, 1962).

appear to some that I am out to make a case for China—and they would think this for an obvious reason. As almost all so-called information about China in the United States has been adverse, any correction of information can very easily be misconstrued. The examination of adverse reports may very easily appear as an attempt to present China in a more favorable light, and I do not see how this impression can be avoided. But if such an interpretation is placed on this book, it would be a wrong interpretation. My purpose is not to examine China but to examine ourselves; to show how step-by-step misleading reports have created deeply set images in our minds and established firmly held convictions that are often unrelated to realities.

Readers of the press in every country must always remain skeptical and vigilant. It is certainly not my intention to suggest that the Chinese press is presenting a less distorted picture of the United States than our press frequently presents of China, and we know how erroneous the statistical information in Chinese newspapers has been (though these errors were often later admitted by the Chinese). The ideas in the minds of the ordinary Chinese about life in America are wildly inaccurate. But we can do nothing about their ignorance while we can perhaps do something about our own. If we do not we shall remain, in the words of the poet, "strangers shouting lies to each other across a sea of ignorance."

In examining reports about China, certain things became clear quite soon. One is that newspaper writers and experts are very prone to draw information from each other. They thus form a kind of self-validating society. One consequence of this is that a single news story can quickly be disseminated and may soon become "hard fact" because of nothing but sheer repetition. For example, millions of Americans today believe that Mao Tse-tung is not only prepared to engage in a nuclear war, but would indeed welcome one because "there would still be 300 million Chinese left." A thorough search through the Chinese press has not revealed any speech or comment of this kind by any Chinese leader. Its origin? A comment by Marshal Tito of Yugoslavia in 1958 at a time when Belgrade and Peking were engaged in verbal assaults against each other. Of several Western correspondents present at the time, only one apparently thought Tito's remark sufficiently interesting to report. But it was quickly seized upon and disseminated. The original remark was embroidered and enlarged. I found that before long it was being mentioned in literally hundreds of editorials and newspaper articles and in analyses by the China experts. It has now become unshakably embedded in our over-all thinking about China.

I had hoped originally to limit the range of my examination to the years since the revolution. But another surprising fact emerged as I began to look through the material. In all the thousands of reports about Communist China appearing in the press there were very few references to conditions in China *before* the revolution. If there was a food shortage or a setback in industry or a change in government policy, these were (if one was to judge by some of the press and specialists) all new phenomena in China and therefore clearly a result of the blunderings or malevolence of the present regime. Many of the correspondents who have been reporting mainland China from Hong Kong and the United States since 1949 had witnessed—and understood the causes of—the downfall of the Kuomintang. Yet it is an astonishing fact that few real attempts have been made to compare the lot of the Chinese today with their lot under Chiang Kai-shek. To the Chinese, a comparison of their standard of living with that in the far more prosperous West is obviously meaningless—the only thing that matters to them is whether they are worse or better off than they were before. Such an avoidance of comparison with China's past is itself a serious omission, for no understanding of China is possible unless we see her in terms of her own historical development.

Finally, I have attempted (not always with success) to keep out of this account a note of personal indignation. There is much to be indignant about when one sees a people among whom one has made one's home and of whom one is fond and proud, given misleading reports and being denied access to information to which they have a right. "Misleading reporting," Walter Lippmann wrote, "is worse than no reporting at all." And I agree. Something large is at issue here—for the reliability of information is the premise on which democracy proceeds. A democracy will not long remain a democracy if the people are kept in ignorance. It is not a question merely of an adjective here, a caption there—that in itself would be of little consequence. But misleading reporting if it continues and is consistent may have a cumulative effect that is disastrous. Even small omissions and small distortions may together result in a single large untruth that will mislead a whole nation. And readers of this book will see that the omissions and distortions have not always been small.

Part I

BACKGROUND TO MYTHOLOGY

The United States is in danger of losing its memory. A nation's memory is its sense of history, and a sense of history cannot be constructed on a basis of misinformation and great passions.

It is not China's remoteness that makes her so difficult for us to understand; it is the intense partisanship that China has always evoked among ourselves. Dispassionate discussion of our relations with China has always been rare. Some years ago almost nothing could be said about the Chinese that wasn't controversial unless it was based on assumptions of their heroism. Today, discussion must be based on assumptions of their malevolence. From our earliest contacts, China has exerted a peculiar fascination for Americans, a fascination compounded both of the highest admiration and the deepest suspicion. Where China is concerned we have never, it seems, been able to disengage our feelings and settle for some middle course.

To understand why this is so we need to go back a little and remind ourselves of our earlier relations with China. In this way we may learn the causes of the intensity of feeling that China still arouses in Americans. We will find too that the misleading reporting about China today has its roots in the misleading reporting about China in the past.

Chapter 1

THE BIRTH OF A LEGEND

The nation which indulges towards another an habitual hatred or an habitual fondness is in some degree a slave to its animosity or to its affection, either of which is sufficient to lead it astray from its duty and interest.

—George Washington

What is the cause of the deep-seated emotion which China has always aroused in Americans? Why the unremitting hostility toward China today?

China's Communism? But why the difference in temper and mood toward the Soviet Union—a much more powerful enemy? Why trade with Russia and not with China? Why permit citizens to travel to the Soviet Union and forbid travel to China? The Korean War? Then why were the American people so quick to forgive the Japanese—an enemy that inflicted infinitely greater damage? Why for a decade has a citizen's view of China almost been a test of his loyalty to the United States? Why is it dangerous for any politician even to suggest that our China policy needs re-examination? Why should a country so far away, so little known, so incapable yet of imposing any threat to America's military security or to her commercial interests, nevertheless have this unique capacity of arousing in Americans such intense emotion?

There are answers to these questions but they will not be found in logic. America's exaggerated hostility to China today has grown out of her exaggerated hopes of China in the past. They are opposite sides of the same coin.

Only a look at the history of U.S.-China relations can provide us with a clue.

American involvement with China reaches back almost to the beginning of our history as a nation. The first American clipper ship sailed from New England to China in 1784, the year after the United States was founded. The tea that was dumped into Boston Harbor came off a British ship that had just arrived from China.

It was merchants who made our first contact with China, but these were quickly followed by the missionaries. At first they came in two's and three's. By 1875 there were four hundred missionaries in China; in 1905, two thousand, by 1918 the number had risen to six thousand and by 1925, eight thousand. Throughout these years two parallel objectives dominated American hopes—to convert the heathen and to exercise political and commercial ascendancy over the affairs of China.

> It would be hard indeed to over-emphasize the extent of the influence of the missionaries in shaping and directing the Far Eastern policies of the United States. . . . Beginning with President McKinley, they received the special recognition from the executive branch of the government. . . . Taft and Wilson in particular were amenable to their influence. What little Wilson knew of the Far East came from his missionary friends. . . .
>
> For many years missionaries, businessmen, and government officials collaborated in the movement to implant American social and economic institutions in China; and of the three the missionaries were by far the most powerful.[1]

Americans represented a very high proportion of the total missionary population. It was not always easy going. Their efforts to convert the Chinese to Christianity aroused the hostility of the ruling classes of China who considered the activities of the missionaries intolerably arrogant—and a threat to the existing order. The missionaries were frequently attacked by mobs even in the treaty ports. The growing anti-foreign feeling in China during the

[1] Richard Van Alstyne, *The Listener* (London: March 23, 1961).

nineteenth century, however, appeared only to heighten the zeal of the missionaries "to win China for Christ."

By 1900 the hatred and suspicion that the Chinese felt toward the foreign missionaries exploded in what we think of as the "Boxer Rebellion." Two hundred foreign missionaries and thirty thousand Chinese Christians were killed. The Western powers responded by inflicting savage reprisals upon the Chinese. Large numbers of Chinese were slain by the allied armies that marched to Peking;[2] great quantities of the finest of Chinese artistic and historic treasures were, on orders of their officers, smashed by the allied troops and indemnities amounting to $320,000,000 were extorted from the impoverished Chinese people. It is horrifying, but revealing of the temper of the times, to read the report of the Rev. Mr. Ament, who had been sent to China by the American Board of Missions to collect indemnities due to the missionary societies.

In an interview on his return to America, reported by the New York *Sun* on Christmas Eve, 1901, Mr. Ament expressed satisfaction that he had not only succeeded in collecting the agreed indemnities, but also had assessed fines amounting to *thirteen times* the amount of the indemnities. (This money, Mr. Ament said, "will be used for the propagation of the gospel.") The Catholics, according to Mr. Ament, were more stringent in their demands for they not only claimed monetary indemnities but also

[2] Many people are confused by the use of the word "Peking" for "Peiping." These names refer to the same city. Peiping (meaning Northern Peace) was the name the city was known by in the Ming Dynasty, but in 1420 the name was changed to Peking (Northern Capital) which it retained until 1928 when Chiang Kai-shek moved his capital south to Nanking and it was known again as Peiping. In October 1949, the Communist government restored the city to its former position as the national capital and it was once more called Peking. It is known as Peking throughout the world except in the United States, in deference to the myth that Chiang Kai-shek is still the ruler of China. To call it Peking would imply that the capital of China is there and not in Taipei on the island of Taiwan.

In 1962, the New York *Times* decided that it was time to fall into step with the rest of the world. The AP and most other papers followed suit. The Voice of America still refers to it as Peiping and I have a letter dated August 21, 1963, from the State Department in which Peiping is also used.

a "head for a head" for each of the Catholics killed in the up-
risings.[3]

I raise these painful memories to remind us of what was then
the normal attitude of civilized Western people toward the
Chinese. It was based firmly on the conviction of Western, Christian, superiority. This assumption of superiority ate like a corrosive
acid deep into the sensitivities of a very proud and ancient people.
To Westerners, the Chinese were uncivilized and almost less than
human. They quite clearly stood in need of God's grace; it was
manifestly America's destiny to lead them to it.

Paradoxically, these punitive expeditions and these reprisals
around the turn of the century ushered in what on the surface
appeared to be the flowering of missionary effort in China. With
the Boxer Rebellion and its aftermath, Chinese resistance to
foreign influence collapsed. They had learned that resistance without strength was useless; from now on they would attempt to
learn from the technically more advanced nations the secret of
their strength. The new relationship between the triumphant foreigner and the thoroughly defeated Chinese produced the kindlier,
more sympathetic image of the Chinese which carried over for
almost half a century.

This new attitude toward the Chinese (Harold Isaacs called
this period "The Age of Benevolence")[4] was sustained in part
by self-delusion. The "remission" of the Boxer indemnity provides a good example of the mythologies that appear destined to
bedevil U.S.-China relations, an example too of how the belief
of "our kindness to the Chinese" continues to the present day.
It may be worth setting the record straight.

In 1908 the U.S. government agreed to remit the balance of
the Boxer Rebellion indemnities still due to America. Succes-

[3] I am indebted to Mark Twain for my knowledge of this interview with
Mr. Ament. When I read of it in Twain's biting essay "To the Person
Sitting in Darkness," I could not bring myself to believe that such an interview had taken place. A search in the files of the New York *Sun* showed me
that Twain had copied the text with meticulous accuracy.
[4] Harold R. Isaacs, *Scratches on Our Minds* (New York: John Day, 1958).
I am greatly indebted to this book for much of the information in this
and the following chapter. Mr. Isaacs' book provides a very valuable account
of the varying images in the American mind of China and India.

sive generations of Americans have been led to believe that this remission was a spontaneous gesture in which we were showing unusual magnanimity to a defeated and contrite enemy. Even in 1959 a China scholar of Professor John K. Fairbank's standing still cites this remission as a matter of great credit to us. According to Professor Fairbank, the U.S. "turned back the money that we received as indemnity for the missionaries that had been killed."[5] The facts could bear a somewhat different interpretation.

With the collapse of Chinese resistance to foreign influence after the Boxer Rebellion, an increasing number of Chinese realized that if their country was ever to establish itself as an independent power it must move into the modern world. Japan, by her victory over Russia in 1905—the first modern Asian victory over a Western power—gained enormous prestige among the Chinese and an increasing number of upper-class Chinese (among them a young man by the name of Chiang Kai-shek) flocked to Japan to learn the secret of her success. It became apparent to many Americans (both educators and businessmen) that unless steps were taken, other countries (especially Japan, Britain, and Germany) might reap the benefits of China's "awakening."

There was, as a result, a growing public demand that something be done to attract Chinese students to the United States, so that they might "act as commercial missionaries." The most influential appeal came from a college president who argued that had the United States acted differently over the preceding years she would "have been controlling the development of China in that most satisfactory and subtle of all ways—through the intellectual and spiritual domination of its leaders."[6]

It was only under pressure that Theodore Roosevelt in 1908 reluctantly agreed to the remission of the *unused balance* of the Boxer indemnity. The act passed by Congress the following year provided that the sum of $11 million be set aside to finance

[5] A symposium, "Foundations of U.S.-China Policy," broadcast on January 10, 1959, by radio station KPFA, Berkeley, California, and subsequently published by the Pacifica Foundation, Berkeley.
[6] Quoted by Jessie A. Miller, *China in American Policy and Opinion, 1906–1909* (Ph.D. thesis, Clark University, 1940).

the education of Chinese students both in China and the United States. It is usually forgotten that the money was Chinese money in the first place, exacted as a punitive indemnity for a historically understandable rebellion and that the sum remitted was the balance remaining after all American damage claims had been more than amply covered.

The sense of kindly benevolence toward a backward people dominated American feelings throughout the earlier part of this century. We came to consider ourselves guardians whose duty it was to lead China toward the benefits of a Christian and of course a safely capitalist world. The missionary activity by this time was not limited to the saving of Chinese souls but had expanded to include medical assistance and the establishment of schools and colleges. By 1925 there existed in China no fewer than 27 mission colleges, and 560,000 Chinese children were being educated in Protestant and Catholic mission schools. There were in that year 700,000 Protestant and 1,400,000 Catholic communicants.[7]

While Christians held many important positions, the influence of the Christian missions on the Chinese people has usually been greatly exaggerated. By 1949, after a century of effort, less than 1 percent of the population had been converted.

Although the missionaries spread more widely through China and in some areas were more intimately involved with the lives of the ordinary Chinese, the traders moved in too.

The United States never moved abroad with the same "empire building" confidence of the British and the Europeans. American diplomacy had therefore to be directed to preventing other nations from turning China into an exclusive preserve. The United States from the first insisted that any privileges China granted to other powers must be extended to her also. Throughout the nineteenth century European nations were—by war itself or the threat of war—wresting from the helpless Chinese all kinds of commercial prerogatives and immunities. America also was able to reap the advantages of these, but with almost no military action and there-

[7] *China Year Book*, 1925–26, Shanghai.

fore with no qualms of conscience. "Hitchhiking" imperialism, one writer called it.

This strategy, that had been insisted on throughout the nineteenth century, was finally formulated in the famous "Open Door Policy" of 1899. Its real intent was concealed beneath all kinds of high-sounding phrases about insuring China's freedom, independence, and integrity. With its primary purpose to see that no one power should dominate China and that the fruits of exploitation should be shared, the Open Door Policy firmly established America's role as China's "protector."

China's domestic development being greatly restricted by regulations imposed by the foreign powers for their own interests, and being militarily impotent, it was a country ripe for exploitation. Throughout the first two decades of the twentieth century Western businessmen enjoyed an unparalleled freedom to establish highly lucrative commerce with China—and they made the most of it.

In the minds of Americans at home during the twenties, the image of the Chinese was nearly always as inferior people—different, dangerous, mysterious, "inscrutable." In America, they ran laundries, they wrote backwards, they didn't go to church, and the men sometimes still wore pigtails.

> Chink Chink Chinaman sitting on a rail
> Along comes a white man and cuts off his tail. . . .

The *differentness* of the Chinese prevented him from disappearing into the crowd; his defense against a hostile environment was to withdraw into his own communities.

Millions of Americans had the image of the Chinese as a sinister figure, imprinted on their minds by a series of very popular films about Dr. Fu Manchu. For Manchu (according to Hollywood publicity) had "menace in every twitch of his finger, a threat in every twitch of his eyebrow, terror in each split-second of his slanted eyes."[8]

> He was revengeful, merciless, adept at obscure forms of slow torture, a master of unknown drugs, and the lord of

[8] Isaacs, p. 116.

a vast army of thugs and slaves ready to do his worst bid-
ding. He was so evil that he periodically had to be killed
off, and was so mysteriously superpowerful that he always
miraculously reappeared in time for the next episode.[9]

While the popular image of the Chinese as a crafty devil was
firmly established in the minds of Americans at home, Americans
in China itself had another attitude toward the Chinese. They
rather liked the Chinese, they enjoyed their life in China, and
they were making money.

It is probably for these golden years up to the Second World
War that the "old China hands"—the businessmen especially—
have the keenest sense of nostalgia. They recall with a wistful
longing the easy life in the treaty ports. For the Westerner it was
a good life. He remembers his clubs, his profits, his polite servants,
his ascendancy and superior position. Americans—and other
Westerners—were members of an elite; they bore no responsibility
to the place or to the "natives"; they could ignore its laws. They
could afford to be expansively kind toward the people around
them. There was a general assumption that the Chinese were
quite incapable of orderly rule or effective administration—so they
should feel grateful to the foreigner for being there to help them.

An interview with a businessman which is recorded in Harold
Isaacs' book summarizes this attitude:

> In my time everybody loved China. The white man was
> respected to a very high degree. We loved the way of life.
> Business was good. The white man was master. It was a
> cheap place to live. There were varying views of the Chinese,
> but generally people were pretty fond of them.[10]

There was, of course, another China and Richard Hughes, correspondent for the *Sunday Times* of London, has reminded us
of it:

> I knew Shanghai when it was the gayest city in the Far
> East—gay, that is, if you were a foreigner or a Chinese
> millionaire. But there were corpses in the street every night.
> 20,000 died a year from hunger, cold and exposure. And

[9] Ibid., p. 117.
[10] Ibid., p. 151.

there were swarms of beggars. And the childish street walkers. And the sweating rickshaw coolies, with a professional life-expectancy of eight years—if they didn't smoke too much opium. . . .[11]

These disturbing glimpses behind the scenes did not discourage the ever-growing number of Americans upon whom China cast her spell. The future looked promising. A strong, united China, grateful for American help, a firm ally across the ocean providing an ever-widening market for American goods, became the national goal. This seemed the natural, the inevitable progression of events.

And in China a generation desperate for Westernization, for modernization, for progress, for some rescue from the miseries of poverty and backwardness, began to see an answer in the American ideal. It was a strangely symbiotic relationship. Its strength lay in the promise each people held out for the other. Its mortal weakness—that this friendship concealed ulterior motives on one side and repressed deeply felt humiliations and grievances on the other. America was "kind" to China—but was hoping for commercial and strategic benefits. The Chinese were dutifully "grateful" to their benefactors, but below the surface bitterly resented Western assumptions of superiority.

Not many of the thousands of Americans, however, living in China during this golden period of the twenties and thirties— the missionaries, the businessmen, the doctors, the teachers, the reporters, and the many who lived there because they liked the way of life and liked the Chinese—not many of these ever paused to speculate whether their affection was reciprocated. Americans were tolerant, easygoing, pleased with themselves for doing China so much good. And there were those, of course, who watched with calculating eye the long-term military and commercial advantages of an alliance with an emerging Asian nation of so vast a size.

That era for long was remembered as "the good old days," but below the surface a growing spirit of nationalism indicated that China was preparing to exert her independence as a nation.

This is not the place to trace the confused political events that

[11] New York *Times*, July 6, 1958.

between 1925 and 1927 brought Chiang Kai-shek to power. As we shall see Chiang had made his deal with the big Chinese and Western commercial interests and had turned on his Communist allies; but even so there were many foreign businessmen who saw in Chiang the first real threat to foreign domination. Many of them even appealed to their home governments to reassert foreign influence, if necessary by strong-arm methods.

But in 1931 the Japanese made their opening move to conquer China—and the whole picture was once more changed. Chiang, who had begun to arouse Chinese nationalist feelings against foreign influence, was now forced to look to the West for support against the invading enemy from Japan.

While Chiang Kai-shek was establishing his bona fides as the proper recipient for American support, he became a Christian—and a new legend was born.

Chiang had married the American-educated Soong Mei-ling, whose family formed part of the Chinese power elite. He embraced the Methodist creed in which she had been raised. To the missionaries Chiang's acceptance of Christianity raised limitless hopes. Many even believed that China would now become a Christan nation. For the first time they could look forward to official support for their endeavors. And in return for this bright promise, the missionaries and their supporters at home gave Chiang Kai-shek and his wife, from 1930 on, their passionate and uncritical support. They were ready to accept his assurances that he was a believer in "democracy"—that his one-party rule was merely a temporary period of "tutelage." They closed their eyes to the ruthless extermination of political opponents, his savage reprisals on his former Communist associates, his intolerance of all who did not give him total obedience, his disregard for the welfare of his people, his nepotism. He was a Christian, his wife was a Christian, the upper ranks of his government were staffed largely by the products of mission schools and American universities—this was enough. From that time on, Chiang's partisans in America began to play a highly influential role in shaping America's China policies.

Thus, during the thirties popular approval of the Chinese flourished. This is the period of Pearl Buck's *The Good Earth* (this novel of China has sold two million copies and was made into a film seen by an estimated 23 million people). Lin Yutang published *The Importance of Living* and *My Country and My People*. The title of Carl Crow's book, *400 Million Customers*, became almost a national byword. The earlier (Boxer Rebellion—Dr. Fu Manchu) image of the Chinese as a crafty, dangerous devil with a knife between his teeth was now quite forgotten. The Chinese were no longer a "faceless mass," but a people

> hardworking, strong, persevering, and able to withstand the most severe adversities, kind towards children, respectful towards elders, all in all an admirable warmly loving character.[12]

The initial Japanese invasion in 1931, in spite of this new image of the Chinese, was met with a certain passivity on the part of the American government and people. The Japanese were engaged more in a "nibbling" operation than in large-scale warfare; and Chiang, instead of fighting them, preferred a policy of "non-resistance" to the Japanese encroachments. President Hoover thought there was something to be said for the Japanese and that "we should in friendship consider her side also." He thought that: "Neither our obligations to China, nor our own interests, nor our dignity require us to go to war. . . ."[13] And meanwhile we were making money shipping war material to the Japanese.

When the Japanese in 1937 began their large-scale attempt to conquer the Chinese, American opinion was finally aroused. Western interests in China were now in danger. Chiang, too, began for the first time to fight back. Day after day the China war was splashed across the pages of the newspapers in America; dramatic newsreel shots of the bombing of Chinese towns were seen by millions of moviegoers. The Japanese sacking of Nanking in 1937, in which thousands of Chinese were slaughtered, revolted

[12] Dorothy B. Jones, *The Portrayal of China and India on the American Screen, 1896–1955* (Center for International Studies, M.I.T., October 1955), Appendix III, p. 36.
[13] R. L. Wilbur and A. M. Hyde, *The Hoover Policies* (New York: Charles Scribner's Sons, 1937), p. 600.

American opinion; and the sinking of the American gunboat *Panay* on the Yangtze River gave the first chill intimation that the United States herself might eventually be involved.

From this time on, the legend of Chiang as the heroic leader was immeasurably strengthened. Western hopes of noninvolvement were pinned on his capacity to resist the aggression of the Japanese. During 1938 an intensive campaign, inspired by missionary organizations and their friends, brought the war to the notice of the public. Committees were formed to boycott Japanese goods; to call a halt to our shipment of war material to Japan; to collect money for medical aid to China. Large advertisements appealed to the conscience and sympathy of Americans. Dispatches from the front were full of accounts that gave a vivid, but usually highly exaggerated picture of the fighting. The Chinese were "fighting against fantastic odds"; they "stood firm through long weeks while superbly equipped Japanese forces shelled and bombed them without cessation."

The flood of popular sympathy which these stories engendered was focused on the figures of Chiang Kai-shek and his wife. They became the very embodiment of all that was heroic, selfless, fearless. Articles in great profusion about them appeared in the press. Missionary and press propaganda concentrated heavily on

> highly favorable accounts of the Chinese government and high Chinese officials . . . they have never failed to point with pride to the fact that a high percentage of the officials of the government have been educated in Christian institutions and that many of them are themselves Christians including Generalissimo Chiang Kai-shek. Madame Chiang has practically become a saint to them.[14]

Time Magazine named Chiang and Madame Chiang "Man and Women of the Year" for 1937.

> But while Japan launched her great adventure without outstanding leadership, China, the victim of the adventure, has had the ablest of leadership. Through 1937 the Chinese have been led—not without glory—by one supreme leader

---

[14] "Missionary Influence upon American Far Eastern Policy," *Pacific Historical Review*, X (September 1941).

and his remarkable wife. . . . He is a salt seller's son, she a bible salesman's daughter. No woman in the West holds so great a position as Madame Chiang Kai-shek holds in China. Her rise and that of her husband, the Generalissimo, in less than a generation to moral and material leadership of the ancient Chinese people cover a great page of history. In China no great moral stigma had commonly attached to graft. . . . For the colossal purchases Chiang had to make he could not afford the normal luxury of graft. To find someone he could trust to purchase war planes the Generalissimo turned at last in desperation to his own wife. She it was who pored over aircraft catalogs, dickered with hard-boiled wire salesmen, and is reported to have had several Chinese officials of her Air Ministry shot to reduce thieving. . . .

If Chiang Kai-shek and Mei-ling can maintain their will as China's will—the same will which said that "any sacrifice should not be regarded as too costly"—Chinese prospects are good.

This week an Associated Press correspondent "somewhere in the Yangtze Valley" . . . was permitted to flash that influenza had bedded the Wife of the Year, quoted the Man of the Year as saying: "Tell America to have complete confidence in us. The tide of battle is turning and victory eventually will be ours!"[15]

The peak of national heroine worship was not, however, reached until 1943 when Madame Chiang Kai-shek came to the United States to plead for more American aid. She had an enormous public success. To millions she appeared to represent in her slight figure all that was most noble, most virtuous, most self-sacrificing, most courageous in the Chinese. When she addressed the U. S. Senate, the Senators "rose and thundered" an ovation for her; and after she had spoken to the House of Representatives, *Time* reported, "tough guys wilted. 'Goddam it,' said one grizzled congressman, 'I never saw anything like it. Madame Chiang had me on the verge of tears'."[16]

But by this time America was at war with Japan too. China was now our official ally. Thousands of GI's, OWI and OSS

[15] *Time*, January 3, 1938.
[16] *Time*, March 1, 1943.

officials, State Department representatives, Air Force crews, correspondents, advisers, "experts" of all kinds were swarming over China. For the first time Americans in large numbers were confronted with the facts. They were able to see for themselves how little the China legend, the image of Chiang's China fostered by the press and official apologists at home, corresponded to realities.

Chapter 2

DOUBLE EXPOSURE
(1941–45)

. . . The image-makers in their simple-minded enthusiasm
had turned China at war into a movie set and had made
the Chinese into plaster saints, including Generalissimo and
Madame Chiang Kai-shek. But China was not a movie set
and the Chinese were not saints, plaster or any other kind,
least of all the Chiangs. This mythology could hardly survive
any live experience, and its passing for many was quite painful.

—*Scratches on Our Minds,* p. 176.

Before World War II ended, two hundred thousand GI's had
become aware that the picture of China presented to Americans
at home was grossly untrue. They arrived in China expecting
to fight side by side with a people united and disciplined by five
years of war. Instead they found a country of vast disorganization
and disunity. Americans hoped that their military presence would
be welcomed by a people struggling desperately against the
Japanese. But they found themselves involved with greedy civil
and military officials, brutalized policemen, and cynical bureaucrats living off a pauperized population.

The "valiant" Chinese army was not at all as pictured by the
politicians and editorial writers at home, but a ragged, exploited
army of conscripts with little spirit to fight for a regime which
they had come to detest. Americans discovered quickly enough
that Chiang Kai-shek was more concerned with maintaining his
position than with fighting the Japanese; that his government was

corrupt, inept, and appallingly insensitive to the sufferings of its people. So little were the leaders able to arouse any widespread popular support that in order to recruit an army at all they were frequently reduced to rounding up young men in the villages and roping them together as in the days of the press gangs in Europe.

There were numerous descriptions of some of the "recruiting" practices which took place in wartime China written by Americans who were there at the time. William J. Lederer has written:

> . . . as early as 1941 I personally have seen long lines of conscripts chained together on their way from their villages to training camps. . . .[1]

And the veteran wartime correspondent Jack Belden reported:

> The basis of all conscription was graft, bribery and influence. Sons of the rich never entered the army; sons of the poor could never escape. An impoverished widow's only son was always drafted; the numerous offspring of the landlord, never.[2]

Two other American reporters—Theodore White and Annalee Jacoby—give us an idea of what conditions in Chiang's army were like during the Second World War:

> China seethed from end to end at a recruiting drive that in brutality, callousness, and corruption matched the worst in her dark record. The suffering was made all the more pitiful by the pious protestations of the government that now at last all things were mending. So many bought their way out of the draft that village heads could not meet their quotas; in order to supply the requisite units of human flesh, organized bands of racketeers prowled the roads to kidnap wayfarers for sale to village chieftains. Army officials engaged in the traffic on their own, and they made no protest no matter how decrepit the recruits' health. In Chengtu a black-market recruit, a trussed-and-bound victim of the press gangs, was sold for $50,000 to $100,000 Chinese, the equivalent of the purchase price of five sacks of white rice or three pigs.

---

[1] A Nation of Sheep (New York: Norton, 1961), p. 44.
[2] China Shakes the World (New York: Harper, 1949), p. 338.

The Chinese did not fear to fight for their country; there was no deficit in patriotism. But they knew what recruiting camps were like. Government regulations could be read with a mirror. Officers were forbidden to mix sand with the rice they fed the recruits; they were forbidden to seize any clothes, baggage or personal possessions a conscript carried with him; they were forbidden to torture, tie up, or lock their recruits in barred rooms at night; they were forbidden to ask families of deserting recruits to pay for the uniforms and feed the soldier got at the induction center. Conditions in combat units were horrible, but by comparison to conditions in induction centers they were idyllic. Recruits ate even less than the starving soldiers; sometimes they got no water. Many of them were stripped naked and left to sleep on bare floors. They were whipped. Dead bodies were allowed to lie for days. In some areas less than 20 per cent lived to reach the front. The week that the stories of Belsen and Buchenwald broke in Europe coincided with the height of the conscription drive in China; the doctors who dealt with the recruit camp about Chengtu refused to be excited about German horrors, for descriptions of the Nazi camps, they said, read almost exactly like the recruit centers in which they were working. Near Chengtu one camp had received some 40,000 men for induction. Many had already died on the way; only 8,000 were still alive at the camp at the end of the drive. One batch of 1,000 inductees was reported to have lost 800 recruits through the negligence of its officers.[3]

And on all sides the Americans were cheated. Graham Peck, who was in China on the staff of the Office of War Information, wrote:

> I think every American who came to Kuomintang territory on war duty has bitter memories of the do-nothing attitudes, and the profiteering which ranged from the prices the U. S. Army had to pay for air fields to the prices GI's were charged in restaurants.[4]

Peck spells out some examples of the fantastic profiteering:

[3] *Thunder Out of China* (New York: William Sloane, 1947), pp. 273-75.
[4] *Two Kinds of Time* (Boston: Houghton Mifflin, 1950), p. 387.

A trading company agreed to sell the SOS [Service of Supply] twenty bicycles for the equivalent of US $700 each. Before they were delivered, the company told the SOS the bicycles had been bought by a Kweilin bank. Later the bank offered them to SOS for US $1350 each.

A company contracted to sell SOS forty auto batteries at US $450 each, delivery within five days. At the end of two weeks the company admitted the batteries had been sold to a bank, which later offered them to SOS for US $750 each.

By oral agreement, SOS arranged to buy twenty-five alternators, at US $8000 each, for an electrical factory in Kweilin. Two days later the plant told SOS that the price was now US $12,000. SOS got other alternators from a firm in Hengyang. Later when it tried to buy more equipment from the Kweilin factory, its manager said SOS had broken one contract with them and "felt indisposed to fill any more American orders."[5]

A month or so after these incidents had come to light, Peck was invited to a dinner party for Lin Yutang (author of the best-selling *The Importance of Living* and other books on China). Lin was visiting his native land after an absence of so many years that wags said his next book about China should be called *The Importance of Living Somewhere Else.* He was, Peck reports, the object of bitter attack by most other Chinese writers for having avoided the tribulations of modern China. He was now back in his own country lecturing his people reprovingly, telling them that any criticism of the Kuomintang played into the hands of the Communists.

When I talked to him about profiteering in Kweilin, he sounded very official. . . . "No wonder the young Americans get in trouble" he said in effect. "They have no understanding of Chinese life or culture. . . . I suggest they do their business through authorized government organizations." When I told this to the SOS officers they blew up. "Sonofabitch" said one. "We didn't think we ought to mention it but those banks we talked about to the press are all Chinese government outfits and the companies we have

[5] Ibid., p. 515.

most trouble with are government-controlled. The private firms give us a much fairer deal. We used to ask for government help in buying, but we found the bastards were just using our information to screw us some more. How's that for culture?"[6]

Peck gives a bitterly memorable description of Madame Chiang's return to China after her triumphal visit to Washington, where "grizzled congressmen," so moved by her speeches, almost wept.

. . . She must have known enough about conditions in China to be conscious that her American triumph was based on fraud. When she returned to China, she seemed to have become a pathologically pretentious woman who, under the surface, was so distraught, uneasy, and at odds with herself that she could no longer make much sense either on the political or personal level. . . .
She was travelling in an American plane. . . . She had been loaned some cargo ships for her baggage, and at the Assam field her things had to be transferred to other planes to go over the Hump. This was done in a rather remote part of the field and the GI's who were doing it happened to drop one crate. It split open and its contents rolled out . . . it was full of cosmetics, lingerie, and fancy groceries with which Madame Chiang planned to see herself through the rest of the war. The GI's were furious, for this was one of the times when the Hump transport was in a bad state, with many American fliers losing their lives to get war supplies to China. The soldiers dropped and broke all the other crates they transshipped. When they had kicked every fur coat and trick clock around in the dust as thoroughly as time would permit they threw the mess into the waiting planes.[7]

At home in America, these stories never reached the public. Not, that is, until the war was almost over. The myth was maintained. Chiang and his wife continued to be the embodiment of heroism.

On the official level, of course, the U.S. government was well appraised by its representatives about the real conditions in China.

[6] Ibid., p. 517.
[7] Ibid., pp. 477–78.

In February 1942, the head of the first American military mission to China, Brigadier General John A. Magruder, was reporting to Washington as follows (a report not made public until after the war):

> . . . referring to the marvelous achievements and abilities of the Chinese army. Such reports are absolutely without foundation. . . . China's military successes are being highly exaggerated by what is being given out in American newspapers. . . . There is grave danger that such continued distortions of fact as to the prowess of China's military forces are spreading about a false sense of security. . . . Such propaganda could lead to grave defects in American war plans, if our own officials should be influenced by it even to the slightest extent.[8]

And, in July, from the American Ambassador in China, Clarence Gauss, came the following (also not published until after the war):

> . . . It is unfortunate that Chiang and the Chinese have been "built up" in the United States to a point where Americans have been made to believe that China has been "fighting" the Japanese for five years, and that the Generalissimo, a great leader, has been directing the energetic resistance of China to Japan and is a world hero. Looking the cold facts in the face, one could only dismiss this as "rot."[9]

In the very month that this report was received from Ambassador Gauss, the Secretary of State issued a widely publicized message to Chiang:

> The American people have watched with deep sympathy and admiration the heroic fortitude and tenacity with which for five long and bitter years the Chinese have fought on against heavy odds.[10]

Wendell Willkie visited China during his wartime whirlwind tour around the world. He, too, added his influence to the myth. His brief visit (wrote Peck),

[8] Foreign Relations of the United States, Diplomatic Papers, China, 1942.
[9] Ibid.
[10] Ibid.

summed up the character of the Chinese capital in 1942 with gaiety and comedy in appearances and tragedies just under the surface, with fine words being spoken about the war and the peace to follow, while both the war and the peace were already being shaped by forces not so mentionable.

. . . never before—not even for the great friend of the Kuomintang, Henry Luce—had surface saving and face-making been attempted on such a scale. Long before Willkie's arrival, the police tore down the worst of the pauper's shacks in the suburb where he was to stay; naturally the squatters were not paid for the homes they lost. In the last few days before he came, the police herded out of the city any beggars and peddlars who looked too wretched to be a credit to the capital of a modern democracy —a great disaster for people who led such a hand-to-mouth existence. . . .

I saw nothing of the later Willkie shenanigans except a plunging of cars through downtown streets. . . . He was kept so busy with banquets, inspection tours and interviews that . . . thoughtful interpretation and analysis were almost impossible. And everywhere he went, the things he saw and the people he talked to had been carefully prepared to make a favorable impression.

. . . Concerning China [in his book One World] Willkie presented opinions which can now be seen as a disservice to America and China . . . his view was almost exactly what the Kuomintang wanted and had so briskly arranged to get. He used his prestige to preserve the old propaganda picture . . . the heroic wartime West and the New China building; the well-trained and loyal armies which needed only arms and air support from America to win; the monumental Generalissimo, his charming Madame, and all the rest of it.[11]

The U.S. all this time, of course, was pouring billions of dollars into China for military and financial aid. In 1942 gold was shipped to Chiang's government as part of a $500 million Treasury loan. A memorandum to the President from Secretary of the Treasury Morgenthau (not published until after the war) provides an insight into how such funds were used and why they were able to do

[11] Two Kinds of Time, pp. 428-30.

so little to help the Chinese people. Most of this loan apparently was sold on the black market for the benefit of officials in the know:

> The Chinese Government issued gold and dollar securities for *yuan* [the Chinese currency] setting aside $200 million of the aid granted by this country for the redemption of the securities. (These securities were sold at an exorbitant profit to the buyers.) I believe the program made no significant contribution to the control of inflation.
> . . . China could use these funds in selling gold or dollar assets for *yuan* although in my opinion such schemes in the past have had little effect except to give additional profits to insiders, speculators and hoarders. . . .[12]

It is an extraordinary testimony to the power of the "Chiang legend," and to the effectiveness with which it was being maintained in America, that an experienced foreign correspondent such as Leland Stowe should arrive in China and be so profoundly disturbed by what he saw. A certain skepticism is part of the essential equipment for any newspaper correspondent, as well as a sophistication that doesn't allow official statements to be taken at face value. But the conditions of China had been so inaccurately presented in the U.S. press that even as shrewd a reporter as Stowe could be appalled at what he found, when he went to China in 1941, just before Pearl Harbor.

> Few disillusionments of mine had ever been greater or more acid than this which I suffered behind China's front.
> I discovered that my vision, like that of almost all Americans, had been seriously blurred by my enthusiasm for the Chinese people's magnificent and incredible resistance to Japan. Somehow you did not pause to reflect that people who fought on and on so marvelously could still be handicapped or betrayed by corruption, selfishness, or indifference among a considerable portion of their governing class. . . .[13]

[12] *United States Relations with China,* Department of State, 1949, p. 489. Henceforth this will be referred to as Department of State "White Paper," the name by which it is commonly known.
[13] *They Shall Not Sleep* (New York: Alfred A. Knopf, 1944), p. 4.

After a struggle with himself, Stowe eventually decided to report what he had found, although he "knew it would come as a tremendous shock to an American public which had come to look upon all Chinese as Sir Galahads and patriots."[14]

It was obvious to those in China that Chiang was more concerned with resisting the growing strength and influence of the Communist Party than he was in fighting the Japanese. Over and over again it was the Communist army that took the initiative against the invading Japanese, and the reluctance of Chiang to engage his army fully against the invaders only further diminished his popular support.

> . . . Increasingly it had become apparent that the Chinese war effort had largely ceased to be an effective factor in China and that to a disturbing extent the Chinese will to fight had vanished. The main Nationalist effort was being concentrated on containment of Communists in the north and in internal political squabbles in Chungking [the wartime capital]. . . .[15]

With the real truth about conditions in China known to official Washington (though not by many of the American people), all thoughts of using Chiang's army for a major military operation against the Japanese were indefinitely shelved.

There were Americans in high places who knew the true conditions in China and tried to do something to correct them. One of these was General Joseph Stilwell, who had been sent to China to be Chiang's Chief of Staff. General Stilwell never lost his confidence that the Chinese would make good soldiers if they were properly treated, effectively led, and given something to fight for. But less than a month after his arrival, he was writing in his diary:[16]

> What a commentary on the Chinese general staff—no preparations, no concern, they just sit and let me go to it. Through stupidity, fear and defense attitude they lost a grand chance to slap the Japs back at Toungee (Burma). The basic reason is Chiang Kai-shek's meddling. . . . I told

[14] Ibid.
[15] Department of State "White Paper," p. 66.
[16] Chicago *Tribune* Press Service, San Francisco *Chronicle*, March 3, 1963.

him in plain words . . . the (Chinese) army and division commanders had failed to obey and I had insufficient authority to force them to obey. . . . They are chislers and grafters. . . .

Chiang Kai-shek has been boss so long, so many yes men, he has the idea he's infallible on any subject. . . . It is patently impossible for me to compete with the swarm of parasites and sycophants that surround him.

That was on March 21, 1942.

On May 10, Stilwell was writing:

C.K.S. double-crossed me at every turn the ——![17]

On June 15:

C.K.S.'s ignorance and fatuous complacency are appalling, the little dummy.[18]

But it wasn't only the little dummy that bothered General Stilwell. On March 4, 1943:

The Chinese Red Cross is a racket. Stealing and sale of medicine is rampant. . . . Higher-ups in army steal soldiers' food.[19]

As we shall see, Chiang Kai-shek's partisans and friends in America were by this time well established and were able to exert a very powerful influence upon America's China policy.

Informed of Chiang's insistence that he be recalled, Stilwell noted in his diary (October 3, 1944):

C.K.S. said that I refused to obey orders. The real reason is that I knew too much about conditions.

On October 19 Stilwell was relieved of his command and re-called to the United States. Thus, for all intents and purposes, ended the career of one of America's finest soldiers.

With Stilwell's dismissal, there was some protest. On October 31, 1944 the New York *Times* printed a dispatch from its correspondent Brooks Atkinson, who said that the removal of General Stilwell represented in China

[17] Ibid.
[18] Ibid.
[19] Ibid.

the political triumph of a moribund, antidemocratic regime that is more concerned with maintaining its political supremacy than in driving the Japanese out of China . . . relieving General Stilwell and supporting his successor has the effect of making us acquiesce in an unenlightened, coldhearted autocratic political regime.

But the few and isolated reports from men such as Leland Stowe and Brooks Atkinson could do little to awaken the American people, so deeply and consistently had the "Chiang legend" been impressed upon their minds.

While the legend of Chiang was maintained for public benefit, Washington *was* receiving accounts of the growing disillusionment of the people and the mounting popularity of the Chinese Communists. Civil war was now reported as a probability. A series of assessments by experienced Foreign Service officers were warning the government of what might be in store.

One such report was made by John P. Davies, Jr. Dated November 7, 1944, it was not made public until 1949:

> Only if he is able to enlist foreign intervention on a scale equal to the Japanese invasion of China will Chiang probably be able to crush the Communists. But foreign intervention on such a scale would seem to be unlikely. Relying upon his dispirited shambling legions, his decadent corrupt bureaucracy, his sterile political moralisms and such nervous foreign support as he can muster, the Generalissimo may nevertheless plunge China into civil war. He cannot succeed, however, where the Japanese in more than seven years of determined striving have failed. The Communists are already too strong for him.
>
> If the Generalissimo neither precipitates a civil war nor reaches an understanding with the Communists, he is still confronted with defeat. Chiang's feudal China cannot coexist along with a modern dynamic popular government [the Communist Government] in North China.
>
> The Communists are in China to stay. And China's destiny is not Chiang's but theirs.[20]

(Never were truer words written; but for this honesty in appraising events in China as they really were, Davies was later to pay

[20] Department of State "White Paper," p. 573.

heavily during the McCarthy period, and in 1954 he was dismissed from the Foreign Service.)

Routine official hypocrisy we will always have, especially in time of war. But this consistent misleading of the American public about the situation in China went far beyond the routine, and far beyond what the necessities of war required. The people of America have a right to feel indignant that they were so misled and with consequences that have been so momentous.

With no protest from the press, indeed with the active assistance of the press, the nation was presented with an account of the war in China that was preposterously unreal and which the government from its official reports should have known was unreal. A picture was painted of Chiang and his wife which concealed the true character of the regime and the wretchedness of the people who suffered under it. The grossly exaggerated claims made on behalf of Chiang and his "heroic struggle" hid from the American people the angry determination of the Chinese people to bring an end to Chiang's social system—to root it out at whatever cost. The information we were given left us as a nation quite unprepared for the depth and force of the hatred which Chiang had engendered among his own people and which finally brought him to defeat.

Those few who warned us were suspect. Some, like General Stilwell, were publicly repudiated and dismissed. And most ironic of all, our official uncritical support for Chiang only enlarged the scope of his ineptitudes and tyrannies by silencing the critics among his own countrymen who might otherwise have ameliorated the worst features of his rule.

After the Japanese defeat, Chiang ruled China for less than five years before his collapse and retreat to Taiwan. These years saw the final corrosion of a whole social system. For a few years, mostly between 1947 and 1949, press reports out of China revealed some of the causes of this corrosion—corruption, graft, nepotism, inefficiency, and military bluster. Books by long-time China correspondents such as Belden, White and Jacoby, Peck and others, probed deeply into the nature of the coming collapse of the Kuomintang.

Thus, for a brief period before his defeat, the "Chiang legend" in America was deeply stained. Some of Chiang's supporters still felt that the Generalissimo was not too greatly to blame, that he was the victim of historic forces beyond the control of any single man; or that he was betrayed by a small group of corrupt and grasping politicians. Some clung to the belief that it was lack of real support from America that betrayed him. While each of these causes may have contributed to his final downfall, the real root of his failure lay within himself.

> Chiang could not understand the revolution whose creature he was except as something fearful and terrible that had to be crushed. He had every favoring grace on his side—the support of powerful allies, the cause of justice, and in the beginning the wholehearted and enthusiastic support of all his people. The people whom he led felt instinctively that this war against Japan was a war against the entire rotten fabric of time-worn misery. When Chiang tried to fight the Japanese and preserve the old fabric at the same time, he was not only unable to defeat the Japanese but powerless to preserve his own authority. His historic enemies, the Communists, grew from an army of 85,000 to an army of a million, from the governors of 1,500,000 peasants to the masters of 90,000,000. The Communists used no magic; they knew the changes the people wanted, and they sponsored those changes. Both parties lied, cheated, and broke agreements; but the Communists had the people with them, and with the people they made their own new justice.[21]

Of all this the American public were almost to the end kept in ignorance.

Conditions of disaster, hunger, and squalor had for so long been an accepted and normal part of our news from China that it never occurred to anyone to lay the blame for these on Chiang. But in the last few years of his rule the truth from China was at last being reported. The curtain for a short time was lifted. And looking through the pages of our newspapers of those years, we can recapture the dreadful realities of Chiang Kai-shek's China.

[21] *Thunder Out of China,* Introduction, pp. xv–xvi.

Chapter 3

CHIANG'S CHINA

—the Communists cannot meet the genuine needs and desires of the Chinese people for economic and social progress.

The President . . . noted that in contrast with the disregard for human rights manifested by the Chinese Communist regime, the record [of Free China] was accomplished without violence to the great traditions and human values which have been cherished throughout history by the Chinese people.

—*Communiqué issued by President Kennedy and
Vice-President Chen Cheng of Nationalist China,
August 2, 1961.*

With these words, President Kennedy, like all Presidents since 1949, added his support to a myth. Chiang Kai-shek is identified with freedom and humanity and the historical tradition of China as against the ruthless dictatorship of the present regime.

Chiang, of course, helps this myth along with his annual promises to "regain" freedom for his people on the mainland. Editorials, articles by "experts," news analysts, and so on, have also helped preserve it. It is only Chiang—so the line goes—who can restore "human dignity" to his people. As recently as mid-1963 newspapers were still talking about "restoring" China to the free world.

Since 1949 mention has seldom been made of what China was really like under Chiang's rule.

And for this very good reason. If we wish to delude ourselves that Chiang represents freedom and democracy, we must not remind ourselves about his past.

Here are some of the facts, and the press did report them.

Chiang started his political life as a close associate of the Russian Communists. In the early twenties he went to Moscow to "meet Lenin, Trotsky and Chicerin, to study Bolshevist strategy, ideology, and revolutionary technique, and to seek aid of a material nature from Moscow."[1]

By 1927 the growing appeal of the Communist movement in China had begun to alarm the bankers and the powerful commercial interests in Shanghai. They offered Chiang a deal. They would finance him and support his political aspirations if he would eliminate his Communist colleagues and break the Communist Party. Chiang accepted. Without warning, his troops turned on their former associates and savagely butchered tens of thousands of them. The "free China" of Chiang Kai-shek, representing "the great traditions and human values" of Chinese history, came to power on the wave of some of the most bloody political reprisals.

> Canton has been quite aptly described as a "city of the dead" since the suppression of the Communist peasant and labor uprisings of Sunday.
>
> Photographs confirm the ruthless slaughter that occurred. There are pictures available of trucks loaded with bodies, piled three and four deep, as they were driven through the streets to burial places.
>
> Long rows of bodies on pavements provided gruesome evidence of the vengeance wreaked upon those suspected of Communist leanings when the Nationalists recaptured the city later in the week.
>
> —New York *Times*,
> December 12, 1927.

That is how Chiang's "free China" began; that is how it continued to the end.

Time goes by quickly and memories fade. Today in our news-

[1] H. F. MacNair, *China in Revolution* (University of Chicago Press, 1931), p. 99.

papers and magazines we see the aging Chiang smiling benevo-
lently for the photographers. It is difficult to recall that under this
man's rule millions were killed and a whole social system went to
pieces. To go back as I have done, to read the newspaper reports from China during the days of Chiang's control, is to look
into a world of darkness and terror and vast human suffering,
matched by a callousness and disregard for human welfare that is
staggering. It only needs a glance at a few headlines, a few reports, to give us a glimpse into the realities of Chiang's China.

THE NATIONALIST TROOPS ARREST
DROVES, ROPE WOMEN TOGETHER AND
TERRIFY HOSPITAL PATIENTS.

. . . stringent methods are being used to see that every
suspicious character, man, woman or child, is placed in cus-
tody. Gruesome tales continue to permeate through from
Canton. . . .

—New York *Times*,
December 16, 1927.

PEOPLE OF SHANTUNG STARVE
AS ARMY PREYS ON PROVINCE

Famine stricken residents of Shantung province, where
babies are selling for a dollar apiece while their parents eat
bark from trees to sustain life. . . .

and a subhead

LITTLE INTEREST SHOWN BY WEALTHY CHINESE

—San Francisco *Call*,
April 22, 1928.

MILLIONS FIGHTING FOR LIFE IN CHINA
CONDITIONS IN REFUGEE CAMPS OF FLOODED
DISTRICT ALMOST BEGGAR DESCRIPTION.
HEAVY DEATH TOLL FEARED.

Conditions in some of the refugee camps . . . have been
revealed by official reports are, in the main, tales of such

horror as cannot be read without a shudder. . . . 20,000 people (in an area on the outskirts of Hankow) fully half of whom are sick, have no place to sleep except upon the soggy ground. Flies are almost as thick as swarming bees. Most of the sick people are suffering from dysentery, and there is no water to drink except what can be dipped from the river and this is stagnant and foul. . . .

—New York *Times*,
October 11, 1931.

CHOLERA KILLS 150,000 CHINESE

—New York *Times*,
September 7, 1932.

NEW NANKING LAW FREES CHILD SLAVES

The new anti-slave statute is recognized, even by the Chinese-language press, as merely another of the idealistic enactments so frequently promulgated by the Nanking [Chiang Kai-shek] Government. With virtually all of the provinces and cities unable to pay operating expenses, and with thousands of schools already closed because there is no money to pay the teachers, there is no money available for the founding of institutions to care for the ex-slaves even if they could be set free.

. . . always on the verge of starvation, there seems to be no way to prevent parents from selling their children into slavery. . . . Since only the well-to-do can afford to keep slaves, the children are probably better off than they would be if they had to starve in the mud huts of their parents.

—New York *Times*,
October 2, 1932.

30,000 CHINESE SLAIN IN MOSLEM REVOLT

. . . at least 30,000 Chinese in Northwestern Kansu province had been massacred . . . by roving bands of Mohammedans attempting to start a revolution against the Nationalist Government.

—AP, December 28, 1932.

36,704 DEAD CHINESE FOUND IN SHANGHAI

Bodies Buried Last Year by Public Benevolent Society Included 33,616 Infants.

—New York *Times*,
March 19, 1933.

In 1935, twelve million were suffering from famine in eight provinces, the victims being reduced to eating bark and roots. And in 1942:

Chinese are dying by the thousands in the battlefield province of Honan where 6,000,000 persons are reported to be on the verge of starvation as a result of one of the worst famines in modern times, missionaries and Chinese officials reported yesterday. . . .

Some 18,000,000 have become famine refugees, and the roads from Honan to Shensi and Hupeh provinces are strewn with the dead and dying. Many are eating grass and the bark of trees and selling their children to persons who can care for them, or leaving them to starve.

"Missionary reports give a stark tragic picture of thousands of stupefied refugees moving along roads in a hopeless search for food and shelter who are likened to a locust scourge as they sweep through drought villages and cause the villages to join them in their tragic trek." writes Harrison Forman of the *New York Times*.

—San Francisco *Call*,
October 1.

In 1943 Honan was hit again, with more than a million dying and five million reduced to eating grass, straw, and certain kinds of earth. In 1944, two million were starving in Hupeh province.

Year after year, in one area or another, catastrophe would overwhelm the lives of millions—and the government did nothing. We should not minimize Chiang's problems, they were heavy and complex. After 1938 the Japanese were occupying a large area of the country; the Communists gradually came into effective control of sizable areas of the north and northwest—and they were appealing to an ever-increasing number of adherents. Chiang was handicapped also by the sense of his own "indispensability" and his determination to have around him men distinguished for nothing but their unquestioning obedience. China's perennial disasters appeared in Chiang's eyes to be an immutable law of nature. Drought and flood, death and disease—that was China's fate. It had always been so. No vision of a new China emerging could energize him or communicate itself to his followers—a China that with the united efforts of her people and with the aid of modern technology might finally overcome her immemorial destiny of suffering.

Chiang's weaknesses were by now well known. His incapacities were blatant and obvious. The ineptitude of his regime was there for all to see. And yet, extraordinary though it may be, the "Chiang legend" continued to exert its spell. Even as shrewd and careful a politician-observer as Congressman (now Senate Majority Leader) Mike Mansfield, who was sent to China by President Roosevelt toward the end of World War II, failed to grasp the depth and extent of the hatred for Chiang that was developing in China; or that his eventual downfall was only a matter of time. Chiang was still China.

Reporting to Congress on his return, Mansfield said he thought the Generalissimo's "newly reorganized Government showed promise of accomplishing sorely needed reforms."

> Chiang is the one man who can make Chinese unity and independence a reality. His faults can be understood when the complexities of the Chinese puzzle are studied . . . and they are no more uncommon than the faults of the other leaders of the United Nations. We are committed to Chiang and we will help him to the best of our ability. He, and he alone, can untangle the present situation because in spite of some of the things he has done he is China.[2]

With the defeat of Japan in 1945 there was a brief period of optimism. British and American businessmen bustled back to Shanghai to reopen their offices and resume their trade. T. V. Soong, Madame Chiang's brother, was in charge of financial administration and the exchange rates set by him enabled these

[2] *Time*, January 22, 1945.

foreign enterprises to make enormous profits for a year or two. Large assets (mostly derived from U.S. aid) had been accumulated in China during the war and generous amounts of foreign exchange were granted for the importation of consumer goods, largely from the United States, and mostly luxury or semi-luxury goods for the wealthier people in the port cities. As China's postwar exports were negligible, this policy resulted in a heavy adverse balance of trade and eventual national bankruptcy.

While it lasted it was good. It was almost like old times.

But it wasn't like old times. For the Chinese by now had had enough. China was getting ready to rid herself once and for all of Chiang and all his gang.

The Chinese are essentially conservative by nature. Once established, a leader in China can count on the support of the people who will give him their loyalty unless he very clearly demonstrates by his ineptitude and injustice that he has forfeited the "mandate of Heaven." For millions Chiang was the national leader, they accepted him as the symbol of national unity. But more and more Chinese were in their hearts deciding that Heaven was no longer on his side.

Just when it was that the people's loyalty to Chiang began to crumble it is difficult to say. By the end of 1943 there was open discontent within his army; but the extent of this disaffection was minimized because of the greater menace of the Japanese.

> The peasants too had their fill of Chiang Kai-shek's government by 1944. His picture hung in government offices in every village, and his name was still a magic symbol, but the men who did his will among the peasants were hated and excoriated. As early as 1942 reports of peasant uprisings began to seep into the capital. These reports— half gossip, half fact—came from everywhere, from areas remote from Communist influence. Discontent was spreading through the hundreds of thousands of villages still under Kuomintang administration.[3]

And it was not only among the peasants . . .

> . . . The universities were suffering the heavy hand of the "te wu," the special secret police of the regime. Sudden

[3] *Thunder Out of China*, p. 131.

and secret arrests, mysterious disappearances, assassinations, a covert reign of terror prevailed in academic circles. Students were suspect, professors watched, freedom of thought, of publication and of speech suppressed. In so far as the choice between totalitarian and democratic government was concerned, it did not exist; the Chinese people groaned under a regime Fascist in every quality except efficiency. The Kuomintang had long lost the peasants; now they had cast away their only asset, the support of their scholars. . . .[4]

The civil war between Chiang and the Communists that followed Japan's defeat can now in retrospect be seen as historically inevitable. And its outcome, too. But at the time the Communist cause appeared hopeless. Chiang, it was thought, could deal with the Communists now that the Japanese were no longer there. His armies were large and well equipped with American weapons. And at first things went well.

Everywhere Chiang had victories. With the aid of American ships and planes, he quickly transported his best troops to all the large cities of North China and Manchuria while Red guerrillas raged at the gates. With ridiculous ease he cleared the countryside around Shanghai and Nanking and drove the vaunted Communist troops north of the Yellow River. "The Communists are babies; they don't know how to fight," said one Kuomintang officer. "The war will be over in three months," Chiang's top-ranking generals declared. American publications echoed these sentiments. . . .[5]

The optimism was soon spent.

Now in 1946 the tune changed. And, ironically enough, it was *Time* with an article on June 10, 1946, which was one of the first to confront the American public with some of the unpleasant facts.

BAD GOVERNMENT

. . . *the news from China was bad—appallingly bad. China was hurtling into economic disaster and political anarchy. Its*

---

[4] C. P. Fitzgerald, *Revolution in China* (New York: Frederick A. Praeger, 1952), p. 103.
[5] *China Shakes the World*, p. 9.

causes: (1) *Communist rebellion*; (2) *failure of the U.S. to send enough prompt aid*; (3) *the corrupt inefficiency of the National Government.* . . .

The most important truth about China is that hardly anybody in China seems to have any faith in the ability of the present Government to run the nation wisely, well or honestly.

Economically, China is decadent, living by an incestuous economy in which public officials sanction, if they are not leaders in, all depraving business practices of the day. It is an economy of printing-press inflation and Government-supported black markets. The inflation's effect on national morale was seen today in Nanking, when China's Supreme Court judges decided to strike for higher wages. They asked the Government to raise the basic pay of civil servants 1,000 times. . . .

The question finally starting to bother Americans in China is "sovereignty for what?" The sovereignty so far is one of greed, ineptitude and Government preserved by force. . . .

An ardently anti-communist American lawyer in Shanghai remarked to me the other night: "The Government is not a government. It is a dirty, venal lot of officials, trying to get what they can while the getting is good. . . ."

The Kuomintang has the military power to preserve itself now, but it cannot forever hold the lid on 400,000,000 unhappy people. If the Americans cannot somehow bring a liberal revolution within the Kuomintang, then it had better clear out. . . .

The present Government has been dissipating, selfishly and with utter callousness, American supplies and money. . . .

That was *Time's* account of Chiang Kai-shek's China in mid-1946.

In 1947, conditions were worse and by the end of that year Americans in China were complaining that business conditions were more and more impossible.

In that year, also, there occurred an event that illuminated, for a short and ghastly moment, the character of Chiang and his regime.

When Taiwan was liberated from the Japanese in 1945, the people there greeted their reunion with the mainland with immense enthusiasm. The islanders were very quickly disillusioned.

Beset by a carpetbagging administration, they found themselves virtually excluded from all government posts, which were given to Chiang's friends from the mainland. And here, as on the mainland, smuggling and black marketeering began to be widespread. Health services, which had been excellent under the Japanese, broke down under Chiang's inefficient rule. Cholera epidemics broke out for the first time in thirty years.

Resentment against Nanking's dictatorial regime became more and more intense. In March 1947 it broke out in widespread demonstrations. The government initially prevented general disorder by agreeing to several "temporary demands"—at the same time secretly sending troops over from the mainland. On March 9 the "Formosan Massacre" began. For nine days Kuomintang troops poured onto the island to take part in a brutal and prolonged attack against defenseless people.

The official account of the massacre, made by the American Ambassador J. Leighton Stuart (printed in full in the State Department's "White Paper," pp. 926–38), makes sickening reading. According to Stuart, on March 8 a Nationalist military commander on the island agreed that "the demands for political reforms in this province are very proper."

Continuing, the White Paper reveals: "Beginning March 9, there was widespread and indiscriminate killing. Soldiers were seen bayonetting coolies without apparent provocation in front of a Consulate staff residence."

Ambassador Stuart's report describes the systematic search and beheading of high school students; the machine-gunning of civilians, the numberless bodies floating in the harbor ("during the end of March and the first part of April. . . . The continuing presence of fresh bodies in Keelung Harbor and other evidence indicate that the elimination of the informed opposition is continuing"), the shots and screams that were heard at night . . .

That was an example of how Chiang Kai-shek dealt with those who asked for "very proper" reforms.

By 1948 American disenchantment with Chiang and his regime was virtually complete—with the exception of the extreme right wing.[6] On May 21, 1948, *U.S. News & World Report* expressed what many others had finally come to understand:

> The Kuomintang Party Government of Chiang consists exclusively of landlords, propertied war-lords and generals of one military clique or another, bankers who profit from wartime speculation and professional politicians vying for power.

As 1948 neared its end, *Business Week*, on November 20, carried an article by a correspondent in Shanghai who wrote:

> Over the years Chiang has alienated almost every economic group in China—peasants, labor, businessmen, and even his own soldiers. He has refused to undertake land reforms, has been unable to establish a sound currency, and is leader of an incompetent and graft-ridden civil administration and army. All these things have combined to deliver China into the waiting arms of the Communists.

The correspondent went on to report that some longtime residents in China—both businessmen and diplomats—hoped for something like the following five-point program for a new U.S.-China policy:

> "1. Use what's left of ECA funds for food relief wherever necessary.
> 2. Tell Chiang that he is finished, and that the U.S. is finished with him.
> 3. Make contact with the Communists as they take over, to see whether it is possible to do business with them. If so, begin trading.
> 4. Maintain similar contact with non-Communist areas, but keep relations on a strictly commercial basis.
> 5. Create a fund to finance legitimate reconstruction projects on a non-discriminatory basis. This fund should be held ready pending evidence of a sincere Communist desire to play ball."

[6] The period of disenchantment did not last long. Soon after Chiang's defeat and flight to Formosa in 1949, the very journals who had been most critical of him once more began to speak of him as "representing the real China," and encouraging the popular belief that the masses in China would welcome his return.

Thus, even some of the more conservative American observers finally had come at last to see what had been obvious to many in China for years.

It has become popular today to describe China falling to the Reds by default—a picture of a war-weary people ready to accept anything in place of the last chaotic days of a victimized and ineffectual Nationalist Government. Whatever element of truth this simple interpretation of the Chinese Revolution has, it fails to look at the causes of the revolutionary tide which was overwhelming China by 1949.

Some idea of what had caused the sweeping away of Chiang Kai-shek and all that he represented is to be found in the words of Jack Belden, a man who looked at China from his own experience—not only in the port cities, but among the peasantry in the vast hinterland:

> . . . Where Chiang Kai-shek had been successful previously in maintaining his rule over the Chinese people, it had been because the despair and the hate of the masses had not been sufficient to stir them out of their traditional apathy. When new conditions arose and the peasantry rose angrily with them, it was necessary that Chiang Kai-shek try to understand both the conditions and the emotions of the peasantry. He failed in both respects; in fact, he did not even try to understand the hearts of his own people. That is part of the inner history of Chiang Kai-shek's defeat and it is also part of the history of American policy in China. Neither the American government, the American press, nor the American people, nor many of their representatives in the Far East in the embassies, the military establishments and the business offices sought to look beyond their own narrow or personal interests toward the heart of the admittedly ignorant, but terribly emotional, bitter men and women of China.[7]

To suggest, as some of our leaders and press have continually suggested since 1949, that Chiang Kai-shek embodies all that is best in Chinese culture and tradition, is a grotesque distortion.

It is an insult to the Chinese people, most of whom loathe

[7] *China Shakes the World*, p. 5.

his name. It is an insult to Chinese culture and tradition. And it is an insult to the intelligence of Americans who know the facts.

How did it come about that the United States within a brief time after his defeat could once more be supporting a man so thoroughly discredited? And be backing him with all the moral, military, and financial influence of our great nation?

To find the answer we must recall the emotional climate of those days and look, however briefly, at a powerful group of Chiang's partisans in America who became known as "the China Lobby."

Chapter 4

THE CHINA LOBBY

No one who knows anything about the way things work
here doubts that a powerful China lobby has brought extraordinary influence to bear on Congress and the Executive.
It would be hard to find any parallel in diplomatic history
for the agents and diplomatic representatives of a foreign
power exerting such pressures—Nationalist China has used
the techniques of direct intervention on a scale rarely, if ever,
seen.

—Marquis Childs, Washington *Post*,
May 5, 1950.

I had forgotten, until I re-read the newspapers of that period,
the extent to which Chiang Kai-shek had forfeited the confidence
of some of his stanchest supporters in America. I have already
quoted the scathing reports by *Time* and *U.S. News & World
Report*, and the article in *Business Week* reporting a suggestion
that we "Tell Chiang that he is finished, and that the U.S. is
finished with him."

One result of this wide disillusionment with Chiang was that
by early 1950 an increasing number of influential voices were
openly urging the recognition of Communist China, and (until
the Korean War altered everything) it was generally taken for
granted that the new Chinese government, rather than Chiang's
group, would represent China in the United Nations.

Secretary Acheson has again assured Secretary-General Trygve
Lie that the United States will not use its veto power to

keep Communist China out of the United Nations. This has been our government's position from the start of the present controversy . . . we have at all times been willing to abide by a majority decision of the Security Council as to who shall represent China in the U.N.

—New York *Times*, editorial,
May 31, 1950.

Even John Foster Dulles, that arch foe of Communist China, in his book published in 1950, wrote:

> If the Communist Government of China in fact proves its ability to govern China without serious domestic resistance it, too, should be admitted to the United Nations. . . .
>
> Communist Governments today dominate more than 30 per cent of the population of the world. We may not like the fact; indeed, we do not like it at all. But if we want to have a *world* organization, then it should be representative of the world as it is.[1]

Only by recalling these attitudes prevailing before mid-1950 can we grasp the magnitude of the change that later took place in public sentiment toward China.

What caused such a tremendous shift of public opinion? In whose interests was it that such a change should take place?

With the loss of the mainland, Chiang Kai-shek became wholly dependent on the United States. From that moment he was a leader without a constituency, a head of state without a country. From then on, his regime had to play at being a great power though it had no power of its own. Chiang Kai-shek had lost his war in China. But one more battle confronted him, and the battlefield this time was in the United States. Chiang's very survival depended on his success in persuading Congress, the Executive, and the American public that it was in their interests to give him money, moral support, and military equipment.

This battle in America he won decisively.

Chiang had two circumstances in his favor. The first: that however rotten his own regime had become, the only alternative gov-

[1] *War or Peace* (New York: The Macmillan Company, 1950), pp. 190–91.

ernment in China was a Communist government. This made it easy for Chiang and his friends to complain that any criticism of the Nationalists was only aiding the Communists. It is only a small step from that to charge that those who voiced such criticism must themselves be Communist sympathizers.

The second circumstance in Chiang's favor was that he had already set up in America a well-financed group of Chinese officials and a number of paid agents who for nearly a decade had made it their business actively to promote the interests of the Nationalist government. Around these representatives and paid agents under Chiang's control, there had gathered an assortment of Americans who for a variety of reasons had sponsored Chiang's cause, and who now, at the moment of his defeat, were more passionately his partisans than ever.

It is not my intention to deal at great length with the activities of the pro-Chiang groups, which collectively have been known as "the China Lobby." But no understanding of our present relations with China is possible without some knowledge of the immensely powerful, usually secret pressures that this lobby was able to exert. *The activities of the China Lobby constituted an alien interference with the processes of government and the formation of public opinion in the United States that had never before or since been attempted on so ambitious a scale.*

What *is* the China Lobby?

Essentially it is a partnership between agents of the Chiang Kai-shek government and Americans who share the belief that Chiang should be given full support by the United States and who, collectively and individually, have exerted political pressure to gain their ends.

The Chinese partners are representatives of a government that relies for its very life on the continued financial and military aid of the United States and which could never hope to regain control of the mainland unless America can be persuaded to champion an all-out war against the Communist regime. Closely controlled and lavishly financed by the Nationalist government, the Chinese partners employ paid lobbyists, public relations experts, and personal persuasion at the highest levels of the American power structure.

The American partners are an assorted lot—honest men deeply concerned with the plight of the Chinese people; businessmen whose aim is to regain the lucrative commercial interests that they lost with the defeat of Chiang; fanatics; and politicians who are ready to use any issue, especially the fear of international Communism, in their hunt for personal power. Never closely knit, but bound by common objectives, these Americans form an amorphous group that on one level has all the skill of the professional manipulator, and on another, can rely on the goodwill of well-intentioned and innocent amateurs.

There has been a consistent attempt, of course, on the part of the supporters of Chiang Kai-shek to deny the existence of any pressure groups acting on his behalf. Taking note of these denials, Cabell Phillips, in a Washington dispatch to the New York *Times*, wrote: "That such a thing as a 'China Lobby' exists is indisputable in the minds of most observers."[2]

Documentary evidence of a China Lobby to meet even the most rigid technical definition is found in a special report issued by the *Congressional Quarterly Weekly Report*.[3] This authoritative journal listed ten registered agents of the Nationalist Chinese government and seven more whose registration had recently been terminated. (There are as we shall see, many other organizations, businesses, and individuals in the United States not registered as foreign agents but actively promoting the cause of Chiang.)

One of the surprising features of the China Lobby is how little has been written about it. Many of its operations, of course, are secret, but even during the years when the Lobby was most influential, much of the American press remained silent. Though sporadic articles by Drew Pearson and others about the Lobby do from time to time appear, there has never been, in any large-circulation journal, anything in the way of a full exposure. *The Reporter* magazine in April 1952 devoted two issues to a very full account of the Lobby's structure and activities, but otherwise,

[2] April 30, 1950.
[3] A special supplement, "The China Lobby: A Case Study," June 29, 1951.

as far as I know, no large-circulation newspaper or popular magazine apparently has brought these alien activities to the attention of the American public in an extended form.[4]

There were two stages in the development of the China Lobby. The first, the World War II phase, was born in 1940 when China stood alone against the invading Japanese. In the summer of that year T. V. Soong, brother of Madame Chiang Kai-shek, arrived in Washington where he remained until 1943. Soong, educated at Harvard and Columbia, had earlier been Minister of Finance in China and later was to become Foreign Minister. By 1940, Soong had already amassed a personal fortune. (By 1944 a former friend estimated his holdings in the U.S. alone at $47 million.) He was a man of great social charm and intelligence, with a flair for exotic and expensive gestures. For example, in the spring of 1946, his wife, to whom he was devoted, fell ill. Soong chartered a private plane in Nanking to fly to Connecticut to pick up a cargo of dogwood of which Madame Soong was particularly fond. The bouquet must have cost between twenty and thirty thousand dollars.[5]

Soong, on his arrival in Washington in 1940, held no official title. But his mission was clear enough—to get more American help for the Chinese government. His major assistant was Ludwig Rajchman, a Pole who had been a League of Nations health expert.

> T. V. Soong and Ludwig Rajchman sized up Washington rapidly when they arrived in 1940. Each of them had a highly developed genius for understanding how the disparate

[4] *The Reporter* magazine ran these articles in their issues of April 15 and 29, 1952. These were in large part part written by Charles Wertenbaker, who was previously Foreign Editor of *Time*.

A longer account of the activities and structure of the China Lobby is contained in a book by Dr. Ross Y. Koen, assistant professor of Political Science at Humboldt State College, California. This book, *The China Lobby in American Politics*, was published in 1960 by Macmillan but has not yet been made available to the public.

Though it has still, nearly three years later, not been reissued for public sale, copies can occasionally be found in libraries.

Both *The Reporter* articles and Dr. Koen's book indicate very careful research and both are profusely documented.

[5] *The Reporter*, April 15, 1952.

parts of a complicated structure like a government bureaucracy fit together. They soon saw that official Washington was a jungle of departments, often with overlapping functions and the usual hostility toward one another. The best way to get something done was to collect influential friends who could circumvent or overwhelm opposition.[6]

Soong made many "influential friends." He developed close contacts with Harry Hopkins (the White House), Henry Morgenthau (the Treasury), and powerful journalists such as Henry Luce (*Time, Life,* etc.), Roy Howard (Scripps-Howard newspapers), and the columnist Joseph Alsop. So close were Soong's associations with important people that he was reported to have once told a State Department official: "There is practically nothing that goes on in your government of which I do not learn within three days." Though he had at this time no official title, he often acted for the Chinese government. There is a story that when an American official questioned Soong's authority to sign a document for his country, Soong replied: "I *am* China."

The activities of Chiang's representatives and agents did not go unnoticed. On May 7, 1947, for example, Representative George Bender (later Republican Senator from Ohio), during a debate on the Truman Greek-Turkey aid program, told Congress of the "intense pressure placed upon our State Department."

> I charge here on the floor of the House that the Chinese Embassy has had the arrogance to invade our State Department and attempt to tell our State Department that the Truman Doctrine has committed our Government and this Congress to all-out support of the present Fascist Chinese Government.[7]

And on August 25, 1949, Representative Mike Mansfield, in the course of a long speech (which I will refer to again later), in which he discussed the misuse of U.S. aid funds by Chinese officials, demanded that the Lobby Investigating Committee:

> . . . investigate the activities of the lobby now brazenly being conducted in this country in behalf of the National

[6] *The Reporter,* April 15, 1952.
[7] Congressional Record.

Government of China and certain personalities connected with it.[8]

A second and far more active phase in the development of the China Lobby had already begun at the end of 1948 when the Chiang regime was beginning to fall apart.

Madame Chiang arrived in the United States on December 1, 1948. It was her job to reorganize Chiang's partisans in this country. Until she left, more than a year later, to join her defeated husband on Taiwan, her task was to mobilize the most influential Chinese in the United States and to promote all the American support that she could.

Operating from the pleasant Riverdale home (near New York, where many wealthy Chinese had homes) of her brother-in-law, H. H. Kung (head of the Bank of China and one of the wealthiest men in the world), Madame Chiang held weekly strategy meetings. The men who attended these sessions fell into two main groups. One, to which H. H. Kung and her brother T. V. Soong belonged, operated from and in New York, and included men of wealth rather than government officials. The other, which worked in Washington, was composed of Chiang's most trusted chiefs of missions.

These two groups represented the inner core of the China Lobby.

> This was no ordinary group of political refugees. The Formosa regime was something more than a standard twentieth-century government-in-exile and something a good deal less than a real national government. It had found shelter on the island of Formosa, but it didn't want and couldn't hope to stay there forever. It had to go back to China or out of existence. The Kuomintang was eager to resume the fight, and its only hope was U. S. assistance on a gigantic scale. . . .
>
> Peace for them was unendurable and unthinkable; at all costs, America too had to be made to see that a third world war was inevitable.[9]

[8] Ibid.
[9] *The Reporter*, April 29, 1952.

The Riverdale meetings hammered out the line of action that the re-energized China Lobby would follow. Chiang's defeat on the mainland must by now have been seen as inescapable. With reports from China bringing almost nothing but news of military disasters, the meetings in Riverdale must often have been held in an atmosphere of tense urgency.

The strategy that was worked out was the only one possible in the circumstances: First and above all, Chiang had to go back and if Chiang was to go back, it was necessary to persuade Americans that a strong and friendly China under Chiang was essential to their own security. To make this acceptable, it would be necessary to convince the American people that Chiang's defeat by the Communists was not due to his own ineptitudes. Chiang was defeated because the American government had failed to give him adequate support, and this because of "treachery" and "betrayal" in the American government itself.

It is probable, judging by subsequent actions, that more precisely defined objectives were also hammered out at these strategy meetings.

Dean Acheson, who as the Secretary of State was resisting the pressures of Chiang's partisans, must go. It was important, also, to discredit General Marshall, for it was Marshall who on his mission to China in 1945–46 had, they believed, attempted to bring about a settlement between the Nationalists and the Communists; it was on Marshall's recommendation that in 1947 $500 million earmarked for China by the Export-Import Bank was allowed to lapse. Then there were the China specialists (both in and out of the State Department)—they, too, had to be removed from positions of influence. These experts had seen the true conditions of China under Chiang. It was they who had urged that Chiang be made to institute basic social and economic reforms, if defeat was to be avoided. These experts, especially those in the State Department, were in a position to exert great influence on national policy. So they, too, had to be removed.

Those, then, were the large and ambitious objectives of the inner core of the China Lobby.

Among the seventeen registered agents paid by the Chinese to help further their plans were the following, according to the *Congressional Quarterly*:

Allied Syndicates, Inc., a New York public relations firm that received $50,000 in fees and $10,000 in expenses from its client, the Bank of China. (The Bank also retained David B. Charney, another public relations expert, at an annual fee of $75,000.)[10]

The Universal Trading Corporation, whose purpose ostensibly was to promote trade between the U.S. and Nationalist China, was listed as a foreign agent working for the Nationalists. This corporation had assets of $21,674,751 in 1949. Another registered agent working for Chiang's government was the China Institute in America, Inc. Henry R. Luce (of *Time, Life*, etc.) was listed as a trustee and an officer of the organization. The Chinese News Service (with headquarters in New York and offices in Washington, Chicago, and San Francisco) was another agent. Its functions included "disseminating of news and information through press releases including *This Week in Free China*." Its operations in the U.S. were under direct supervision of the Ministry of Information of the Nationalist government. The Central News Agency was another registered agent, which was wholly owned by the Nationalist government. It listed total expenditures between 1945 and 1951 as $1,114,355; but Senator Wayne Morse, during the MacArthur hearings, drew the attention of Congress to this agency which, Morse said, between 1946 and 1949 was alleged to have "spent in the neighborhood of $654 million to influence American public opinion."[11]

The Nationalists supported two Chinese-language newspapers in the U.S. One of these, *Chinese Nationalist Daily*, stated that its purpose was to serve as the "official organ" of the Kuomintang and answer all criticisms of the Chinese Nationalist government by newspaper editorials and articles.

An individual listed by the *Congressional Quarterly* as being an agent of the Nationalists was William J. Goodwin, who in

[10] New York *Times*, April 30, 1950.
[11] U. S. Congress, Senate Committee on Armed Services and Committee on Foreign Relations. *Hearings, Military Situation in the Far East*, p. 2117.

1948 worked for the National Resources Commission of China.
His salary was $30,000 and he received $28,857 in expenses. From
July 1949 to March 1950 he received $25,000 as an agent for the
Chinese News Service, plus $9,776 in expenses. He was also listed
as a lobbyist with Congress. The Washington *Post* of September
18, 1949, threw some light on Mr. Goodwin's activities:

> In less than two years, according to Justice Department
> records, Goodwin has contracted for $65,000 from the Na-
> tionalist Government, first to get help from the United
> States, then to influence leaders of thought and urge them
> to approve larger measures of American support and material
> aid.

The Reporter, too, discussed Mr. Goodwin's activities:

> In an interview with Edward R. Harris of the St. Louis
> *Post-Dispatch* . . . Goodwin estimated that he had en-
> tertained about a hundred Congressmen a year, converted
> at least fifty of them to support more aid for Nationalist
> China. . . . At one of Mr. Goodwin's dinners for Con-
> gressmen, a high [Chinese] Embassy official briefed a group
> of Senators on the reasons why W. Walton Butterworth . . .
> should not be confirmed as Assistant Secretary of State.[12]

Some of these paid agents injected themselves directly into the
political life of America. For example, Mr. Leo Casey, an employee
of Allied Syndicates, Inc., a registered Chinese Nationalist agent,
went to California to help Richard Nixon in his campaign against
Helen Gahagan Douglas in the race for U. S. Senator from California.

> Mr. Casey organized an "Independent Voters Commit-
> tee for Nixon." He worked hard, he says, to attract the
> Negro vote, on which Mrs. Douglas, a liberal, was counting
> heavily. Since Mrs. Douglas had also been a sharp critic
> of the House Un-American Activities Committee, he also
> played up Mr. Nixon's part in the investigation leading
> to the conviction of Alger Hiss. His job well done and
> Mr. Nixon elected, Mr. Casey went back to New York.[13]

According to *The Reporter* Mr. Casey was shocked when he

[12] *The Reporter*, April 15, 1952.
[13] *The Reporter*, April 15, 1952.

learned after his return that his trip to California was for "the China account."

One of the busiest American members of the China Lobby was the late Mr. Alfred Kohlberg. Mr. Kohlberg was the head of a successful, $1 million a year, business that imported textiles from China. Kohlberg in time became an important figure in the China Lobby. He, too, gave support to politicians with the "right" views about Chiang. The *Congressional Quarterly* Special Supplement reported that he made a large campaign contribution to Styles Bridges (R.-N.H.) in 1948. Kohlberg subsidized a journal called *Plain Talk* (later the *Freeman*), through which he attacked the Institute of Pacific Relations, of which he was a member, the "pro-Soviet group" in the China section of the State Department, General Marshall, Owen Lattimore, General Stilwell, Henry Wallace, and others. After withdrawing from the Institute of Pacific Relations, he set up a competing organization: "The American China Policy Association."

> Through his China Policy Association and his magazine *Plain Talk* (later the *Freeman*), through his friends and fellow enthusiasts . . . Alfred Kohlberg was rapidly becoming a principal peddler of pro-Nationalist propaganda. Above all, he was spreading . . . his uninhibited version of the State Department "conspiracy." And so, in the winter of 1949–1950, not long before Senator McCarthy's first barrage, T. V. Soong sought out Mr. Kohlberg.[14]

And money for all this?

There was never a shortage of funds as far as the China Lobby was concerned. Before Chiang's defeat enormous sums of money were being transferred from China to the United States and were made available for pro-Chiang activities.

And—ironically—most of this money came from the United States in the first place!

On August 25, 1949, Representative Mike Mansfield addressed himself to this issue on the floor of the House of Representatives.

[14] *The Reporter*, April 29, 1952.

Into the Congressional Record he read an article from the *U.S. News & World Report* to be published the following day:

> "The effort to find out what really happened to the $4,350,000,000 of American taxpayers' money given to China since 1941 is leading investigators to great personal fortunes amassed by a few Chinese.

> "Story behind the White Paper is that a few Chinese highly placed in Generalissimo Chiang Kai-shek's Government have built up fortunes running into hundreds of millions of dollars. They are fortunes comparable to those made by Americans in the period of this country's industrial growth. But Americans, owing to United States law, no longer can acquire wealth in the amounts amassed by Chinese who profited from United States aid to China.

> "On the receiving end of the aid was a one-party government dominated by Chiang Kai-shek and small cliques of his relatives and friends.

The *U.S. News* article cited the case of the $220 million shipment of U.S. gold which turned up in the hands of insiders who made hundreds of millions in profits. It also referred to $200 million in U.S. currency sent to redeem Chinese savings certificates—insiders grabbed up the savings certificates and got hold of the U.S. dollars. Its story as read into the Congressional Record continued:

> "Automobile and truck parts, radio and electrical equipment, blankets and GI rations even blood plasma, which was sent from the United States to the Chinese Army were sold by and to civilians. Wealthy Chinese whose connections inside the Nationalist Government enabled them to divert these supplies from military channels reaped handsome profits. Some of the Material was actually purchased by Communist agents.

> "United States relief supplies and economic aid to Chinese cost American taxpayers more than $2 billion. But much went to profiteers. . . . Rice supplied by the U.S. for famine relief was resold to rich Chinese.

> "Taking out the profits made from United States aid to China was an operation that began about 1946 and still continues. Hundreds of millions of dollars in gold and

foreign currency were smuggled out through British Hong Kong and Portuguese Macao. More was carried by Chinese with diplomatic passports carrying Chinese government pouches. Huge fortunes were assembled in Zurich, Buenos Aires, New York, San Francisco and other cities out of reach of the Chinese people whom the United States sought to help. Most owners of the fortunes have fled China too."

Having quoted this article, Mansfield demanded an investigation:

> I suggest that this committee seek to determine whether American money, originally appropriated to aid the Chinese Government, illicitly diverted to private use by the method described above, is actually used to promote new legislation for aid to China by which more money would be made available.
>
> I suggest that this committee inquire into whether American money provided to help China, but siphoned off for private use by the method described above, is being used to finance attacks on our Secretary of State and other officials charged with continuing our relations with China.[15]

Other critics also asserted that the China Lobby may have been using U.S. aid funds to further its purposes. Senator Morse, during the MacArthur hearings (p. 2117), spoke about the Nationalist officials and generals who made fortunes in graft on American loans and that it was:

> reasonable to assume that some of this money is being used to finance propaganda . . . chiefly to promote more money going to Chiang and Chiang forces. This suggests to some a closed circuit of American dollars flowing from Congress to the Nationalists and back again in the form of alleged activities for still more money for Chiang.

Senator Morse in this speech also referred to the $654 million alleged to have been spent by the Central News Agency to "influence American public opinion."

In the summer of 1949, $800,000 was transferred from Formosa to New York for financing the work of the China Lobby. And further funds were made available not long after that.

[15] Congressional Record, August 25, 1949.

> Ever since 1949, the official financing of the Lobby has centered largely in Washington. . . . Before Madame Chiang left the United States early in 1950, she arranged for a fund of more than a million dollars, then under the direct control of the Chinese National Resources Commission, to be put at the disposal of Counselor of Embassy Chen Chih-mai. General Pee, the military attache, who reports directly to Chiang Kai-shek, also draws large funds independently of the Embassy.[16]

The China Lobby, it is quite clear, was never short of cash.

Thus Chiang Kai-shek, though defeated by his own countrymen, could look with some confidence toward America. His wife's presence there for over a year had brought new vitality to his supporters. Objectives had been defined, strategy planned. The members of the inner core, many of them Chinese of exceptional intelligence and of high standing, some of them Chiang's own relatives, had established close contacts with men at the very pinnacle of the American power structure. His agents, public relations experts, and lobbyists, skilled in the methods of influencing people, were employed and busy—and there was almost limitless money available for their activities. And around this inner core of Chiang's supporters were Americans of all kinds—well intentioned private citizens, publishers of large circulation journals, writers, businessmen, politicians—ready and anxious for all manner of reasons to promote the cause of Chiang and his Nationalist regime.

But Chiang in his moments of wildest optimism could never have dreamed how successful his Lobby would be. Nor would they have been so successful if their period of supreme effort had not coincided with a mood of bewilderment and bitter recrimination that just then was sweeping the United States.

While it is true that in the last few years of his regime there was growing disenchantment with Chiang, the "loss" of China nevertheless came as a tremendous shock to the American people. Americans simply could not bring themselves to believe that the

16 *The Reporter*, April 29, 1952.

Chinese, however rotten their leadership, could have preferred a Communist government.

With Chiang's defeat came tumbling a century of American hopes. The years of service of so many well-meaning Americans—all for nothing. The bright dream of one day bringing the Chinese into the Christian community—gone for good. The carefully calculated expectations of building a friendly China as a bulwark against Russia—now meaningless. The banks, the oil companies, the special commercial privileges, the profits, all now to be abandoned. And the vast China market made available to our Communist enemies rather than ourselves.

The true nature and deep roots of the Chinese revolutionary movement had never been fully grasped in America. Lack of information had left the American people unprepared either to intervene in sufficient strength to thwart the revolution, while that was still possible (if it ever was), or to accept the final result when it came. Americans had for so long accustomed themselves to thinking of the Chinese as their friends, they felt they had done so much for China, they had such high hopes of her future, that it had never really entered their minds that one day the Chinese might have other plans of their own.

How true was it that we could have "saved" Chiang if we had tried harder and had given him more?

Walter Lippmann summed up the opinion of the generals this way:

> On the prospects of Chiang and his government, the judgment of all the generals was the same. None thought that Chiang would win, all were convinced that Chiang was losing the civil war. Marshall's estimate supported Stilwell's and Wedemeyer's supported Marshall's and Barr's report confirmed the estimate. The generals differed, however, on what to do about Chiang. Stilwell's conclusion was that we should abandon him. . . . Wedemeyer's conclusion . . . was that we should take charge of the Chinese government and of the civil war. Marshall's decision . . . was that we could not abandon Chiang but that neither could we take over his powers, his responsibilities and his liabilities.
>
> —New York *Herald Tribune,*
> September 8, 1949.

But whatever America might or might not have done—it was now too late. Our friends had now become Communists, and to Americans at this time all Communist movements were mere extensions of Soviet power. So to disappointments and bitterness there was added a component of fear. The defection of a quarter of the world's population to the camp of the enemy was a shattering national blow.

Within a year of Chiang's defeat G.I.'s were dying in Korea before Chinese guns, with sixty-five thousand American casualties in the first year. As hopes of a quick victory in Korea faded and bitterness and frustration grew, an ever-larger number of Americans turned their anger on their own officials. The spokesmen for the China Lobby they felt were right after all. Chiang's defeat, and all that flowed from it, could have had only one cause—betrayal and treason in Washington. The conviction of Alger Hiss in 1950 (though he had been out of public service for four years and the activities about which he committed perjury had occurred thirteen years earlier) added to the fears of a Communist conspiracy within our own ranks.

And it was during this period of bewilderment and mutual recrimination that Chiang's partisans and expert manipulators gained a powerful ally.

On January 7, 1950 an obscure Senator from Wisconsin by the name of Joe McCarthy was dining with three companions (none of whom knew him very well) at the Colony Restaurant in Washington. McCarthy had been elected in 1946. His reputation was uninspiring.

He had got himself involved with some dubious lobbying practices.[17] He had had a brush with the Wisconsin Department of

---

[17] For example, one week before the Senate Investigating Committee began investigating the Lustron Company, that had borrowed $37,500,000 from the Reconstruction Finance Corporation, Senator McCarthy (a member of the Investigating Committee) received a check for $10,000 from the Lustron Company. This was ostensibly for payment of a pamphlet (the rate of payment works out at $1.43 a word, something of a world record) which it turned out later McCarthy did not write. Full details of this and other McCarthy shenanigans can be found in the exhaustively documented book, *McCarthy: The Man, the Senator, the "Ism"* by Jack Anderson and Ronald W. May (Boston: The Beacon Press, 1952).

Taxation.[18] Word of his questionable practices was beginning to circulate in Wisconsin. McCarthy, very rightly, realized that unless he did something to endear himself to his constituents in Wisconsin his election next time might not be as easy as his first had been.

Richard Rovere, in his excellent book *Senator Joe McCarthy*,[19] describes this dinner at the Colony and how McCarthy confided to his companions that he stood in need of a dramatic issue for the 1952 election. One of his companions

> suggested that McCarthy come forward as a champion of the St. Lawrence Seaway. McCarthy said he didn't think that would do. He asked the others what they thought about some up-to-date variant of the Townsend Plan—a hundred dollars a month pension, say, to everyone over sixty-five. The others disapproved—too demagogic, they felt. Father Walsh [one of the four] then suggested Communism—its power in the world at large and its capacity for subversion. McCarthy seized upon the idea at once and at once began, according to one of the participants, to vulgarize. "That's it," he said. "The government is full of Communists," he said. "We can hammer away at them."[20]

A month later, on February 9, Joe McCarthy spoke to a group of ladies at the Ohio County Women's Republican Club at Wheeling, West Virginia. And with that speech began McCarthy's brief and terrible passage across the pages of American history.

> "While I cannot take the time (said McCarthy at Wheeling) to name all of the men in the State Department who have been named as members of the Communist Party and members of a spy ring, I have here in my hand a list of two hundred and five that were known to the Secretary of State as being members of the Communist Party and who nevertheless are still working and shaping the policy of the State Department."[21]

[18] McCarthy had filed no returns with the Wisconsin Department of Taxation on stock market earnings in 1943, claiming that in that year he was not a resident of Wisconsin but a tail-gunner in the South Pacific. The Department forced him to pay up $2677.
[19] New York: Harcourt, Brace, 1959, pp. 122–23.
[20] Ibid., p. 122.
[21] Ibid., p. 125.

The witch-hunt was on!

The speech, based on a brazen falsehood, was itself an extraordinary performance, and it seems that no one was more surprised than McCarthy at the furor it caused. Challenged to justify his charges, he attempted to do so on the floor of the Senate.

It was, Rovere wrote,

> a flabbergasting performance, lasting from late afternoon almost until midnight . . . McCarthy, growing hoarser, redder, and less coherent, shuffled about the idiotic "dossiers" that were spread untidily over two desks and that were plainly as foreign to him as they were to other Senators. Scott Lucas interrupted sixty-one times, mainly in a futile effort to make McCarthy straighten out his mixed-up figures. Brian McMahon . . . made thirty-four vain attempts to have McCarthy submit to a testing of his claims against reason and evidence. . . . Other Senators tried, too, but it was useless. He would not explain, he would not amplify, he would not qualify. . . .[22]

It was this man who, incredibly, from then on for four fateful years, dominated the American political scene. "No bolder seditionist," wrote Rovere, "ever moved among us—nor any politician with a surer, swifter access to the dark places of the American mind." He stamped with his name a whole appalling era of our history, and many of the suspicions and fears which he kindled are smoldering with us still. Abroad his name became associated with all that was considered evil in our American society. By riding roughshod over accepted practices, all established values, McCarthy in these few years inflicted incalculable damage to the democratic structure and the decencies of American life. He disregarded the Constitution. Operating within his senatorial immunity, he dragged into the mud the names and reputations of some of the finest and noblest of men. He usurped judicial authority and executive function. Because of McCarthy innocent men and women found their lives ruined, their careers in shambles. His power was such that he was able to challenge, without basis, the loyalty of men in the highest offices of the nation, and before his threats even the mighty military establishment groveled.

[22] Ibid., pp. 133–34.

He held two presidents captive—or as nearly captive as any Presidents of the United States have ever been held; in the conduct of the nation's affairs, Harry S. Truman and Dwight D. Eisenhower, from early 1950 through late 1954, could never act without weighing the effect of their plans upon McCarthy and the forces he led, and in consequence there were times when, because of this man, they could not act at all. He had an enormous impact on American foreign policy at a time when that policy bore heavily on the course of world history, and American diplomacy might bear a different aspect today if McCarthy had never lived.[23]

What gave McCarthy his extraordinary power? *He had the ear of the people.* Though for four years he failed to identify a single Communist, his voice expressed the hidden suspicions and unconscious frustrations of millions. McCarthyism was bipartisan and McCarthy had more admirers among manual workers than any other group. To many (in the words of one of his great supporters, Fulton Lewis, Jr.), "McCarthyism is Americanism." At one time 50 percent of the American people had a "favorable opinion" of this bully and fraud, and another 21 percent had "no opinion" of him. And with this fantastic support of the people behind him, he managed to degrade the political life of his nation. For four years attention was riveted on matters of "loyalty risks" and "security clearances," "loyalty oaths" and "treason," and administrations vied with each other to see which would dismiss the largest number of unworthy civil servants.

> "We are kicking the Communists and fellow travellers and security risks out of the Government . . . by the thousands," the Vice-President of the United States said. It happened to be a fact that not one certifiable Communist had been disclosed as working for the government—though quite possibly there were a few. But this was not the worst of it. The worst was that McCarthy and McCarthyism had led us to think that the health of the state was war against clerks of dubious patriotism.[24]

The China Lobby and McCarthy needed each other.
The pro-Chiang partisans had been denouncing Communism

23 Ibid., p. 5.
24 Ibid., p. 18.

for years, but they had never captured the public's imagination. Kohlberg had talked loudly and long about the "Communist conspiracy in the State Department," but he reached only a relatively small audience. Here at last was a man "with guts enough and dumb enough," as Kohlberg was to phrase it later, "to accuse the makers of foreign policy of being traitors."[25]

Soon after McCarthy's outburst at Wheeling, Kohlberg met the Senator for the first time. McCarthy had the headlines and needed ammunition. Kohlberg had never made the headlines but had all the ammunition that was needed. The Senator was soon furnished with all of Kohlberg's articles, releases, and charges. And McCarthy made use of them. And Goodwin, the foreign agent, also boasted that he had "helped materially" to lay the groundwork for McCarthy's attacks on the State Department.[26]

> To right wingers of all shades all over the country, China suddenly, under Senator McCarthy's impetus, became the magic issue that might finally provide the road to power. . . . Throughout 1950 and 1951 the chorus from the Right and even from some sections of the Center and Left grew shriller and shriller. Kohlberg could well be pleased with his part in preparing the score. "I am proud," he declared, "to have given Senator McCarthy a small part of the information he gathered for his fight. . . ." A year later he had only one reservation about the Senator. "He doesn't go far enough," Kohlberg remarked. "He's too cautious about using his information."[27]

In their book, *McCarthy: The Man, the Senator, and the "Ism,"* Anderson and May draw attention to the McCarthy-China Lobby relationship. The "press and the public were so blinded by the fireworks of Joe's broadsides," they wrote, "that no one seemed to notice where he was getting his ammunition."

> With startling regularity, the key targets of Joe's attacks turned out to be State Department officials who had opposed the Open Pocketbook policy toward Nationalist China. Certain men had questioned the ability of Chiang's demoralized

25 *The Reporter*, April 29, 1952.
26 *McCarthy: The Man, the Senator, and the "Ism,"* p. 198.
27 *The Reporter*, April 29, 1952.

armies to defend the Chinese mainland; they had reported that American aid money was being diverted into the pockets of corrupt Nationalist officials. And they ended up on McCarthy's Red list.

As scraps of information bubbled to the surface, it became clear that the campaign against Chiang's critics had originated with the "China Lobby."[28]

Those who were even remotely connected with the "loss" of China were especially singled out. The campaign to discredit the China specialists and scholars outside of government service was carried on by McCarthy and the China Lobby unceasingly for four years, and the reputation and influence of many of them were destroyed.

Even more prolonged and bitter attacks were leveled at the China specialists in the State Department. For having written, in the course of duty in China, factual reports about the growing strength of Communists, and the true conditions in the areas under Chiang, career officers were pilloried for being "pro-Communist." Some of the most highly trained and intelligent Foreign Service officers were subjected to humiliating attacks and indignities. Some had to submit to as many as eight loyalty hearings. Before long nearly all the career officers in the State Department who had been critical of Chiang Kai-shek were suspended or fired or had resigned. Almost none of the China-trained experts remained in positions where they could have used their knowledge and experience to modify U.S. policies. From the China Lobby-McCarthy alliance, the Foreign Service of the United States received a wound from which it will take many more years fully to recover.

It is generally conceded today that McCarthy could never have gained his brief but horribly destructive ascendancy if the newspapers had not bestowed publicity on him so lavishly. He did not, it is true, receive much active editorial support. What help of this kind that he got from the press came mainly from the Chicago *Tribune*, the Washington *Times-Herald*, and the Hearst chain.

[28] *McCarthy: The Man, the Senator, and the "Ism,"* pp. 191–92.

Nearly all the other papers were openly opposed to McCarthy and his tactics.

But it was not support but publicity that McCarthy thrived on —and the press gave him plenty of it. During his period of power the name McCarthy appeared more often on the teletyped stories coming into newspaper offices from Washington than the name of any other Senator. For long stretches at a time, the press made him the central figure in American politics—and McCarthy on his part did his best to provide the press with headlines.

The press was caught in a peculiar difficulty—which McCarthy was shrewd enough to use for his own ends. His charges *were* news, though they might also be lies. As Walter Lippmann once wrote:

> McCarthy's charges of treason, espionage, corruption, perversions are news that cannot be suppressed or ignored. . . . When he makes such attacks against the State Department or Defense Department it is news which has to be published.[29]

But, of course, it was also news that a United States Senator was lying and defrauding the people and the government—but that news did not, until long after, reach the headlines.

> The American press was simply not set up so that it could feature a "McCARTHY LIES" story alongside a "McCARTHY SAYS" story.[30]

The difficulty may be real, but in the light of all the damage that McCarthy brought, the excuse seems lame.

Thus by skill, by luck, by money, by ruthlessness, because of the shock of Chiang's defeat, because of the bitterness of the Korean War, because of McCarthy's help when his help was powerful, Chiang Kai-shek's partisans succeeded to a great extent in controlling America's China policy.

It is in any event a fact that both Secretary of State Dean Acheson and his immediate predecessor General Marshall testified during the Senate hearings on Far Eastern policy that they would

[29] Quoted by Rovere, *Senator Joe McCarthy*, p. 166.
[30] Ibid.

never so much as *consider* the recognition of Communist China
or support its admission to the United Nations.

> They assured the Senate that the very idea of recognition
> was so abhorrent to them and to other American diplomats
> that it was never even *discussed* in the Department of State,
> which simply was not the truth. Pressed further, they made a
> pledge, which they were in no position to keep, that the
> United States would never offer recognition. Deception,
> stupidity, stubbornness, and a commitment in perpetuity—
> these were the lengths to which McCarthy and McCarthyism
> drove these intelligent men.[31]

And at this point the rudder jammed.

Our China policy became immovable, and has remained immovable to this day. Our China policy, after more than a decade,
is not only immovable but also, on any effective political level,
almost undiscussable.

Why?

At least part of the answer lies in the fact that *the China Lobby
still exists*. Under different forms, and with a somewhat different
cast of characters, the influence of Chiang's supporters in America
is still immensely powerful, and no doubt funds for its activities
are still available in ample supply.

At the end of the Korean War a bipartisan organization—as
it were, a lobby within a lobby—was created to oppose Communist China's representation in the UN. Its title, effective but misleading, is the Committee of One Million against the Admission
of Communist China to the United Nations. This Committee is
now one of the principal spokesmen of those who espouse the
cause of Nationalist China.

Professor Urban Whitaker, of San Francisco State College, spent
a year in 1961 as a Rockefeller Fellow studying the China question.
After two long interviews with Mr. Marvin Liebman, Executive
Secretary of the Committee of One Million, he was able to throw
some light on its activities and policies.

> For years the Committee of One Million has existed mainly
> on public relations. It has never had a million members. Its

31 Rovere, *Senator Joe McCarthy*, p. 14.

own official history states that, as of 1961, it had only 6,000 contributing members. For all the suggestiveness of its clever name, the committee finds it appropriate to print no more than 25 to 35 thousand copies of the various brochures it publishes from time to time. It does not appear to be short of funds, however, and has long been one of America's most effective pressure groups. Its most powerful instrument is its promise to focus the full emotional power of anti-Communist public agitation against the candidacy of any person opposing the committee's views on China.[32]

If this Committee fails in preventing Communist China's representation in the UN it has its next step already planned. It will then create a new movement—The Committee against U. S. Participation in the United Nations.

Not only is Liebman's office the center of a right-wing lobby that has been largely responsible for disorienting our China policy, but it is the center of a well-financed plan to destroy the United Nations [The inference being that the withdrawal of the U.S. would, in effect, destroy the U.N.]. . . . Here is a deep and disturbing indication of the residual McCarthyism which continues to hamstring our national energies and to put a halter on our democratic tradition.[33]

And if there are those who feel that this is all a little farfetched, that no group operating from an office in New York can really have much of an influence on the foreign policies of a great nation such as ours, they should remind themselves that this is only the outward and visible operation of powerful forces that still work largely in secret.

Even as I am writing this chapter in mid-July, 1963, a Senate committee has just released a transcript of hearings on some of the less public activities of the Lobby. And in doing so it has revealed once more the extent and effectiveness of its ramifications.

On March 25, 1963, the Senate Foreign Relations Committee, investigating the activities of nondiplomatic representatives of foreign principals in the United States, heard testimony that a New York public relations firm, the Hamilton Wright Organization, a registered agent for Nationalist China from 1957 to the

[32] *The Nation*, October 7, 1961.
[33] Ibid.

end of 1962, contracted to receive as much as $300,000 in an 18-month period from the Chiang Kai-shek government. For what? On this point the testimony is absolutely clear: to write and distribute stories, news articles, photographs, and movies that would create a favorable image of Nationalist China in the minds of the American people.

To read the transcript of the Senate hearings[34] provides the same combination of fascination and shock as a good detective story. From it one can reconstruct in one's mind quite vividly the methods and techniques that might be employed by experienced professionals paid to influence the public.

The document containing the official terms of the contract between the Hamilton Wright Organization and The Republic of Free China for one year (October 1, 1958, to September 30, 1959) is reproduced in facsimile (all 23 pages of it). Reading these terms and seeing all that the Wrights promised to do, one feels that they certainly earned their fee. We learn, among many other things, that six "newsreels" will be released simultaneously to NBC-TV, CBS-TV, ABC-TV, etc., and that the Wright Organization guarantees that half of these releases will be used. Under the contract a minimum of 3000 still pictures were to be taken, and hundreds of the best of them were to be offered to the leading news-photo syndicates. (A single picture might then show up in as many as 500 newspapers.) The Wrights promised to make color pictures too, to prepare Sunday picture supplements for syndication to sixty Sunday newspapers; they promised to write twenty newspaper feature articles, each to go to two hundred newspapers—and many of these articles would appear under the names of members of the syndicates or under the names of the staff writers of the newspapers that used them.

Senator Fulbright drew attention to one clause in the contract in which the Wright Organization "guaranteed" that:

> In 75% of the releases, neither the editor of the newspaper —nor the newspaper reader—HAS ANY KNOWLEDGE

[34] Activities of Nondiplomatic Representatives of Foreign Principals in the United States. Hearing before the Committee on Foreign Relations, United States Senate, Part 7 and Part 10. (U. S. Government Printing Office, 1963).

WHERE THE MATERIAL ORIGINATED. Only the editor of the syndicate knows. In some instances, we syndicate our material direct to newspaper editors.

(The capitals were in the original contract.)

Under the quiet, probing questioning of Senator Fulbright, the Wrights (father and son) testified that at one time or another a number of news syndicates, publications, and networks were furnished with material supplied free by these paid agents.

Though the contract stated that in 75 percent of the releases neither the editor or the newspaper reader would know where the material originated, though the syndicate would, the Wrights strenuously argued in their testimony that most of the editors *did* know where the material was coming from.

MR. WRIGHT, SENIOR: Every release that goes out from our office says: *From the Hamilton Wright Organization, 30 Rockefeller Plaza.* and underneath it says: *Officially for the Government of Free China.*[35]

It was testified that for several years the Wright Organization employed a Mr. Don Frifield at a salary of twenty-five thousand dollars a year to write articles on the Orient, and that these articles were generally favorable to the Chiang government.

THE CHAIRMAN: To whom, after he wrote an article, did he [Frifield] submit it?

MR. WRIGHT, SENIOR: He submitted them to North American Newspaper Alliance, to other syndicates, to newspapers direct, Sunday newspapers, on the basis of being free, and they could reject or accept it.

THE CHAIRMAN: Did they in fact?

MR. WRIGHT, SENIOR: They published a tremendous lot and requested more articles.[36]

[35] Hearings, p. 790.
[36] Ibid., p. 789. But in a letter to Senator Fulbright, the editor of North American Newspaper Alliance, Inc., pointed out that the only stories by Frifield that NANA distributed were non-controversial and not connected with U.S. policy toward China, and more of his stories were rejected than accepted (Hearing, Part 10, pp. 1500–1).

THE CHAIRMAN: Was this part of your representation of China?

MR. WRIGHT, SENIOR: Yes.

MR. WRIGHT, JUNIOR: Yes.

THE CHAIRMAN: And these articles were generally favorable to China?

MR. WRIGHT, JUNIOR: Yes, indeed.

MR. WRIGHT, SENIOR: Some of these articles were irrelevant to China. They talked about the Far East because editors requested stories that didn't have China in it all the time. They talked about Hong Kong; the refugee situation in the Far East.

THE CHAIRMAN: Did the editors who used these articles know they had been written and paid for by a representative of a foreign government?

MR. WRIGHT, SENIOR: Definitely, yes.

Later in the testimony Senator Fulbright returned to Mr. Frifield's activities.

THE CHAIRMAN: Did Frifield write for the New York Herald Tribune News Service?

MR. WRIGHT, SENIOR: Yes, indeed.

THE CHAIRMAN: And you think they knew he was employed by you?

MR. WRIGHT, SENIOR: Absolutely. I have many friends over there.[37]

. . . .

THE CHAIRMAN: The net effect of this was the New York Herald Tribune was accepting pieces prepared by a paid foreign agent,

[37] Later, Mr. James G. Bellows, editor of the New York *Herald Tribune*, released a statement declaring that "according to our correspondence, it was not known" that Frifield was a paid writer for "a China Lobby firm," that organizational and personnel changes had since occurred, and that the *Herald Tribune* staff "is watchful at all times that unlabeled, sponsored material should not be handled as news in the newspaper or on the news service." (Hearing, Part 10, p. 1501). Mr. Frifield subsequently filed a statement with the Committee which included a letter from the former editor and manager of the *Herald Tribune* News Service at the time of Frifield's writing, stating that "we were fully aware" of Frifield's association with Hamilton Wright and further noting that the Frifield material was edited by the news staff and accepted "on the basis of merit."

and they were accepting them and giving them to the public as if they were objective news stories?

MR. WRIGHT, SENIOR: That is done every day in the week. That is done by the Associated Press; that is done by the United Press; that is done by Fox Movietone News. It is done constantly.

MR. CHAIRMAN: Can you give me another example?

MR. WRIGHT, SENIOR: Yes. I showed you examples of the New York Times. I showed you examples in the magazines, pictures in the National Geographic Magazine. They know we are doing this work all the time.

But here again, Mr. Chairman, the big thing is, is it news or is it propaganda? They decide whether they like it or they don't like it. If they don't like it, they don't accept it.

THE CHAIRMAN: Well, in reading your proposals to the Government of China, your purpose was to influence the political image of China. That was part of your objective, and that is what these stories were largely directed toward, were they not?

MR. WRIGHT, SENIOR: I do not agree with that. I think these stories were directed to show the way of life, the institutional way of life of China, for example.

THE CHAIRMAN: That only goes to the method. The objective was to create a favorable image.

MR. WRIGHT, SENIOR: We are getting back to this same discussion we had before.

THE CHAIRMAN: That is correct.

MR. WRIGHT, SENIOR: As to what do you call politics or what do we call political propaganda, hard core political propaganda. My answer to that is "No."

THE CHAIRMAN: But the whole point that we come back to is that Mr. Frifield is employed by you, and he writes a story favorable to the Government of China. Under the law, the public who reads this is entitled to know that this was written by a paid agent and not just a newsman. That is what the law says.

MR. WRIGHT, SENIOR: But the law does not demand that the New York Times publish a story or publish credit that this story has been accepted from a paid representative of the foreign government under the Justice Department law. This has never been; this law has never been defined and never been executed to that extent.

THE CHAIRMAN: Do you think if it required that, then it would stop?

MR. WRIGHT, SENIOR: It would stop us. It would put us out of business in 24 hours.[38]

Later, there was this testimony:

MR. WRIGHT, SENIOR: You think we are deceiving the public?

THE CHAIRMAN: Yes.

MR. WRIGHT, SENIOR: You think when we give a story to Life magazine we are deceiving the public?

THE CHAIRMAN: I didn't say in every case.

MR. WRIGHT, SENIOR: You think when we give pictures to the Associated Press we are deceiving the public?

THE CHAIRMAN: When you write a story that is favorable to your client and you fail to identify it as having been written by one paid to do it, I think this is a form of deception.

MR. WRIGHT, SENIOR: What about the motion pictures?

THE CHAIRMAN: Well, it would be the same way, unless you would identify that these are made by a person employed—

MR. WRIGHT, SENIOR: Who cares?

THE CHAIRMAN: To make them.

MR. WRIGHT, SENIOR: Who cares?

THE CHAIRMAN: Well, the Federal Government cares.

MR. WRIGHT, SENIOR: The public doesn't care.

THE CHAIRMAN: They passed an act for it. The Congress passed an act requiring it. That is who cares. I didn't pass it. It has been on the books.

MR. WRIGHT, SENIOR: Let us talk about this a little more because this is going to go very far. Suppose 20th Century-Fox—we ask 20th Century-Fox to put a label on their film like you are suggesting and they say, "No, we won't do it. We didn't produce the picture. You did. You turned it over to us for $1."

Where do you stop and start?

[38] Ibid., pp. 793–94.

THE CHAIRMAN: Well, as the law now stands, I think it requires that this be identified as produced by an agent of a foreign government.

It strikes me that is the simple requirement of the existing law. It does not say you cannot do it.

MR. WRIGHT, SENIOR: This would kill it. They wouldn't use it.

THE CHAIRMAN: Why not? If it has any inherent—

MR. WRIGHT, SENIOR: Because they will not sell propaganda to the theatregoer. How would you like it if you went into the Radio City Music Hall with your family and you sat down to see a show, and a short subject comes on about Hawaii headed by 20th Century-Fox, and you say, "Isn't this a wonderful picture," cinemascope, color, beautiful beaches, beautiful sand, fishing, sports, and then at the end of it it says, "This has been presented by the Hamilton Wright Organization, a paid representative of the government of Hawaii, distributed by 20th Century-Fox"? You would get up and raise hell about it.

THE CHAIRMAN: I wouldn't raise near as much hell than if it wasn't there and I found out later I had been taken in by a piece of propaganda that wasn't true.

.   .   .   .

MR. WRIGHT, SENIOR: We say that on all our films, film of the Hamilton Wright Organization.

THE CHAIRMAN: Well, whenever you do there is no objection.

MR. WRIGHT, SENIOR: We say that. But 20th Century-Fox will not say that; Warner Bros. won't say that. Every picture of ours that goes out as one of our pictures; in addition we have this new tag on there that Mr. Lenvin asked to go on.

I don't know how far you are going to go with this Hollywood crowd in asking them to put it on. . . .[39]

I have quoted enough from these Senate hearings to convey the essence. Perhaps the final touch came after the hearing was concluded, when the Senior Wright, according to the Washington *Post* on July 11, 1963, complained that he had been "treated

[39] Ibid., pp. 819–20.

with a great deal of embarrassment. There's nothing sacred," he said. "It's like going into a man's drawer and reading his love letters."

These hearings would indicate that the China Lobby still existed (at least until the end of 1962); that large funds were still spent in promoting a favorable image of the Chiang Kai-shek government; and that the U.S. press was aiding the dissemination of Chiang's propaganda.

I have in this chapter attempted to indicate the pressures that have been exerted in the U.S. on behalf of the Chiang Kai-shek regime. This, quite obviously, is not the full story of the China Lobby. Much still remains hidden, much will never be fully known. But I have said enough, I hope, to remind ourselves how McCarthyism and the China Lobby at one time interacted and mutually supported each other; and how some of the U.S. press has allowed itself to be used for propaganda paid by Chiang Kai-shek and his partisans.

There were many other factors that shaped American policy toward China. The activities of the China Lobby must be seen in relation to the broad mosaic of historical events. It seems clear, however, that Chiang Kai-shek, by means of his paid agents and with the help of his supporters, with the use of money and with the support of items published by the U.S. press, exerted an extraordinary influence upon public opinion and the official policies of the United States.

Part II

A TEST OF THE NEWS

So far in this book we have reminded ourselves of the history of American involvement with China. We have seen how all kinds of erroneous reports about Chiang Kai-shek and about events in China were disseminated during the war, and how Chiang and his partisans have attempted to influence American public opinion.

But what can we test the news against? What constitutes accurate reporting? There is as yet no single definitive account of what has happened in China since the establishment of the Communist regime, and it may be many years before such an account can be written. But this does not mean that there have not been some decisive happenings in China during the last fourteen years about which there is now little or no dispute. (There is no dispute, for instance, that since 1949 Mao Tse-tung's government has continually been in effective control of China.) And while on less clearly observable facts there is no absolute measurement of accuracy, we are able to compare what we have read in our press with the eyewitness reports of other Western correspondents, industrialists, scientists, doctors, and economists, who have been able to travel to China and see what is going on there. And finally, of course, we can ask ourselves which reports in the American press have been self-contradictory, which have survived the test of time, and which have been proved mistaken by subsequent events.

In this section I shall apply these tests to American accounts of some of the more important developments that have taken place in China since the revolution.

Figure 1 A UPI photograph correctly captioned as a group of slain Viet Cong in South Vietnam.

Figure 2 This picture, which is just a part of the UPI photograph above, was printed with this caption: "Pitiful is this refugee from Red China, one of many who collapsed from exhaustion. . . ."

Figure 3 An example of a wrong translation of Chinese characters. In the American magazine which reprinted this Chinese poster, the Chinese caption was translated as: "Under the leadership of the Communist Party and Chairman Mao, to make China the richest and strongest socialist nation." A correct rendering would be ". . . a rich and strong socialist nation." There is a big difference in undertone.

Figure 4 Another example of an erroneous caption. This photograph was published as a Chinese "recruiting poster" calling for army volunteers. It is, in fact, an advertisement for a movie.

How About What You Don't Have?

Figure 5 It would be assumed from this cartoon that it was the Chinese who were preventing U. S. newsmen from traveling to China. For the real facts in a confused story, see Chapter 18.

The Great Wall of China

Figure 6 Cartoons such as this one firmly convinced the public in the U. S. that the refugees coming into Hong Kong in May and June 1962 were starving. Two weeks before this cartoon appeared, both the British and U. S. governments had officially stated that the refugees showed no signs of malnutrition.

Chapter 5

WHEN THE RUSSIANS TOOK OVER CHINA

The Background

In December 1949, not many weeks after the establishment of his new government in Peking, Mao Tse-tung went to Moscow to negotiate a "Treaty of Friendship, Alliance and Mutual Assistance" with the Soviet Union. China, after two decades of civil war and occupation by the Japanese, and a long period of misrule by Chiang Kai-shek, was in need of economic help and she turned to the one country that was likely to give it to her.

Subsequent events have shown us that the help the Soviet Union was prepared to give to the Chinese government was generous. Under the terms of the treaty negotiated by Mao in Moscow, a considerable number of Soviet technicians were to be dispatched to China during the next decade to set up factories and train Chinese in modern technology; many complete manufacturing plants—some of them very large—were sent from the U.S.S.R. and set up in China; an enormous amount and variety of essential equipment was provided to enable the Chinese to begin their industrialization. Blueprints, machinery designs, and technical data were given apparently without stint. Machine tools, trucks, locomotives, weapons, agricultural machinery, and geological and electronic equipment were provided in vast amounts.

It is a matter of historical fact—and the Chinese are the first to acknowledge it—that China's remarkably swift recovery after the civil war and the rapidity of her industrialization would have been quite impossible without the assistance provided by the

Soviet Union. All this flowed from the treaty that was being discussed by Mao Tse-tung in Moscow.

Nor was this all. Under the Yalta agreement of 1945 (while Chiang Kai-shek was still in power) the U.S.S.R. had demanded that the Chinese port of Dairen be internationalized, that Russian control of Port Arthur be re-established, and that the Chinese Eastern and South Manchurian railroads should be jointly controlled by Russia and China. Within a few years the Soviet Union renounced these rights which she had successfully claimed at Yalta. Port Arthur and Dairen subsequently were returned to the Chinese and the railroads that had been run as a "joint enterprise" were placed under exclusive (by then Communist) Chinese ownership and management.

Almost a decade later the Russians and Chinese found themselves engaged in a bitter dispute, but in the period we are discussing there was little evidence to suggest that there existed anything but the closest collaboration between the two great Communist nations.

A study of some of the items appearing in the American press during the early 1950's provides us with a classic example of how totally misleading speculation can be. It is true that very little direct information was available—the Russians and Chinese did not let us in on their discussions and plans. That was natural enough and was to be expected, and it was natural enough that our national curiosity was aroused as to what was going on in those discussions in Moscow. But what is not natural is to present speculation as if it were news, especially when the speculation turns out, as in this case, to be 100 percent wrong.

We can see here how some of the reporters, columnists, the China "experts" take their cues from each other; unanimity provides a measure of assurance. I maintain that we can also see how a myth, once it is firmly established, can linger on for almost a decade in the face of overwhelming evidence that disproves it.

But if the original surmise is wrong, it does not matter how many writers repeat it, or how distinguished they are, or how "authoritatively" they express it, or how learnedly they can make speeches about it, or how much the government itself lends official support to it—it will remain false, and the public will to the extent to which the error has been disseminated be deluded.

Let us now turn to see some of the things the public was being told about Sino-Russian relations at the time of Mao's visit to Moscow and after. With the facts now available to us, it is a legitimate generalization to say that almost everything said about Sino-Russian relations at this time by the press, the government, the columnists, and the "experts" *had no basis in reality.*

The Story

> . . . what is happening in China is that the Soviet Union is detaching the northern provinces of China from China and is attaching them to the Soviet Union.
>
> —Secretary of State Dean Acheson in a speech to the National Press Club, January 12, 1950.

Mao was in Moscow. Dire predictions were headlined across the country. Eminent columnists wrote of "secret codicils" and editorials warned that another country had fallen into Stalin's hands. The fact that Mao had gone to Moscow in December 1949 and that the treaty was not signed until February was used as grounds for much speculation as to the harsh terms that the Russians were demanding of the Chinese.

The Secretary of State in the speech quoted above was specific. Outer Mongolia,[1] Inner Mongolia, Manchuria, and Sinkiang province (in all, about a third of the area of China, the press dutifully reported) was being taken over by the Soviet Union.

The New York *Times,* on January 22, 1950, editorially accepted the accuracy of Mr. Acheson's impeachment.

[1] The fact that Outer Mongolia had been a republic for almost a quarter of a century did not prevent Mr. Acheson including it as part of the China that was to be "detached" by Russia.

He stated that the Soviet Union was "attaching" areas in northern China, and they can certainly be attached without the formality of annexation. Outer Mongolia is already so "attached" by every standard. The Russian domination of the "autonomous" border area of western Manchuria and northern Inner Mongolia is obvious. The control of all Manchuria through the use of the railway network and the major part of it is already far advanced.

But this was really an old story—Mr. Acheson merely provided the official endorsement. On February 14, 1949, C. L. Sulzberger, Paris correspondent and foreign affairs expert of the New York *Times,* was reporting:

> In northernmost China the Soviet Union, continuing the traditional eastward drive of Russian imperialism at the expense of Marxist ideology, is in the process of assuming direct control over a vast area extending from Turkestan across Mongolia and Manchuria to the Pacific Provinces of the U.S.S.R.

In the same year, on November 22, Arthur Hays Sulzberger, president and publisher of the New York *Times,* and Henry R. Lieberman, the *Times* correspondent recently returned from China, were addressing the fifteenth annual luncheon for automotive and industrial executives in Detroit. Mr. Lieberman informed the executives that the Chinese Communist revolution, "particularly in Manchuria, has been 'hi-jacked' by Russia."

With the Secretary of State's endorsement, the "take-over" story was given a new lease on life. On January 22, 1950, the New York *Times* added a further ominous note:

> . . . the general pattern indicates at least the possibility that Communist China may sooner or later receive some sort of compensatory offer from the Soviet Union. . . . Expansion in the South may be Red China's recompense for submitting to Russian expansion in the North.

Where, one must ask, did the New York *Times* find its evidence for this "general pattern" of horse-trading between Stalin and Mao? From the *Times* bureau in Moscow, where the negotiations were being conducted? I could find no report from there. The only published material I could find as a possible source for this editorial was a UP dispatch from Formosa printed a few days earlier. According to this report, Yen Hsi-shan—a notorious warlord from northwest China, then Premier of Nationalist China—declared "that the Chinese Communist leader Mao Tse-tung had 'swapped' huge areas to Russia for Chinese Communist domination of southeast Asia." Whether the *Times* accepted this undocumented (and untrue) statement from one of Chiang Kai-shek's henchmen as a basis for an important editorial, I do not know, but the editorial would seem to have been consistent with the statement.

Mr. Christopher Rand had cabled the New York *Herald Tribune* from Hong Kong on January 19, 1950, that to dominate a part of China, Russia would have to dominate it all.

> It is believed here that Soviet Russia has much the same designs on the fringes of North China that Czarist Russia had: It wants to dominate them piecemeal, as Secretary of State Dean Acheson has recently suggested. Times have changed, however. Especially China has become much more unified than in Czarist times. This means that to dominate some parts of North China it is probably necessary to dominate the whole country.

The State Department on January 25 issued "background material, based on the large accumulation of reports and data available to this Government." The full text of the "background material" was carried by the AP and reported in the New York *Times*. In addition to repeating the Secretary of State's earlier statement the text declared that in Manchuria:

> . . . the Soviet Union has placed the richest industrial area of China firmly behind the Far Eastern segment of the Iron Curtain. . . . Soviet strategic detachment from Chinese control is in progress in China's northern provinces as it is in certain European areas and, as in those areas, may be expected to proceed by carefully planned stages.

The State Department named names and places:

> The Sha Ho Kon Vehicle Manufacturing Works, the Dairen
> Shipbuilding Yard and the Dairen Sugar Works are all under
> Soviet military control.[2]

The *Herald Tribune* on January 27, under the heading IM-
PERIALISM IN CHINA, ran an editorial:

> The deadly nature of the thrust implicit in Secretary Ache-
> son's charge of . . . Soviet alienation of Chinese territory
> . . . the evidence that the Communist regime in Peking is
> the tool and abetter of the process (foreign imperial dom-
> ination) is more than serious: it is lethal. . . . This exposure
> of the actual march of the new Russian imperial exploitation,
> and of its Chinese tools and agents, is as deadly a weapon
> as any now remaining to us for the combat of Communism
> in the vast mainland Chinese areas which it has submerged
> in chaos and disillusion. . . .

But the *Times* was not to be outdone.

SOVIET SAID TO ASK FOR FULL CONTROL OF 7 CHINA PORTS was
the banner headline given to a Paris dispatch by C. L. Sulzberger
on January 29. According to Mr. Sulzberger's sensational disclosure, not only were the Russians now demanding full control of
seven northern ports,[3] but they were pressing the Chinese for
three additional concessions: A labor force of five hundred thousand Chinese; increased shipments of food, especially grain ("from
the rich Province of Manchuria—although disorganized and ravaged China faces the imminent threat of a disastrous famine");[4]
and finally far-reaching concessions were to be made to "minority"
groups and in the very areas Mr. Acheson was detaching from
China!

[2] In reply the Chinese (according to a January 30 report to the New York
Times by Mr. Tillman Durdin) said the State Department's "background
material" was "shameless fabrication." A few days later the New China
News Agency said that not only did the State Department manufacture
Russian control but it even invented places. According to the New China
News Agency, there was no such place as Sha Ho Kon, where the State
Department had conveniently set up a "Vehicle Manufacturing Plant."
[3] One of the ports up for grabs, as listed by Mr. Sulzberger, was "Li Fu-chen
believed to be Haichow." There is no port called Li Fu-chen; and this is
probably a garbled version of the name of a Vice-Premier, Li Fu-chun.
[4] Manchuria has never been a Chinese province, but the northeastern section
of the country comprising a number of provinces. Actually the term "Manchuria" does not exist in Chinese but was invented by foreigners.

In return for all this, according to this remarkable story, the Chinese were demanding huge financial help and arms shipments. Mr. Sulzberger reported:

> Latest advices indicate that the Chinese negotiators have not yet acceded to these demands. They have been countering with requests on an almost equally ambitious scale.
> The result is that the bargaining that is going on . . . is on a basis of Oriental bazaar trading almost without historical precedent.

According to this astounding revelation from Paris, if the Chinese were forced to knuckle under and grant Moscow "the requested rights over their northern ports, they would concede the U.S.S.R. absolute control over the Yellow Sea."

In this front-page dispatch, Mr. Sulzberger managed to turn up much surprising news: Mao was not happy about the negotiations and so Chou En-lai and a "second wave" of Chinese delegates had to be called in; Mao may have fallen "seriously ill"; Moscow wanted the "most independent-minded leaders of Communist China to be absent from their country at the time" so that it would afford "more opportunity for a pro-Soviet faction . . . to consolidate its political position quietly while the limelight currently is focused on Moscow. . . ."

An amazing scoop—almost as if Mr. Sulzberger had had a private line from Paris right into the Kremlin!

On January 31, 1950, the New York *Times* reported that State Department officials generally gave credence to the Russian demand for seven Chinese ports as disclosed by Mr. Sulzberger. The State Department press officer, Michael J. McDermott, told a news conference:

> The reports seem to be in line with Secretary Acheson's speech that Russia was in the process of taking over in North China areas.

On February 13, 1950, the Sino-Soviet Treaty was signed.

No mention of one-third of China being "detached"! No seven ports handed over! No five hundred thousand Chinese laborers to be sent to Russia! It was left to Mr. Sulzberger three days later to explain why—under a four-column, front-page headline:

SECRET CODICILS TO SINO-SOVIET PACT SAID TO GIVE RUSSIA KEY PEIPING POSTS AND LARGE FORCE OF CHINESE LABOR.

Specific indications were received here tonight that secret codicils to the new treaty of alliance between the Soviet Union and the Chinese People's Republic had been signed by representatives of the Moscow and Peiping Governments.

In this long dispatch, Mr. Sulzberger in effect repeated the Russian "demands" that earlier he had announced were being made on China—though he scaled down the number in the Chinese labor force to three hundred thousand. But he added some new secrets. A Soviet mission was to be established in the security and administrative branches of the Chinese government; Russian political commissars were to be installed in large Chinese army units under the guise of officer training programs; the Kremlin had prepared personnel, trained in Tashkent, to take over the administration of Sinkiang province.[5]

But where, one must ask, did Mr. Sulzberger obtain all his remarkable information? What were his sources? We can search in vain for any indication as to how trustworthy his informants might be. "Specific indications were received here tonight," he tells us.

What were the "specific indications" and where did they come from? He doesn't tell us. Instead, Mr. Sulzberger, *in this one dispatch alone*, used these as "sources" for his "specific indications": "it is understood"; "it is reported"; "responsible information that became available in Eastern European capitals," "satellite sources," "it is considered logical," "information available in interested capitals," "there is an inclination in certain quarters," "such circles speculate," "the following reliable information," "Peiping is understood to have urged," "However, it is

[5] Following Mr. Sulzberger's disclosures of these "secret agreements," the New York *Times* quoted Chiang Kai-shek's representative at the UN, Mr. T. F. Tsiang, who assured the American public that "the Chinese Communists had 'sold' Manchuria and the province of Sinkiang to the Soviet Union under secret clauses in the Moscow-Peiping treaty."

reported," "it is furthermore reported," "are said to," "it is believed," "is understood to have made," "no concrete information is yet available. . . . However, it is known," "it is understood that," "it is understood" (again), "Moscow is said to," "it is reported that," "it is believed," (again) "it appears that," and "to date no reliable information has been received."

Thirty years earlier in their analysis of reporting about Russia, Walter Lippmann and Charles Merz had some harsh things to say about the use of vague sources. They thought that even more misleading than government statements that were not statements of fact were *anonymous* statements. Phrases such as "government and diplomatic sources," "reports reaching here," "it is stated on high authority that," place the reader at the mercy of opinion that he cannot check. Behind such phrases could be almost anybody— a minor official, a dinner table conversation, hotel gossip, a paid agent. "It is time to demand," they wrote, that the correspondent "identify his informants sufficiently" so that readers can judge the nature of the report. "He need not name the individual source but he can 'place' him."

However vaguely they were disclosed to the reader, the New York *Times* itself clearly had faith in Mr. Sulzberger's sources of information. An editorial on February 16—the day the story appeared—stated:

> . . . the published agreement does not tell the full story but is supplemented by secret agreements which . . . would admit Soviet forces to Chinese bases and into the China Sea athwart our own Pacific lines of communications. . . .
>
> For while making China another Soviet satellite, the Kremlin has managed to disguise this fact . . . the agreement itself is full of hidden traps. . . .

Three days later, the New York *Times* editorially dismissed the treaty's stipulation that "Russia would withdraw from control of Port Arthur and the Manchurian railways." (In fact, the Russians eventually did withdraw.)

> Presumably the Kremlin believes that by that time puppetry will be so firm in Manchuria that nominal control can be a dispensable fiction.

The same editorial shrugged off the meagerness of Russian economic aid to China ("the real meat of it must lie in the undisclosed agreements. This is the window-dressing. . . .")

> Nevertheless, even if the agreement is taken in its precise value it is hard to see how China has made any substantial gain. The Chinese have sold out their chances to be independent. . . . If Mao was horse-trading in Moscow he took a trimming. . . .

In May, reporting from Tokyo, Mr. Sulzberger was still handing over Chinese real estate to the Russians.

> The Soviet Union is now engaged in the first stages of a long-range program to integrate North China into the economic structure of the U.S.S.R. with indications that political absorption of that vast area may be an ultimate goal.
> . . . there is ample reason to believe that Moscow's eventual desire . . . is to take over the entire enormous region between Vladivostock and the central Asia republics [a mere 2500 miles!] in order to construct a "land bridge" between the Maritime Provinces and Alma Ata.

It was not only the New York *Times* but other influential papers and the press generally which were confidently reporting the take-over of China. The specialists and scholars, on the other hand, appeared a little more hesitant to reach such sweeping conclusions. Their reports were generally safely ambiguous—they covered the subject "from all angles," leaving a series of possibilities so that whatever eventually happened they would not be too wrong. But they did not hesitate to soberly weigh the prospects of Russian domination of China.

Thus, for example, we find a leading specialist on Sino-Soviet relations, Dr. Robert C. North of Stanford University, referring to Sulzberger's findings which reported "Mao had agreed to furnish a large labor force for work in Siberia, had accorded key positions in China's army, secret police, and Communist Party to Soviet advisers, had consented to place seven Yellow Sea ports under Soviet supervision in case of war, and had 'sold' Sinkiang to the Russians."[6] While this noted authority did not accept the

[6] Robert C. North, *Moscow and Chinese Communists* (Stanford, Calif.: Stanford University Press, 1953), p. 267.

full accuracy of these reports, he nevertheless thought them of sufficient importance to deal with them as a serious possibility.

When on March 26, 1950, it was announced that the Russians and the Chinese had set up joint oil and mineral companies for the development of Sinkiang province, and that both countries would split the costs and share the proceeds, it brought forth a flurry of "we told you so's." The New York *Times*, still hot for China's take-over, in an editorial a few days later referred to Sinkiang "now within the controlling orbit of the Soviet Union. . . . This type of generosity . . . can more accurately be called merely the economic prelude to annexation."

Mr. Acheson, who had "detached" Sinkiang from China back in January, was still, at a news conference on March 31, insisting "that the Soviet Union was moving 'on a grand scale' to detach Sinkiang Province from China." (New York *Times*, April 1, 1950).

Not one of these assertions was correct. All of Inner Mongolia, Manchuria, and Sinkiang province have remained completely under Chinese control. No Chinese labor force was sent to the Soviet Union. No ports were handed over. No Russians were given positions in the Chinese secret police or Chinese army. Russia, though she has driven some hard bargains, has never at any time, attempted to deal with China as if she were a "satellite." In the case of the joint development of Sinkiang's oil and mineral resources, the Russian share was later turned over completely to the Chinese. (The French correspondent and author, Mr. Tibor Mende, who visited Sinkiang in 1960, found that vast province likely to become one of China's principal industrial centers. "Sinkiang, according to all evidence," he reported, "is a showplace in multi-national relations for the rest of China."[7])

Russia's "annexation" of one-third of China was so well established by the press accounts that it became, to many, a matter of historical fact. Here are a few quotations to show this happening.

[7] *China and Her Shadow* (London: Thames and Hudson, 1961), p. 207, and Part Three, Chapter 3, "Sinkiang, the New World Beyond the Jade Gate," pp. 214–29.

An AP message from Taipei, May 23, 1950, quoting Chiang's Defense Ministry, reported that four hundred thousand Soviet citizens were settling in Manchuria and thirty thousand Soviet advisers and technicians were attaching themselves to the Peking government.[8]

Dr. Ivar Spector of the University of Washington's Far Eastern Department, in one of a series of articles which appeared in the Seattle *Times* of June 4, 1950, wrote of Soviet encroachment in China and informed his readers that this process had gone so far that the Chinese were going to adopt a Russian alphabet.

A report from the UP correspondent in London on June 13 concerning the appointment of a new Soviet ambassador to Peking. "It was believed here that Panyushkin may seek to prolong Russia's grip on Manchuria."

"Michael Straight, editor of *The New Republic*, said yesterday that Chinese Communist troops probably were ordered into Korea by Soviet officials and their 'Manchurian puppets' without the consent of Mao Tse-tung, Red China's chief of State. . . ." (UP, Washington, November 10, 1950.)

. . . we can tell our friends in China that the United States will not acquiesce in the degradation which is being forced upon them. We do not recognize the authorities in Peiping for what they pretend to be. The Peiping regime may be a colonial Russian government—a Slavonic Manchukuo on a larger scale. It is not the Government of China. It does not pass the first test. It is not Chinese. It is not entitled to speak for China in the community of nations.

—Dean Rusk, Assistant Secretary
of State for Far Eastern Affairs,
May 18, 1951.

"It is now more than two years since Secretary Acheson declared that the Soviet Union's policy on the Asiatic mainland was one of "attachment." . . . The currently reported developments are a part of that process of attachment. If Mao Tse-tung doesn't know what the Kremlin is doing he is

[8] The best estimates have shown that the Russians never sent many more than ten thousand technicians to China between 1950 and 1960. This was confirmed in a conversation I had in September 1960 with Mr. Sapronov, Senior Counselor at the Embassy of the U.S.S.R. in Peking.

not wise enough to lead a nation. If he does know, and con-
nives at it, he is not honorable enough to deserve the respect
of his innocent followers." (New York *Times* editorial, August 18, 1952.)

As the years went by and the promised "annexation" of China
did not take place, a few lone voices were heard, suggesting that
perhaps it might not occur at all. Writing from Hong Kong on
September 20, 1955, Mr. A. T. Steele was reporting to the New
York *Herald Tribune*:

> Signs of cooperation between China and Russia have been
> far more numerous than evidence of disharmony. . . .
> There is no visible evidence to bear out the view that Pei-
> ping is "taking orders" from Moscow. On the contrary, all
> outward signs are that the Peiping government is very much
> its own boss. . . .

But these assessments were in a distinct minority.

The Saturday Evening Post, in its issue of May 19, 1956, quoted
a well-known French correspondent to the effect that it looked "as
though the men in Peking have stopped even trying to remain
Asian. They are forcing their people to absorb the West in a new
way—the Russo-Communist Marxist type of western civilization."

Similar stories of a China under Russian domination continued
almost until Sino-Russian differences became so obvious that
further talk of this kind became quite meaningless.

The consequences of these erroneous reports were momentous.

To understand the full implications we must go back and see
what the conditions were at the time.

Probably not many people now remember that between the
establishment of the new Chinese government in October 1949
and the outbreak of the Korean War in June 1950, influential
voices were being raised suggesting that the United States should,
like Britain and other Western nations, accept the Communist
victory as a *fait accompli* and come to terms with this reality by
recognizing Peking. It was still possible at that time to argue for
the recognition of China without being considered subversive; in-

deed, throughout the country widespread discussion was taking place as to the wisdom or otherwise of recognition.[9]

Closely tied to the question of recognition was the question of China's representation in the United Nations. It seemed very possible at this time that the Peking government would be accepted as the real representative of the Chinese people, and as at this time no one was suggesting the creation of "Two Chinas," this would have meant the automatic withdrawal of credentials from the government of Chiang Kai-shek. As early as January 28, 1950, the New York *Times* was reporting that "two more members of the United Nations Security Council—Egypt and Equador—may withdraw recognition next month from Nationalist China and supply the necessary votes to seat a delegation of the Chinese Communist regime. . . ."

The seating of Communist China in the United Nations and that government's recognition by the United States, were, of course, precisely what those supporting Chiang Kai-shek in Washington most wished to avoid (see Chapter 4, "The China Lobby"). It was during this time—when recognition of Communist China and her admission into the UN both seemed possible, and even likely—that speeches by Secretary of State Acheson and editorials in influential papers such as the New York *Times*, disseminated the stories that the Chinese government was a "satellite" in the grip of the Soviet Union and that great parts of China's territory were being taken over by the Russians.[10]

One of the main purposes of granting diplomatic recognition to Communist China was to prevent her from becoming exclusively dependent on the Soviet Union. This story that China was already in the grip of the Soviet Union, and was even being dismembered by the Soviet Union, must have greatly influenced

[9] For example, a large conference called by the World Affairs Council in San Francisco, with representatives of the State Department and others present, voted by a large majority for the recognition of Communist China.

[10] It was not only in a single speech that Mr. Acheson made this charge. He repeated it in a press conference (reported in the New York *Herald Tribune*, February 16, 1950): "The Russians will attempt to use the treaty [of alliance with China] to make China as abject a satellite as Hungary or Romania."

those who might otherwise have been in favor of establishing normal relations with her.

The New York *Times* itself expressed it at this time in an editorial not long before the war in Korea started:

> It [the Communist regime] has sold out, to Soviet Russia, vast properties and rights of the Chinese people themselves, and, again, in the words of the State Department, "placed the richest industrial area of China firmly behind the Far Eastern segment of the Iron Curtain." In these circumstances it is both our right and our duty to wait for further evidence before we recognize the Communist regime as a genuinely sovereign government. . . .

The New York *Times* then drew the logical editorial conclusion—*no recognition of China!*

Thus, at a moment of great historical decision which enormously influenced America's future, the people of America were being misled by accounts of events which were untrue.

The consequences of this are with us still.

Chapter 6

THE STARVING CHINESE

We have seen with what relative equanimity the Western press reported the perennial famines that were such a tragic feature of prerevolutionary China. Hundreds of thousands of deaths by starvation would occur in one part of China or another every year; and in bad years more than a million people would die. Those are the brutal facts.

The descriptions of those who have witnessed these famine conditions in China are horrifying to read: the population in wide areas reduced to eating bark and grass, small children, while they still had strength enough to crawl, attempting to alleviate their pain by eating dirt and sand; while quite often landlords would surround their loaded granaries with armed guards until the more fortunate peasants in desperation would sell them their remaining land, their tools, and mortgage years of future toil in exchange for just enough food for survival. Certain Western missionary and charitable organizations would attempt to give such help as lay within their power—but this could mitigate the condition of only a few engulfed in these disasters.

For the most part, though Westerners did not minimize the appalling human suffering involved, these famines were accepted as a tragic but inescapable fact of Chinese life. Brief reports of the worst famines would appear in the Western press; occasionally a three- or four-line dispatch would mention that famine conditions were reported from such or such a province; often large areas would be stricken without any mention. So accustomed had the world become to starvation in China that it rarely caused headlines. The reports, such as they were, were matter-of-fact in tone, with no accompanying editorials or thundering criticisms of the Nationalist government.

With the establishment of the new government in Peking in 1949, two things happened.

First, starvation—death by hunger—ceased in China. Food shortages, and severe ones, there have been, but no starvation. This is a fact fully documented by Western observers, is acknowledged by the Western embassies in China, and is known, of course, to the highest official intelligence in our own country. No Western reporter who has traveled there, none of the resident Western correspondents who live there, no one who has ever traveled through the Chinese countryside and talked to the peasants has any doubts at all that this is true. The indisputable fact is that the famines that in one area or another constantly ravaged the farmlands of China, and the fear of starvation, which for so long had haunted the lives of the Chinese peasants, are today things of the past.

This tremendous fact of historic significance and the influence it has had upon the Chinese people's attitude to their government has been almost wholly ignored by the press. Indeed, the press has helped to create an image in the public mind of a China suffering more than it has ever done before. How many Americans, for instance, would believe a report like this?

> The truth is that the sufferings of the ordinary Chinese peasant from war, disorder and famine have been immeasurably less in the last decade than in any other decade in the century.[1]

The newspapers in America that I have studied conveyed quite an opposite impression. For an answer to this we come to the second change that happened as a result of the Communist victory in 1949.

[1] *The Times*, London, April 18, 1962.

From that time on the press—which until then had scarcely treated the very real farm problems of Nationalist China as news—began to take an inordinate interest in the food conditions inside China. The reason was clear. To many in the West it appeared that the most likely source of threat to the Peking government lay in a revolt of the people against it—a revolt arising from massive famine conditions. Signs of food shortages were seized upon, enlarged, exaggerated. Endless speculation took place, even within the most learned circles, as to how long it would be before the peasants would revolt.[2]

In May 1962 an unusually large number of Chinese refugees flocked to Hong Kong, and the overwhelming impression given in the newspapers was that it was starvation that drove them there. As we shall see (page 101), other accounts and official British government statements attest to the fact that the refugees were not suffering from malnutrition, nor did any of them seek political asylum or claim that they were fleeing Communism as such. The primary reason for this sudden flow of refugees in May 1962 appears to have been the reluctance of peasants who had become accustomed to city life to be sent back to the farms "to help agriculture." Food shortages and the general discomfort of life at this period were undoubtedly some of the causes for this exodus, but not starvation.

By reiteration impressions are deeply embedded in people's minds. I am convinced that for almost fifteen years, the great majority of the American public have been led to believe that conditions of almost perpetual famine have existed in China. And that this has been so largely as the result of mistakes by the Chinese government.

Let us examine in greater detail how this impression has been created—about a country whose improvements in its food conditions, as I and others found them, has probably been one of its greatest achievements.

[2] See Chapter 9.

1950 — FAMINE IN RED CHINA—There seems little doubt now that famine in China this year will be catastrophic . . . the situation will be more critical than at any other time in a half century. (New York *Times*, editorial, March 26.)

1951 — *Food riots* are reported among peasants. *Famine, floods* are back again. (*U.S. News & World Report*, March 16.)

1952 — Shanghai is a city of hungry millions. (UP, Taipei, June 23.)

1953 — FAMINE IN RED CHINA: . . . there is no hiding the fact that multiplied millions of Chinese are starving. (New York *Times*, editorial, June 24.)

1954 — Red China's leaders are already tightening controls, increasing rationing measures, and trying to prepare against the pressures of starvation. (*Time*, May 10.)

1955 — RED CHINA IN GRIP OF SPRING FAMINE: Signs of a spring famine in Communist China are filtering from the mainland. (Tad Szulc, Hong Kong, New York *Times*, April 24.)

1956 — RED CHINA BESET BY SPRING FAMINE (headline, New York *Times*, March 27.)

1957 — The threat of famine stalks millions of Chinese again this spring. (AP, Hong Kong, May 13.)

1958 — Troubles are piling up fast in Red China. Peasants are deserting the collective farms. Cities are packed with hungry, jobless millions. . . . (*U.S. News & World Report*, April 4.)

1959 — FAMISHED RED CHINA SLAVES STEAL PIGS' SLOP (headline Hong Kong dispatch, New York *World Telegram and Sun*, June 25.)

1960 — In face of the hunger that stalks mainland China for the third straight year. . . . (*Time*, August 22.)

1961 — Red China Hunger Reported Stirring Opposition: Taxed to the limit of their endurance by the tightest rationing of food in the modern history of China and near-famine conditions in some areas, the Chinese are reported to be reacting to the situation by rejecting Government regulations and even organizing anti-Government movements. (New York *Times*, April 15.)

1962 — Communist China is a land of massive malnutrition and hunger. Three successive years of poor harvests have reduced the food available to most Chinese to little above the barest subsistence level. (Harry Schwartz, New York *Times*, April 22.)

1963 — March and April will be the months to watch. It is then that food stocks will be lowest. Unrest among Chinese peasants is expected. Revolts are likely. . . . (*U.S. News & World Report*, January 7.)

The appearance of such reports in news sources was not halted even in 1957, the year that China had the largest harvest in its history. I was in China that year. I covered thousands of miles and everywhere saw evidence of the bumper crop. Not long after I returned to the United States, *Time* Magazine (November 11, 1957), in its news columns on Red China inquired, "Famine on the Way?"

Throughout the 1960–62 period, when famine reports were being given large play by the nation's news sources—papers, radio, and TV—there were other accounts and evidence that indicated that such famine reports were grossly exaggerated. On neither of my visits to China did I find conditions anywhere near as bad as had been painted in our press. In 1960 I traveled through areas in China—and reported this in *Awakened China*—where food rations were very tight indeed. But I saw no signs of serious malnutrition, and people who had lived and worked in China during the real famines in the past constantly reminded me that whatever food problems present-day China was facing, they bore absolutely no resemblance to the past.

Reuters, from their bureau in Peking, reported the food shortages, but never described them in terms of "famine" conditions (and some of these less drastic accounts appeared in our press). Competent and experienced European reporters also wrote accounts in China very different from the prevailing press reports about the disastrous conditions there. I feel sure that official Washington intelligence was well aware that the situation in China was not as disastrous as was being pictured.[3]

The press did open its correspondence columns, however, to some writers who wished to present a different account of conditions in China. An example of this was a letter written to the Editor of the New York *Times* on May 5, 1957, in reply to an editorial entitled, GUNS AND BUTTER, which had appeared on April 27. The writer of the letter, Professor Alexander Eckstein, is no sympathizer with Communism. He collaborated with Professor W. W. Rostow in his book, *Prospects for Communist China*.[4] This, in part, is what Professor Eckstein wrote:

> You very correctly point out that the emphasis in all Soviet-bloc planning, including Communist China, continues to be on heavy industry. However, you carry this conclusion much too far in an attempt to show that Chinese food production has badly lagged or declined so that ever-greater masses are exposed to starvation. The figures you cite to support this conclusion are grossly misleading. . . .
>
> . . . all of the available evidence would tend to support the conclusion that food production on the Chinese mainland has grown appreciably in recent years. At the same time the efficiency of food distribution has been greatly improved. As a result, the Chinese Communist regime is in a position to quickly alleviate or prevent local famines which have been traditional in China throughout history.
>
> Thus there is no evidence to support the often-held conclusion that China in recent years has been subject to repeated mass starvation.

A letter to the editor of the New York *Herald Tribune*, following some of Mr. Joseph Alsop's accounts of mass starvation on the mainland in the spring of 1961, is another attempt to correct a false impression. The writer, Sybil Cookson, of Sussex, England, quoted her own experiences as well as those of a friend "who has lived in Shanghai for many years."

[3] On December 31, 1960, the Pittsburgh *Press* reported, "Red China Famine Doubted by U.S." According to a UPI story from Washington, "Press officer Joseph W. Reap said, 'We are not aware of any Chinese Communist reports of actual famine conditions.'"
[4] Professor Rostow was one of President Kennedy's principal advisers on foreign policy.

Having recently undertaken a three weeks' tour of China —visiting six cities and many country districts—my husband and I were astonished to read Joseph Alsop's recent report from Hong Kong suggesting that there is widespread famine in China and even a likelihood of a revolt against the present regime.

This report was based on information supplied by refugees, a small minority of disaffected persons, and I can only suppose that their stories have been embellished by propagandists eager to discredit the Peking government. In any case they are quite contrary to our impression formed in China itself last autumn. We were allowed to travel where we desired—in crowded streets, stores and holiday resorts. We visited communes, schools and technical colleges, hospitals and homes for old folk. Nowhere did we see any signs of disaffection, much less of famine, despite a disappointing harvest.

Having seen reports of "famine in China," Mrs. Cookson wrote to a friend who lived in Shanghai. The following are extracts from her friend's reply:

That China during 1960 experienced the severest and most widespread natural calamity of the past century is a fact. . . . To say that China is experiencing a famine is grossly untrue.

During the many years I have lived in China, I know what famine under the old regime was like when natural calamities were not as severe as those in 1960. Then famine refugees streamed into the cities, hoping to pick up a bit of work and perhaps a bowl of soft rice . . . at a relief kitchen . . . many existed by combing the garbage pails of the families who had food. . . .

People throughout the country have been and still are cooperating in their efforts to be sparing with food and to avoid waste, so that the supply will go round for all.

Other attempts to correct erroneous accounts of conditions in China were not so successful in reaching print. In the New York *Times* on September 10, 1961, Mr. Tillman Durdin, the *Times'* China expert, wrote of "mass discontent," "apathy," "mounting deaths," and mentioned a report by a British M.P. of a daily intake of six hundred calories. The medical absurdity of this should be obvious—no human being, let alone a whole nation, can long exist on six hundred calories.[5]

I have before me a copy of a letter written on October 2, 1961, by a Chinese-speaking British doctor, J. S. Horn, F.R.C.S., addressed to the Editor of the New York *Times* and challenging Mr. Durdin's article. Dr. Horn had just returned home to London after a leisurely journey through central China. "As a doctor," he writes, "I should be quick to notice signs of malnutrition and a daily intake of 600 calories would rapidly produce severe symptoms. Yet the general health of the people appears to be good . . . I found the problems resulting from successive years of severe drought were being tackled with energy and confidence."

A careful search through the files reveals that apparently the New York *Times* never printed this letter.

These isolated attempts to bring the facts to the attention of our newspapers made no difference at all. Throughout 1961 the press published a fairly steady flow of reports of starvation in China.

Red China is in heavy trouble this time. "Natural calamities," crop failures, famine are only part of it. . . .
—*U.S. News & World Report,*
February 20

The population of China is starving. The starvation is methodical and rationed, but it is not even slow starvation.
—Joseph Alsop, New York *Herald Tribune,*
September 13

Things are going from bad to worse inside Communist China. They can get catastrophic. . . . It's a land of hunger. A major disaster in the making; the Reds soon may be fighting for their lives.
—*U.S. News & World Report,*
October 2

[5] Mr. Joseph Alsop also reported six hundred calories as being the average daily intake—see Chap. 9, "Mr. Alsop's China," p. 178. See also Edgar Snow's chapter on this Alsop report, entitled, "The Year the Chinese Disappeared," in his book, *The Other Side of the River* (New York: Random House, 1962).

The story of starvation inside China . . . is far grimmer than the outside world has been told.

> —Drew Pearson, San Francisco *Chronicle*,
> November 5

. . . the sour-tasting new soy sauce is said to be made of human hair.

> —*Time*, December 1

In the spring of 1962, when the number of refugees from nearby Kwangtung province suddenly increased, newspaper headlines and reports escalated the famine and starvation in China to its full height. Again at this time some voices were raised directing the public's attention to other facts—but the words were scarcely heard in the general clamor. In the House of Commons on May 22, the British Colonial Secretary said: "There is little evidence that the Chinese refugees attempting to enter Hong Kong were suffering malnutrition."

> (*May 28*) *U.S. News & World Report*: "ASIAN MYSTERY: The MASS FLIGHT FROM RED CHINA. Deepening the mystery is the character of the refugees. Many are described as healthy men and women, aged 20 to 30 and showing no signs of malnutrition. . . ."

> (*May 30*) New York *Herald Tribune* reported from Washington that Assistant Secretary of State Averell Harriman had stated that the refugees were "not starving. In fact, they did not show physical evidence of malnutrition."

> (*June 11*) *The New Republic* carried an article from Hong Kong by Jacques Jacquet-Francillon: "Another hypothesis widely circulated throughout a part of the Western press on both sides of the Atlantic also fails to hold water: the famine theory. The refugees whom I saw and the many I was able to question were not people who had fled a land in the grip of real famine. There were no 'living corpses,' as they have too glibly been described. They arrived at the border in a state of exhaustion from four to five days of trudging the roads; but most of them had some food left."

These officials and eyewitness accounts made little impact. They were far outweighed by the huge and steady stream of hunger stories.

(*May 15*) AP reported from Hong Kong: "Refugees rounded up by Hong Kong patrols today claimed that hundreds of Chinese have died of starvation while trying to reach the border. One said it was impossible to get enough to eat to keep alive in his village. . . .

(*May 19*) AP reported from Hong Kong: "Some 3,000 to 5,000 more refugees from hunger-ridden Red China streamed across the border before dawn yesterday."

(*May 27*) Tillman Durdin, in the New York *Times*: "The migrants in fact were fleeing grim conditions of hunger. . . . ". . . It is now no longer considered absurd for observers of the China scene to talk of the possibility of a break-up of the Communist regime or revolt against it."

(*June 18*) *Newsweek* spoke of "the 60,000 hungry workers who swarmed out of China last month. . . ."

(*June 24*) The San Francisco *Chronicle*, in a report from its Hong Kong correspondent: "How many refugees from hungry Red China fled into crowded Hong Kong last month? . . . the truth is anybody's guess."[6]

By July the sudden flow of refugees was over and no longer of general interest to the American press. The stories about the "famine" in China were finally grinding to a halt, though they continued off and on until almost to the end of the year. But *U. S. News & World Report* (which had written on May 28 about the deepening mystery of the refugees—"Many are described as healthy . . . showing no signs of malnutrition") now provided its readers with a new report. On July 9 it ran a bold headline: THE FAMINE MAKERS—A REPORT ON WHY RED CHINA IS STARVING.

[6] The real number of refugees was, indeed, "anybody's guess." "22,000 from the beginning of this month" (*Wall Street Journal*, May 18); Since May 1, "some 30,000 or more" (AP, Hong Kong, May 22). "An estimated 100,000 refugees had escaped to Hong Kong in recent weeks" (*Wall Street Journal*, May 28). "From the first of May until the 25th, 60,000 Chinese were shunted back and forth" (*Newsweek*, June 4).

And (just in case its busy readers did not have time to read the article itself) things were summed up in a subheading: HERE IS THE INSIDE STORY OF WHAT REALLY IS CAUSING THE FAMINE IN RED CHINA. THE CAUSE: COMMUNIST BUNGLING.

Thus, in spite of authoritative denials, statements from British government and U.S. officials, and eyewitness reports, the American public was left with an over-all impression that it was the "famine" in China that was the cause of the refugees.

Two days after *U. S. News & World Report* had run its "inside story of what is causing the famine in Red China," one of Britain's most eminent and respected businessmen addressed the Royal Asian Society in London. Mr. John Keswick has known China for a great many years—long before 1949—and has returned there a number of times since. The subject of his address was a visit he had just completed to China.

> In the towns there were the usual crowds, and to the casual traveller's eye, they certainly did not appear to be starving, as has been reported in some of the press of the Western world.[7]

It was during the summer of 1962—when our papers were running endless stories about China's famine conditions—that I received a letter from a UN official—Mr. Chang Kuo-ho—who, with his American wife and three children, had recently visited his relatives in China. Mr. Chang wrote on July 4, 1962:

> From April 14 to June 1 we were in China. We spent one week in Hangchow, enjoying its quiet beauty and then went to Shanghai for five days. From thence we went to Peking where we spent a month and a half.
>
> After having seen so many of my relatives and friends in China I feel I can fully substantiate your view that "up to and including the present food shortage there has been no starvation in China." My father, aged 70, receives 27 catties

[7] In this address Mr. Keswick described his journey by train through the fertile deltas of the Canton and Pearl rivers. "It runs comfortably, cleanly and on time." *U.S. News & World Report* on July 23, in its page devoted to "Washington Whispers," referred to an unidentified "Chinese businessman just out of Red China: Troubles there are deep and deepening in every conceivable way. For example, a train trip that took three days just a short time ago now takes eight days."

[approximately 35 pounds] of staples—rice, flour and/or other grains in varying proportions—a month; so does my brother, an engineer. The ration coupon required for each meal in a restaurant is usually four ounces, about a bowl and a half of rice, sometimes with a mantow (steamed flour roll). Laborers, of course, get more; a high-school student gets 33 catties [approximately 43 pounds]. Top level intellectuals receive additional coupons for other necessities and for better quality goods.

What is new is the introduction of "high class" commodities on the market, from refreshments up to say a bicycle or a radio. This has encouraged people to save both their money and coupons for something they really want, rather than spending their money always on food. The stores also have some goods to show on their counters. A few years ago it very often happened that as soon as a shipment arrived it was gone in a matter of hours. You referred to this in your remark that the Chinese are "concentrating on improving the quality of their products and increasing their diversity and range."

As far as our own living conditions were concerned, we could not have wished for more. We paid 1.50 yuan (60¢) for a portion of Keh-fon (blue-plate special) and three portions would usually suffice for the five of us, three of whom are children. (The children had a Western breakfast every now and then for a treat.) The standard of hospitality remained on a very high level. We were treated by our friends and relatives to many sumptuous dinners both in Shanghai and Peking. These were still seven or eight course affairs. It seems that in a restaurant coupons are required only for the consumption of staples—rice or flour. The trick, therefore, was to order a big dinner so that nobody wanted to eat any rice or mantow.

The fields around Shanghai, Hangchow and Canton, such as we could see, seemed in excellent condition. When we were in Hangchow it was the season for cabbage, wheat, broad beans and rape, and the fields could not have looked better, with glorious patches of gold in lush green. We detected a note of caution about the expected harvest. People were restrained in their estimates. The wheat fields around Peking were low when we arrived but were waist-high when we left.

This letter from a UN official is only one of many that I received from Westerners in China—visitors and residents—during the "famine" period. Quite obviously these correspondents were in no position to judge the over-all food conditions merely from their personal and therefore limited observations. But the letters did not convey an impression of a desperate and hungry people in the midst of a grim crisis.

At a time when most sources of public information in the United States were giving accounts such as those quoted, the *Far Eastern Economic Review*—a conservative and reliable businessman's weekly published in Hong Kong—carried an article (issue of December 28, 1961) of quite a different order. It was written by Gilbert Etienne, assistant professor at the Graduate Institute of International Studies, Geneva, who had recently returned from China.

> The study of present-day China constitutes above all a lesson in prudence and caution. Eye-witness accounts by foreigners are few and often embody a bias either too favorable or too hostile. . . .
>
> Evidence gathered from non-communist informants as well as our own observations enable us to confirm that it is wrong to speak of real famine, or, as some have done, of general famine. Districts where the situation was particularly serious were pointed out to us, but the conditions there are far from the mass starvation that China has known in the past. Rationing is very strict, though distribution between areas where there is a surplus and those deficient is much better arranged than in the past. . . .

And not quite a year later, when the worst of the shortage was past, one of Britain's most knowledgeable diplomats, Mr. Malcolm MacDonald, had something to say after his return from a visit to China. Mr. MacDonald, son of a former Prime Minister, who has served as U. K. Commissioner-General in South East Asia, British High Commissioner to India, British Representative to the Geneva Conference on Laos, and Governor-General of Kenya was reported as follows in the New York *Times,* which was one of the instances of a different assessment:

He voiced the opinion that the Chinese people and the Government were in a confident but not complacent mood. He noted reports that the second 1962 harvest was better than in the last three years. . . .

"In the old days hundreds of thousands or even millions would have died," he said. "The first effective organization for the distribution of food in China's history had prevented starvation in the last three years," he said.

Comparing conditions in China with those prevailing in 1948, when he last visited the country, Mr. MacDonald said that the standard of living, although low in contrast to industrial nations, was "remarkably improved."

He said the Government had learned from mistakes made during the "great leap forward" instituted in 1958, and had less optimistic goals. The result is that "national economic development is going forward again." (New York *Times*, November 4, 1962.)

On January 1, 1963, this editorial appeared in *The Times* of London:

> . . . For two years past the words famine and starvation have been bandied about and there have been those who even foresaw the fall of the present regime in China because of bad harvests and the failings of the "great leap forward." . . .
>
> . . . Most of the dispute over how much food Chinese have been eating in the past three years centres on the evidence of refugees who cross the border into Hong Kong. Many of the experts question this evidence, arguing that the refugee is sometimes biased, rarely accurate, usually interested in painting an adverse picture. . . .
>
> . . . one reason for general discontention in China could be the fact that a relatively efficient rationing system now spreads the burden whereas in the early decades of this century deaths by starvation in China would run into the hundreds or thousands every year in some part of the country and would exceed a million once in a decade on the average. But there were few "observers" eager to report the fact in those days. . . .

By the spring of 1963 there was abundant evidence that a marked and general improvement in the food conditions of China had taken place. On April 11, 1963, the *Far Eastern Economic Review* devoted many columns to special reports on the food situation from Shanghai and Peking. (American correspondents in Hong Kong made little or no reference to these reports.)

From the magazine's Shanghai correspondent came this account:

> When staple food and cotton became short due to bad harvests, the Government introduced a strict uniform rationing of them throughout the country, but kept the prices down at the original minimum, compatible with the earnings of the larger section of working people. . . .
>
> The scheme gave full protection to the wage earner in the lower bracket of pay. . . .
>
> At present, meat, fish, poultry, eggs, vegetables, etc. are obtainable from the co-operatives in cities in unlimited quantities and without restrictions of any kind, at about double the price of rationed supplies, which continues as heretofore. . . .[8]
>
> Since November last year there has been a substantial reduction in prices of meals in all restaurants, and especially for coffee, cocoa and chocolates: for those items reductions ranged from 50 to 80%. . . .
>
> . . . Coffee and cocoa (with sugar added) are being sold to the public through food stalls at Yuan 0.1 and 0.12 a glass, [approximately 4/10¢ U.S.] and chocolate is sold in the form of candies and sweets in wrappers, on cakes and in bars. . . .
>
> . . . the milk drinking habit among the coming generation, and especially as nourishment for babies and children is now almost universal in cities. In recent years the shortage of fresh milk was acutely felt. . . .
>
> Now the supply has resumed the normal level to regular customers, and bottled milk has become available from provision stores. Recently, after a long absence, butter has appeared on the market. . . .
>
> . . . Lately tinned foodstuffs of pork, chicken and duck meats, fish and vegetables have become available in free sale, as well as various preserves, jams and fruit juices. . . .
>
> While the easier food situation is evident in Shanghai and other large cities, persons returning from visits to their rel-

[8] This is basically the same system that was followed in Britain during wartime rationing.

atives in the interior all proclaim that locally produced food-stuffs are plentiful in the country, their prices are generally lower there than in cities and that commune members with reserved land at their disposal to cultivate are well off.

And an article by Colina MacDougall, citing an official Chinese (Hsinhua) dispatch, reported as follows:

> The Chinese government is taking good care that there should be no immediate recurrences of the serious shortage of vegetables which hit the country in 1961 . . . Peking residents at least now have an abundant supply of vegetables all the year round, even in winter months. . . .
> The average daily supply for the city . . . over the last year was 2,500 tons, which probably means at least a pound of vegetables per head per day. . . .
> Peking reports that all these vegetables were grown in hot-houses, since for four months a year the climate is too cold for outdoor cultivation. . . . The area under hothouses, is said to have increased 20 fold since 1949. . . .
> . . . communes deliver by lorry and cart to more than 1,000 vegetable markets and larger restaurants in the city. This system too has ensured a steady income to the communes and Peking claims that their earnings have risen 50% in the past five years.

But, apparently, firmly implanted concepts take a long time to change even in the most official circles. Six weeks after these reports, and others, were available, Mr. Chester Bowles was still following the "starving Chinese" line. In a talk at Stanford University on May 20 Mr. Bowles—who had been Under Secretary of State, and was soon to take up his post as Ambassador to India—was still referring to "a hungry Communist China," which,

> . . . unable to get the help it needs from Russia to feed its multitudes, [China] will probably try to expand within the next few years . . . China is in a pretty grim situation. . . . The only choice open to China is to make a grab for the rice fields of Southeast Asia. . . .

and he spoke of the Chinese as "people who live on fifteen hundred calories a day."

Two days before Mr. Bowles made his speech, another report about China was circulated by the AP to papers throughout the country. By this time, after nearly three years, stories about China's "starvation" and "famine" had all but petered out. The "collapse" so confidently predicted just hadn't happened. In the press, an occasional story, such as this AP dispatch, was appearing. The report was by Mr. Richard P. Lister, a British author and former industrial metallurgist who had just returned from China:

> China is vast and we saw only a fraction of it. All the same you cannot spend half a day in Naples without knowing the deep poverty or a morning in Stockholm without seeing that the Swedes are thriving. In the China we saw, there were no signs of despair. There were poverty and hard living but the people seemed to have enough to eat and enough to wear. Above all, they had hope. Things were getting better and they could see that happening. . . .
> Floods, harvest failures, international complications all appear to be things to be overcome rather than moaned about. Do they worry about overpopulation? Indeed not. For the moment it's perhaps a blessing. . . .
> . . . output of food is increasing at a spectacular rate. Floods are being brought under control, irrigation is improved and the organized labor of the village commune does lift the individual from the despondency of fruitless toil.
> The Chinese seem as confident of the future as they are of their place in the scheme of things today. Perhaps even more so. (San Francisco *Examiner*, May 19, 1963.)

But the constant reiteration by our press of the "starvation" stories made an impression that could not be corrected by occasional accounts such as these. The image retained in the minds of most Americans is of a China whose people live in conditions of almost perpetual hunger.

Chapter 7

THE MATHEMATICS OF SUFFERING

I. The Cost of Progress

The world we live in today, with all its marvelous achievements, is still a world in which the life experience for most people is one of prolonged suffering.

The facts are sadly familiar to us. Between one-third and one-half of the world's population suffer malnutrition.[1] Every day some ten thousand people die of malnutrition or starvation—more than at any time in history; in India alone fifty million children will die from lack of food in the next ten years.[2] Two-thirds of the human race have an average per capita income equivalent to fifty or sixty dollars a year. Seventy percent of the food-growing families of the world still use wooden ploughs or hoes, the least efficient tools for raising food; and only 2 percent possess power implements.[3] A college graduate in India is lucky if he can find work that will pay him more than five dollars a week. Only a very small percentage of the world's people have access to a hospital when they fall ill. The electricity generated in the whole of the Indian subcontinent would be insufficient for the needs of New York City. Women in the United States spend more *on cosmetics* than the combined total of the national budgets of all the African countries that have won their independence since the war.

[1] Reuters report of the First International Congress of Food Science and Technology, London, September 18, 1962.
[2] *Newsweek*, June 17, 1963, reporting on the World Food Congress held in Washington under the auspices of the UN.
[3] *Die Weltwoche*, Zurich, September 6, 1958.

The facts shock us, and then numb us. What the statistics represent is so far outside our own experience that we can make no identification with the human realities behind them. We cannot *feel* what it means to be this poor. But whether we can feel it or not does not alter the fact that this is the world we live in. Those of us in the advanced Western countries represent a small and favored minority—15 percent of the world's population, consuming 55 percent of the world's goods. And there are hundreds of millions of human beings who are determined that it isn't going to remain that way!

How is a poor country to become less poor?

To begin to lift itself up out of poverty, squalor, and illiteracy, a nation needs to save. An irrigation pump, a school, a bicycle factory, a road, an iron plough, cannot be obtained unless someone has saved money to buy it with. *There is no other way.* And for a nation whose people are barely surviving, saving means suffering, and with suffering come social tensions and unrest. The suffering and social tension are less if the people understand their collective goals and if the effort is shared equally, and in these circumstances pride, the sense of joining in a common struggle, and mutual support is greatly enhanced. The social tension is great when the suffering is unequal and when one class of people not only are escaping the suffering but are actually benefiting from the suffering of others.

Western progress came with suffering. Britain led the world in industrial emergence—but at what a frightful human cost! The suffering in Britain was not shared equally by all. It is not long ago, as history goes (in the lifetime of my grandfather) when children of seven and eight were sent down the coal mines of South Wales and girls of nine worked fourteen hours a day in the textile mills of Lancashire. From their present position of economic security the British forget—they probably wish to forget—their own dark legacy.

Two generations or more of British working people were sacrificed to enable Britain to save and to advance: farmers and shepherds and village craftsmen were herded into the dark slums of the industrial cities to live in conditions that would not today be permitted for animals. This appalling human exploitation enabled a relatively few people, a single class, to get rich, and from their savings more factories and mines and mills and railroads and ships could be built. Britain built an empire on the accumulated wealth of a very few—and with the empire the burden of suffering was shifted somewhat from her own island people to those abroad whom she had subjugated and was in a position to exploit. Because the suffering was not imposed equitably but with injustice, the social tensions at home in Britain's Industrial Revolution were great. The rise of Britain as an industrial power was marked by continual riots, unrest, and savage reprisals—and at times the firing of rifles by a well-fed army on defenseless and despairing workers. And Britain in its day had its refugees—hundreds of thousands of them, fleeing to the colonies, to America, to anywhere where life seemed to offer something better than the unspeakable conditions in that emerging industrial nation.

Britain became rich and powerful, but the effects of those times and the class antagonisms which they engendered are deep within her society still.

And the United States?

The United States began its life under extraordinary favored circumstances. Here were vast farming lands as yet untouched, and below the ground almost limitless natural resources quite unexploited. And above all, the wealth of the British upper class was available for the early capitalization of American industry. With the exception of the indigenous Indian population which was dispossessed, America might have been spared the suffering that would otherwise have come in its period of industrial growth.

But in spite of these uniquely favorable conditions, America did not escape her share of human suffering. In using Negro slavery and Mexicans for its agrarian development (and cheap imported labor from Europe for its industries), America also inflicted its share of injustice and misery on others. The "internalized colony" of the Negro population, as far as cheap labor is concerned, served the same purpose as Britain's colonies overseas.

And with slavery, there emerged two social-economic systems within America so disparate and contradictory that only a savage and prolonged civil war could again unify the country—and the six hundred thousand dead of that war must be added to the human cost of American advance.

We need to remind ourselves of these historic facts, not to feel guilty or wring our hands, but to enable us to understand some of the extraordinarily difficult problems that today face the underdeveloped countries of the world. And we mustn't forget that the emerging countries have no exterior "colonial" people and resources to exploit, nor an internal slave population, which so significantly helped the development of the British and American economies.

There are several other essential and inescapable conditions that must be met if backward countries are to advance, and one of them is the fullest possible mobilization of the surplus that has accumulated in the hands of the wealthier classes. In some backward countries there is in fact no shortage of surplus. Twenty-five percent of India's national income, for example, is at the disposal of a minute and largely unproductive strata of the population. (A London *Times* dispatch from New Delhi—see page 141—reported that about 1 percent of India's population earns nearly half the national income.) In Latin America vast revenues today find their way into the hands of a very small elite, revenues which if prudently used for the advancement of the national economies would enable these countries to make a start on the road to economic development and social regeneration.

However, such mobilization of existing and potential economic surplus is bound to meet with the determined opposition from the property-owning strata, the "small class, whose main interest is the preservation of its wealth and privileges."[4] *The fundamental challenge that faces all backward countries* is to overcome the implacable resistance of the class that at present enjoys the possession of power and wealth. Until this challenge is faced and met there

[4] United Nations, *Measures for the Economic Development of Under-developed Countries*, 1951, par. 37.

is almost no possibility of a genuine program of economic and social progress.

As their position is progressively challenged, the ruling elite in backward countries tend to increase their measures of repression. Waste, extravagance, corruption, absentee landlordism, and disregard for the welfare of the people characterize nearly all of these countries. The ruling groups are prepared to squander vast sums on sprawling bureaucracies and on large military establishments the sole function of which is to keep the regimes in power and to provide the instruments of repression. Under these conditions the peaceful transformation of a country from a state of squalor, stagnation, and oppression toward an advancing social democracy becomes impossible. Hostility and desperation mount and the people are at last left with only one recourse—the physical removal of the elite that has for so long oppressed them. What at one stage might have been accomplished peacefully can at a later stage be done only with violence.

To overcome the resistance of a repressive ruling class, to mobilize all existing surplus capital, and to save—these are the three basic problems that confront every backward country, in Africa, Asia, or Latin America. These three essentials represent the inescapable costs of economic growth. Some countries are as yet unwilling to meet these costs, or, if the people themselves are willing, they are still too weak to overcome the resistance of those defending their positions of power and privilege. Other countries, such as China, have understood these realities and have been prepared to act on them. China recognized, as Russia did, that no progress was possible until their regressive ruling classes had been overthrown. They recognized also that no progress was possible without the mobilization of all existing savings, and that further savings could only come through work. And, finally, they recognized the obvious fact that if the hardship and effort that are inevitable during the early stages of primary accumulation were to be equitably shared, the economic direction must be centralized.

Both Russia and China, once their regimes were established, took immediate steps to improve the social conditions of the people. They expanded educational opportunities, improved public health and medical facilities, and gave security for the old. But at the same time the basic rule of national saving was never forgotten—that during the period of primary accumulation the people's per capita production had to rise more rapidly than their per capita consumption. In other words, the individual's standard of living could improve, despite greatly increased work, only relatively slowly.

One of the extraordinary features of life in China today, as I found when I was there, is the extent to which this basic economic lesson is understood by even the humblest peasant. He knows that he is expected to work harder than ever before and he knows why improvement in his standard of living can at this stage rise only relatively slowly. Because this first lesson in economics has been explained and re-explained to the masses of people in China, because they can begin to see around them the benefits deriving from collective saving, and above all because the people themselves have insisted that the work and effort be shared equally by everyone, there has been significantly less social tension in China during the past decade than Russia experienced in the equivalent stage of her "primary accumulation."

Today the Russian people are finally reaping the rewards of forty years of effort and denial. They submitted to a system of austerity, economic discipline, and forced marches to higher production goals because *this is the only way a very backward country can advance itself*. The inequitable class exploitation that enabled Britain to industrialize and advance would not be tolerated today by any country in the world. Russia has passed its stage of primary accumulation and her people are now enjoying a rapidly rising standard of living. If she maintains her present rate of increase and we do not increase ours, the Russian people will—in the lifetime of our children—be enjoying the highest standard of living in the world, with the most comprehensive system of social security. This is what an extremely backward nation can do if it comes to grips with the essential economic laws which govern economic growth.

But as Professor Gilbert Etienne—who has studied the Chinese efforts at firsthand—has written in his very careful account of the Chinese economy:

> The scope of their task was much greater and the lack of capital much more serious than faced the Russians in 1927, which prevents the Chinese from drawing inspiration too closely from the Soviet pattern for growth. For lack of capital, human investment and mobilization of the masses were undertaken much more systematically than before 1957. . . .
>
> The method of application may be criticized but, at the heart of the problem, experiments observed in other Asian countries lead us to think that clear and decisive progress will remain uncertain if Asia limits itself to classic methods of financing, whether Soviet or Western. Somehow or other it is necessary to stimulate more efficiently the energies of the masses. . . .
>
> To sum up . . . the great leap certainly does not lack interest. On the contrary it deserves careful study for even in non-communist underdeveloped countries certain Chinese lessons might be taken note of . . . it is useful to ponder the stern struggle of the Chinese at a moment when certain Asian and African countries tend to see in foreign aid the key to every problem, and suppose that all that is required is a fair distribution of the resources of the globe. . . .[5]

It is true that those countries that already have an accumulated surplus, and have gained knowledge in industrial techniques, can help the underdeveloped countries to mitigate the inevitable hardships that come when a poor country begins to save. But no amount of aid from outside can be a substitute for the basic savings that can come only from the energies of the indigenous population. India, for example, in the past ten years, has received in aid $6.5 billion dollars—a prodigious sum. But until India finds ways of releasing the latent energies of her own people, and to tackle the problem of primary accumulation, all that this foreign aid can do, at best, is to prevent the total disintegration and collapse of the Indian economy; it cannot in any significant way advance it.

There is an understandable reluctance in the West to face these

[5] *Far Eastern Economic Review*, December 28, 1961.

hard requirements of economic growth in less-favored countries. America historically never went through the period of feudal suppression that today has so many people in its grip. We have nothing in our own national experience to help us feel the helplessness and fury that is moving those who wish to break their chains. Our own revolution—led by a cultivated and politically conscious upper class—is far behind us; we shrink from the thought of social tension and violence. We hope that by providing some of our own surplus capital, our technical knowledge, and our goodwill, economic advance can be promoted sufficiently quickly to prevent the hungry masses from breaking into violent action.

This hope is not likely to be fulfilled. We are placing altogether too much reliance on foreign aid. It will require far more than aid from abroad before economic and social advance is possible in the poor countries of the world. The necessity—understood by the Chinese—of finding ways to release the energies of their own people, rather than to rely on foreign aid, is slowly being acknowledged.

For example, an editor of *The Christian Science Monitor* wrote an article on March 20, 1963, after returning from a visit to Asia, in which he asked (italics mine):

> . . . what of the race between Communist and non-Communist standards of living? What of the race between India and China?

His own answer was:

> *It is best not mentioned in a loud voice . . . The kind of agricultural drive that the Communists themselves attempt, the all-out effort with the entire country mobilized to propel it, is India's and South Asia's next and greatest need.*

II. The Cost of Stagnation

> . . . the undeniable material accomplishments of the Chinese Communists have cost dearly in terms of human freedom and human dignity.
>
> —Robert C. North
> (*Moscow and Chinese Communists*, p. 264)

With this statement, Dr. North added his support to a tired cliché which even by 1953 had been repeated a hundred times and which has been heard a thousand times since. Whenever a scholar like Dr. North, or a newspaper writer, is confronted with undeniable evidence of progress in China, the use of this cliché makes it appear that it would have been better if no progress had been made at all.

> . . . the high price in human lives and human misery that the Chinese people have had to pay for Chinese Communist achievements.
>
> —A. T. Steele, New York *Herald Tribune,*
> September 16, 1956.

> The Chinese Communists have forced agriculture ahead by a series of power drives . . . the human cost was nightmarish.
>
> —Editorial, *The Christian Science Monitor,*
> March 13, 1962.

There are many others.

Even before reaching page one of his "history" of the early years of the Chinese government, the scholar Richard L. Walker (see Chapter 4, "The China Lobby") murmured the usual incantations: "The cost of the tremendous task of remaking China in the Soviet image has been unbelievable in terms both of human and of cultural destruction." Throughout his book Mr. Walker appears to be obsessed by "human costs" in China—"a cost in human destruction which staggers the imagination."[6]

Another scholar, Dr. Y. L. Wu, wrote about Peking's early problems "in managing and expanding a rather confused and lethargic economy" (a quaintly restrained description of Chiang Kai-shek's corrupt and rotting economy in 1949), and "the human suffering and sacrifice its policy has exacted."[7]

[6] *China Under Communism—The First Five Years* (New Haven, Conn.: Yale University Press, 1955), Introduction p. xii and 153.
[7] *An Economic Survey of Communist China* (New York: Bookman Associates, 1956), Introduction p. 3.

Tillman Durdin, several years later in the New York *Times* for April 27, 1958, cabled from Hong Kong:

> Peiping says impressively high production is being achieved. . . . But the effort that is being put forth by the Chinese people must be somewhere near the limit of human endurance.

(A week later, on May 4, *The Times* headlined a Reuters dispatch, not from Hong Kong but from China itself, which presented quite a different picture: SUNDAY IN PEIPING IS A DAY OF JOLLITY, STORES, CAFES, BATHHOUSES AND THEATRES CROWDED—REDS FIND REST USEFUL.)

And *Time* Magazine on December 1, 1961, in nearly ten pages of text and pictures on the subject "Red China—The Loss of Man," presented a picture of almost unrelieved catastrophe, but managed to detect "some gains."

> But whatever the gains, they do not begin to offset the price imposed by Peking through oppression and misery. Today no one can be sure how many people share this misery. . . .

It is a disturbing fact that none of these commentators and scholars have suggested possible alternative policies that might have been open to the Chinese government. Most would say, no doubt, that to have returned to the appalling conditions under Chiang would have been unthinkable; and they might generally agree that the first achievements of Mao's government were impressive. The mobilization of the energies of the people, the stabilization of a runaway inflation, the steps taken to equalize food supplies, the reconstruction of rundown factories, the distribution of land to the peasants, the great advances in public health, and the expansion of educational facilities—all these were vital if yet further disasters were not to fall upon the Chinese people. From the moment that the Communists took over, the widespread starvation that had become a recurring nightmare of Chinese life became a thing of the past. And yet these accomplishments, we are told, were achieved only at a "human cost" so terrible that they outweighed the benefits they brought.

Press and scholar alike repeat the cliché but provide no clues as to what the government could have done. Dr. North takes pity on the Chinese for their loss of dignity and freedom. What dignity and freedom did they have to lose? Neither dignity nor freedom is possible when life is dominated by the most elemental anxieties of survival.

Is it possible that some of those who now talk of the "human cost" of China's progress are unconsciously expressing nostalgia for the China that they knew? For the Westerner, as we have said, life was good in the old China. He remembers the good food, the gracious houses, the polite servants. He may remember wistfully how much the American dollar could buy. His was a life of easy ascendancy. He did not need to feel a responsibility for the people or the country. And within this narrow circle of privilege, life in China must have exerted an extraordinary charm.

I have noticed that many of those who recall their life in China and talk most of the "human cost" that has been paid for today's achievements tend to remember not the children scratching in the garbage heaps, the tiny bundles—the dead infants—in the streets, the coughing rickshaw men, the disease, the dirt, the appalling squalor. They remember—it is natural enough—the gay parties and the flowered dresses at the Shanghai race course (in the enclosure reserved for foreigners), the Sunday picnics in the Western Hills outside Peking, the dinners in the courtyard under candlelight, the leisurely tiffins at the club, the quiet talks with refined and Westernized Chinese friends. Those who recall this life must do so with a certain anguish, knowing that it has all been quite swept away. Is it just possible that this is the "cost" they speak of?

The great mass of the Chinese have no such memories and no nostalgia at all for the China that is gone. Talk to a Chinese today about his "loss of freedom" and he would laugh in your face.

As I wrote earlier:

> When a Chinese worker or peasant says he is freer today than he has ever been in his life, he means it. And he sounds as if he means it. Perhaps he doesn't mean it in our way, for he has never known the particular forms of political and

social freedom which have been the product of our own historical past and which are the fruit of our relative physical security.

A Chinese uses the word "freedom" in a very personal down-to-earth, non-theoretical sense. He is not talking about abstractions but experience. He means that he is at last free to eat, and not to starve; he is free of the landlord and moneylender; he is free to develop skills and to exercise talents which would otherwise have remained hidden; he is free to send his children to school, and when they are ill there is a doctor who can help to make them well; he is free to look at the future with hope and not with despair. For him these are all *new* freedoms. And it's not such a bad list!

As for dignity, I think it is very probable that the forty million people of minority races in China who for the first time are enjoying complete political and social equality with all others, would say their dignity has been enhanced, not lessened. The Marriage Law . . . released the women of China from the miseries of a very degrading feudal system.[8]

I would like to see Dr. North ask a young woman of China today if she feels her "human dignity" has been infringed!

Before our professors, whether or not they have ever been in China, express too much solicitude about the fate of the "individual" and the loss of his freedom and dignity, they might pause a moment to recall that the freedoms and "individualism" we enjoy did not arrive out of thin air, they did not come out of nothing.

The liberties and political democracy we have today *had to be fought for*. They are the result of a good many years of bloody trial and error—first in Britain, then extended to the United States. Many brave men sacrificed their lives to achieve them. Those who talk so easily of the "free world" should remember, and perhaps with a humility that does not come easily, that our favored condition on this planet is still sustained at the expense of others. What our professors choose to call our "human dignity" is possible because of our relative affluence, an affluence based even today largely on exploitation of peoples in less-favored lands.

And for those who forget this and who pin their hope for the

[8] *Awakened China*, pp. 388–89.

underdeveloped countries on aid, this extract from an article in *Bulletin of the Atomic Scientists* by a Pakistani may be a useful reminder:

> But why are we poor? Mostly no doubt through our own follies. But let me humbly suggest that it may partly also be that we are financing some of the prosperity of the rich. Year after year I have seen the cotton crop from my village in Pakistan fetch less and less money; year after year the imported fertilizer has cost more. My economist friends tell me the terms of trade are against us. Between 1955 and 1962 the commodity prices fell by seven per cent. In the same period the manufactured goods went up by ten per cent. Some courageous men have spoken against this. Paul Hoffman called it a "subsidy, a contribution paid by the underdeveloped countries to the industrialized world." In 1957–1958 the underdeveloped world received a total of $2.4 billion in aid and lost $2 billion in import capacity (through paying more for the manufactured goods it buys and getting less for what it sells), thus washing away nearly all the sums received in aid.[9]

The scholars in the China field before 1949 expressed very little concern over the lack of freedom there or the monstrous injustices of the social system under Chiang Kai-shek. Nationalist China's stagnation brought forth no sympathy for the "human dignity" of the Chinese people then. And it strikes much of the world as a little ironic that those who cry the loudest about the loss of freedom and dignity in China are members of a society that prevents a large section of its own people from enjoying any dignity at all, and where soldiers carrying rifles have to accompany small children to school lest they be stoned by mobs.

As Max Horkheimer astutely observes, throughout history "the value of the individual has been extolled by those who had an opportunity of developing their individualities at the expense of others."[10]

It is not often that I find myself in philosophical agreement with the late Mr. John Foster Dulles, but even he appeared to have a

[9] April 1963. "Diseases of the Rich and Diseases of the Poor," by Abdus Salam.
[10] *The Eclipse of Reason* (New York: Oxford University Press, 1947), p. 178.

closer grasp of the realities than our professors with their talk about
the "loss of freedom and human dignity."

> We can talk eloquently about liberty and freedom, and
> about human rights and fundamental freedoms, and about
> the dignity and worth of the human personality, but most
> of our vocabulary derives from a period when our own soci-
> ety was individualistic. Consequently, it has little meaning
> to those who live under conditions where individualism
> means premature death.[11]

But if (as I believe) there has been a serious failure on the
part of those who have reported on events in China to present
thoughtful alternatives to the programs which they have so severely criticized, they are guilty also of another failure. Nowhere
do they attempt to place the Chinese experience in any kind of
relation to what is going on in other parts of the world (with the
exception of India, which I will deal with presently).

There *is* a cost to be paid for progress—no one can possibly
deny this; but a cursory view of other underdeveloped countries
might have reminded these writers that perhaps there is a much
grimmer price to be paid for *not* progressing.

In reading accounts of other underdeveloped areas one is aware
of a wholly different tone of voice to the one used when our
writers deal with China. Here there is no high moral indignation,
no singling out of government leaders for blame, or if they are
blamed they are never spoken of, as the present Chinese leaders
so often are, as if they were totally evil men.

At about the same period when the press was devoting a tremendous amount of space to describing the "famine" and "starvation" in China, *Newsweek* (August 27, 1962) contained this account of South America:

> Just a few hours by jet from New York or Chicago live
> more than 200 million people in the vast reaches of Latin
> America, and it is doubtful if one-tenth of them know what
> it is like to go to bed with a full stomach. The great cities
> glitter opulently—Rio de Janeiro, Buenos Aires, Mexico
> City; but beneath the glitter and in the hinterland are odious

11 *War or Peace* (New York: Macmillan, 1950 and 1957), p. 257.

and despondent slums where liquid-eyed Indian children scrounge for scraps and handouts while their parents labor for wages of twenty cents a day or less. This is the wasteland of the Western hemisphere, a land of misery whose poverty is as stark as any in the world. Here the nearest thing to peace is a kind of embittered apathy, and the only known order is confusion.

On August 20, 1962, the Los Angeles *Times* was describing how "750,000 live in tin and packing crate shacks in slums on Buenos Aires fringe." On November 15 of the same year a New York *Times* editorial dealt with Peru:

> A little news item from Lima, Peru, tells a potentially big story. It is about Indian peasants—8,000 of them—in the old Inca capital of Cuzco, high in the Andes, clashing with the police. They were expressing a protest, the specific motivation of which was less important than the general discontent that pervades the southern part of the Peruvian highlands. . . . They live in such poverty as to be outside the money economy, and are not only illiterate but do not speak Spanish.
>
> This is the kind of problem that the Alliance for Progress is trying to alleviate by encouraging land reform. In Peru, with its very small, hereditary land-owning class and a military junta that is doing little or nothing, it is hard to achieve such reforms. The social structure has changed relatively little in the last four centuries. Now, for the first time, the people are learning that their poverty, illiteracy, and disease are based on social injustice. The Communists preach revolution; we preach evolution through reforms under the Alliance for Progress.

A week later the New York *Times* editorial column spoke of riots in Chile:

> . . . Anyone doubting Chile's difficulties need only read the frank and courageous pastoral of the Chilean Bishops issued on September 18. Two sentences will explain the basis for such discontent as the Santiago riot demonstrated: "Serious statistical studies, based on official sources, tell us that one-tenth of the Chilean population receives about half of the national income, while the remaining nine-tenths must

subsist on the other half. This means that a great part of the working class does not receive wages commensurate with the norms of social justice."

. . . As with other such situations in Latin America, help and understanding from the United States are required—and time.

One cannot help but compare the note of understanding solicitude adopted in this editorial with the tone of voice of an editorial —also in the New York *Times* (December 30, 1960)—dealing with "Famine in China."

. . . Moreover, we may suspect that the system of People's Communes, with its fantastic effort to reduce the individual Chinese peasant to the status of a work ant in an ant colony, has played a role in the present catastrophe.

From the Philippines came a report in *The Christian Science Monitor* (January 8, 1963):

According to government statistics, there are at present about 1,000,000 Filipinos totally unemployed, and another 3,000,000 under-employed. Of a population of 29,000,000 some 5,000,000 are earning from $48 to $60 a year; 20,000,000 are earning from $75 to $250 a year; and four million are earning more than $250 a year.

Philippine Secretary of Finance Rodrigo Perez said that the statistics "mean that 25,000,000 [i.e., 86% of the population] are worrying about where their next meal will come from.

And in *The New Republic*—an editorial on January 5, 1963—a report on Brazil:

. . . the nation's 10 million landless farmers earn between 25 and 50 cents a day, and face starvation in a bad crop year. . . . 80 per cent of the arable land held by 2 per cent of the proprietors. . . . From two to four infants out of ten in the northeast die before they are a year old. . . .

These few reports are enough to give us a terrible glimpse into what happens in the countries that have not yet been able to lift themselves up from their basic poverty—here we can see the human price that is exacted for *not* progressing.

Substitute the names of the countries and the cities and we would see China before the revolution—but in China on so much vaster a scale. The French correspondent, Robert Guillain, who is a sharp critic of today's regime, nevertheless recalled the conditions of the past:

> Before, it was appalling—that truth predominated over every other. Poverty, corruption, inefficiency, misery, contempt for the people and for the commonweal, these were the elements that made up the most wretched nation on earth. And I knew China then.[12]

We need these reminders of the past, these tallies of the cost of stagnation, if only as milestones to see the prodigious distance the Chinese have come. Twenty thousand bodies, on average, picked up off the streets of Shanghai every year (37,000 in 1933); three million lives lost in 1931 in central China through flood and famine; over a million in 1942 in Honan province. And the landlords hoarding grain while babies ate grass and roots. And young girls sold to slavery or prostitution so that at least they would eat. Areas the size of France with virtually no doctors, and rickshaw men with a professional life-expectance of eight years. . . . *This was the China of the past, but it is not the China of today.* This was the price the Chinese people were paying for stagnation, until with indescribable efforts they rose and shed their nightmare past.

In the light of these historic facts, one must ask: By what right do our well-paid writers and our comfortable scholars now presume to tell us that the Chinese people have paid too high a price for their advance?

III. *The Indian Way vs. the Chinese Way—A Case History of Self-Deception*

Two Asian nations, both preponderantly peasant, both with vast populations, both attempting to lift themselves up from a condition of immemorial poverty—and both with new but very

[12] *Le Monde*, Paris, quoted in *The Long March* by Simone de Beauvoir (The World Publishing Company, Cleveland and New York, 1958), p. 485.

differing forms of government. It is little wonder that our newspapers like to see these two great people as engaged in a "race," the outcome of which will either help or damage us in the cold war struggle.

Differences of physiological conditioning, of resources, of climate, and countless differences of social tradition, make this concept of a "race" largely meaningless, but nevertheless the comparison is there and some useful lessons may be learned from it.

And, of course, for a host of reasons, we want India to "win."

The outlook has never been promising; but when the relative rates of progress discourage us we are assured that though material progress in India has been slower, it is being achieved more democratically, more "humanely," with less authoritarian control, with greater stability, and that in the end India will far outdistance a China that has progressed only by driving its people forward "to the edge of endurance" and at a "frightful human cost."

If we believe this, we had better wake up.

I have been to both countries. I have walked through Indian villages and Chinese villages. I have seen the advances in technology in both countries. I have talked with students and teachers, and writers, peasants and workers, and at length with both the prime ministers. I have watched the children playing in the city streets and studying in their schools. I have walked through the slums of Calcutta and the slums of Shanghai—the very worst of them.

And I say we had better stop kidding ourselves.

I know as certainly as I know that I am writing this book that if the press and the politicians continue to tell us that India under her present system will eventually win this "race" with China, or that her way is more "humane," or more stable, or more orderly, or likely to meet more nearly the spiritual and material aspirations of human beings—then I say they are using words with little relation to reality.

India is "freer," yes. For the very few. It is a more decentralized, more pluralized society. More lethargic. Much more easygoing. For the privileged much more comfortable. In the universities the

British liberal tradition has taken firm root. You can spend delightful days with young university students in stimulating speculation over the widest possible range of topics, in a way that is not possible in China today. I don't for a moment want to minimize the value of these things and I would be sad to see them sacrificed.

But the issue is not quite so simple as it sounds.

The Indians in their university may read Burke and Bentham and Locke and Thoreau—they are very bright and intellectually ingenious, these young Indians—but they appear curiously unrelated to the teeming life of India. I was brought up sharply one day talking with a small group when one of them said: "How *bored* we are with our own country!" and I noticed the "we" and looked quickly at the others, and in their expressions I could see nothing but agreement. A remark like that might have been heard in the days of the Kuomintang, among those of the wealthier Chinese students who had lost hope in the future of China. But it is utterly impossible to imagine a Chinese student saying it today. A Chinese student is not unrelated to the life around him, he is *involved* in it—involved personally, directly, emotionally. His own likes and dislikes are secondary and almost irrelevant to him, for the central fact of his experience—the fact which gives his life meaning and which has released his abundant energy—is precisely this involvement with his people and his country.

So we are confronted once more with that crucial equation in the strange mathematics of suffering—and perhaps it has no final answer—how are we to balance freedom for the very few against poverty and stagnation for the many?

But this question, when it confronts actualities, appears somewhat theoretical. The reality is that the average child of a peasant or worker in China today has better health, better food, a better chance for education, greater security, and is likely to live longer, than the average child of an Indian peasant or worker. If he is musical or has a gift for writing or painting, he stands a far greater chance of finding opportunities to develop his talents. If he becomes a scholar or technician he will never—as happens so often in India—find his skills unwanted.

In material development, in technology, in industrial production —the advantage lies decisively with China. Here are a few facts. The press largely ignores them, but we had better not.

Item. Though left in 1947 by Britain with a more advanced industrial base, India by 1962 had increased her steel production only to 3,707,000 metric tons. China that, prior to 1949, had never produced more than two million tons of steel had, by 1960, increased production to 18.4 million metric tons,[13] *five times the production of India* (or about twice the Japanese steel production at the time of Pearl Harbor).

Item. China's grain production in 1962 was estimated at 185 million metric tons;[14] India's grain production for the same year was eighty million metric tons.[15] Allowing for differences of population, this indicates that China's per capita grain production was 56 percent higher than India's.

Item. By 1960, India's rate of investment was barely one-tenth of her national income; in China it was three times higher.[16]

Item. China's rate of industrial growth in the decade before 1960 was about three times faster than during the same period in India.[16]

Item. India's investment has been assisted by foreign aid which, up to August 1962, amounted to more than $6.5 billion;[17] China's investment came almost entirely out of her own current production.

The Christian Science Monitor, in an editorial on March 13, 1962, entitled "Red China Reappraised," made one of the rare

---

[13] *Far Eastern Economic Review,* April 18, 1963.

[14] At the time of this writing, China has given no official figures for the year 1962, but the New York *Times* (February 4, 1962) reported an estimate by experts in Hong Kong of 185–90 million tons. *The Christian Science Monitor* on the same day reported estimates of 180–85 million tons. I have taken the mean figure.

[15] A report from New Delhi, *The Times* of London, March 11, 1963.

[16] Tibor Mende, *China and Her Shadow,* p. 262.

[17] The U.S. share alone was $3.952 billion between July 1945 and mid-1962. (Report by Presidential Advisory Committee on Foreign Aid. New York *Times,* March 22, 1963.)

references to these comparisons with India (and this at a time when the press, including the *Monitor* itself, was talking of China's "famine" and speculating about her "collapse"):

"The Great Leap Backward" is a much used current phrase enjoyed by all.

. . . a quick check of any newspaper file will confirm this one-sided flow of information. Weaknesses of Chinese Communism are played up. Its accomplishments too often ignored.

. . . Growing evidence suggests that China is moving ahead far more rapidly than India into economic development. . . . Comparisons by individual industries and even by crops are equally impressive.

Though statistical comparison with China is not often made, reports in the press (until the border fighting began in October 1962) were voicing increasing concern about the health of India's economy. Something was clearly going very seriously amiss in spite of $700 million-a-year aid from this country. As early as 1960, India's Finance Minister was warning that India's resources were almost at rock bottom and that there was no scope for running them further down. He also said that India would have to depend wholly on foreign aid for the financing of development plans.

The danger is that such assistance may replace ordinary trade . . . leaving the Indian economy chronically dependent on American aid. . . .

Indian sales abroad have expanded only 3% in the last decade. . . .

—*The Wall Street Journal*,
June 22, 1962.

For the past three years . . . production of food grains in India has been static. . . . The population . . . now multiplies at a rate of 11 million a year. The rate of acceleration is still mounting.

There is in India a general lack of a sense of urgency about the food problem . . . the yield of India's fields has increased only fractionally, if at all, in the past 30 years.

—From a special report on
India's agriculture, *The Times*
of London, March 11, 1963.

. . . production far short of plans and in some cases even declining. . . . Profits from nationalized industries: Target $950 million. Actual profit $5.4 million, .03 percent of investment.

—Reporting on the first year of India's Five-Year Plan, *Newsweek* (July 9, 1962).

India's Finance Minister is chasing through the capitals of Europe in pursuit of $220,000,000 to finance the second year of the 3rd Five Year Plan; meanwhile India's liquid assets have been dropping inexorably to new all-time lows.

Barron's, July 16, 1962.

Considering India's many troubles, it seems clear that foreign aid for a program of accelerated industrialization may raise as many problems as it is intended to solve.

—*The Wall Street Journal,* June 22, 1962.

Today India's foreign exchange reserves have practically disappeared and there is no money to pay for maintenance imports. . . . India is increasing, not decreasing, its reliance on foreign capital.

—*The Christian Science Monitor,* November 15, 1962.

These are indications of a foundering economy.

Some savings, some advances there have been; but the effort, the sacrifice involved, has been unequally applied. In a feature story entitled "Social Injustice in India," *The Wall Street Journal* on July 16, 1962, reported that the production of things needed by the poorer people has been increased very little (matches, 1.1 times; cotton cloth, 1.4 times; soap, 1.8 times), while the production of things used for the wealthier people, items that are mostly just "curios" to the poor, has been increased by much more (radios, 5.9 times; sewing machines, 9.6 times; rayon yarn, 21 times). The needs of the well-to-do, a fraction of the population, have in the words of the report, "been very well looked after." While the price of foodstuffs rose by 48 percent, the prices of luxuries and semi-luxuries "remained comparatively steady until recently, when some relatively slight increases occurred."

Not everyone in India is poor. A report from Bombay in the San Francisco *Chronicle* on December 31, 1962, described how a father (an aluminum merchant) spent sixty thousand dollars on his daughter's wedding—"scented water was sprayed even on the lamp posts"; how a cloth merchant spent forty thousand dollars on his sixty-fifth birthday celebration, and how a former maharaja threw a "wedding party" costing fifteen thousand dollars for the "marriage" of his pet dog. While on April 15, 1963, a report in the same paper tells us that Calcutta is a:

> . . . city of incredible extremes: extremes of human degradation superimposed on extremes of vast wealth. The wealth belongs to the enormous business firms. . . . Their proprietors (still mostly British) maintain a standard of elegance in their homes which is probably equalled only by Texas oil barons. Yet only a mile away, the impoverished huddle in their packing-case shelters and brush their teeth in gutter water.

Another aspect of social injustice—age-old and difficult to eradicate—is India's system of castes. Though abolished by law nearly two decades ago, discrimination against the "untouchable" still continues.

> . . . the centuries-old practice of discrimination against the lowly Untouchable caste has faded in India's major cities. But in the rural villages where most of the country's 453 million live, segregation of Untouchables is still widespread—and often violently enforced.
> Age-old restrictions [include] bars against Chamars using umbrellas, riding horses or sitting on carpets. . . .
> 64.5 million [one-seventh of the population] Untouchables [are] . . . barred from temples, forced to use special teacups in teashops, and frequently refused service by barbers. . . .
> —*Newsweek*,
> February 11, 1963.

It is almost axiomatic that when a backward nation attempts to advance without a basis of social and economic justice, tensions and violence will result. India is no exception.

I remember when I was in India in the summer of 1959, I noticed a not-very-prominent account in the papers of a riot in

Calcutta. On August 30 twenty thousand people rioted in Nagpur. The next day, and for four consecutive days, raging mobs surged through the streets of Calcutta—a mass riot that was only subdued after troops and police opened fire, leaving many dead. (I could not help thinking at the time what our press would have made of this incident if it had occurred in Shanghai and not in Calcutta! It would have been another indication of Chinese Communist "brutality," and, of course, another sign of the "imminent collapse" of the regime.)

This tragic event in Calcutta is not an isolated incident. Mr. Bradford Smith, who spent two years in the Quaker International Center in New Delhi, wrote an article in the February 10, 1962, issue of *The Nation* entitled "Chronic Violence in India." He said that hundreds of organizations hold meetings in praise of *ahimsa* (non-violence).

> Yet India is plagued with outbursts of mass violence that often get beyond the power of the police to control. No day passes without some news of a mob conflict. . . .
>
> The Government of India is engaged in a desperate race with time, to see whether it can raise the standard of living sufficiently to maintain democracy as the accepted means of solving its problems. . . .
>
> The social friction generated by poverty, ignorance, linguistic differences and the caste system are . . . increasing rather than lessening.

In 1962, *U.S. News & World Report* (which has often predicted the "collapse" of the government in Peking) sent a correspondent to India. His report on Calcutta was published on September 24. I have been to Calcutta; I have seen these same sights; *and I can honestly say that nothing like this exists in China today.*

CALCUTTA: CITY OF NIGHTMARES

Just look at Calcutta, and you get an idea of the problems that India faces. Filth and poverty are a way of life. Sudden death is commonplace.

. . . as yet, all the aid given by the United States and Russia and all the efforts of the Indian government have not yet succeeded in reversing the downward trend. . . .

Walk through one of the more than 3,000 officially des-
ignated slums, and you see why Prime Minister Nehru once
called Calcutta a "nightmare city."

I toured a slum known as "The Garden of the Litchi." A
trade-union official was my guide. We walked through a maze
of dark alleys, wide enough for only two people. Under foot
was mud, garbage, cow dung, even human excrement.

We turned into small courtyards where large families live
in tiny, windowless, dirt-floored cubicles. The drinking water
there comes from shallow wells. "We tell them, 'Boil the
water,' but few do it," my guide said.

Near the wells are the privies. They are supposed to be
emptied by "Untouchables," lowest group in India's caste
system. Some privies are neglected for weeks, months. You
can see where they have overflowed into ponds of greenish,
scummy bathing water.

Pot-bellied youngsters, curious to see a foreigner, swarmed
out. "Long live the red flag!" they shouted at us. "Victory
to the Communist Party!"

That is the India we do not often hear about when we talk
about the "humane" Indian way to progress.

It was left to an American Ambassador, J. Kenneth Galbraith,
to express the brighter side of things. Speaking to the House
Foreign Affairs Committee in Washington, the Ambassador to
India claimed that "India today is one of the success stories" of
Asia. "Red China, by contrast is a failure." The reason for this
success? Mr. Galbraith said: "Aid, including in a very substantial
measure American aid, has made this possible."[18]

A rather more profound analysis of India's situation came to my
attention not long after I had read Mr. Galbraith's report on
India's "success story." A comparison of Japanese and Indian development showed little cause for the kind of optimism expressed
by Ambassador Galbraith:

> It is, of course, risky to generalize about a sub-continent.
> But it is broadly true to say that Indian agriculture cannot
> achieve its potentialities without a social revolution. In most
> areas, the land reform has failed in what should have been

[18] *U.S. News & World Report*, May 7, 1962.

its primary object: to give the peasant an incentive to improve the land and increase productivity. If he is not a sharecropper, forced to give an average of 50 per cent of his yield to men who in fact, if not in law, are landlords, he is at the mercy of the moneylenders, charging interest rates up to 200 per cent. Laws passed to end abuses have remained very largely a dead letter and the local government officers have not power to interfere. Hence the peasant does as little work as possible; India's greatest source of productive energy remains untapped.[19]

This report was in a foreign journal.

Many heart-rending accounts of the appalling conditions in India appear in our press, but the writers never really reach the heart of the matter. Nor do these correspondents and editorial writers seem aware that the condition just described—the non-use of India's greatest source of productive energy, her people—is precisely the problem that China has successfully tackled.

The same report from the *New Statesman* continues:

Indian planners dismiss western criticism of their attitude to agriculture on two grounds. They point out that production has in fact increased from 50 million tons of foodgrains in 1951 to nearly 80 million tons today; and that, in any case, the U.S. will always make good deficiencies from her surplus. . . .

The argument that the U.S. will always rescue India from a shortage of basic foodstuffs not only makes nonsense of the plan's express object of securing self-sufficiency, but misses the whole point. The primary object of an agricultural revolution is not to raise food production but to draw the villager out of the self-contained world of subsistence living and into the monetary, consumer market. At present, more than half the population of India lives, for all practical purposes, outside the economy—indeed, outside civilization as we in the West know it. Half the sub-continent is completely cut off from the process whereby wealth is generated. Yet under the second plan, agriculture got only 11 per cent of the budget; even under the third plan it gets barely 14 per cent.

Moreover, such measures as the government is taking

[19] *New Statesman*, London, June 1, 1962. "The Tortoise and the Hare," by Paul Johnson.

to promote rural advances tend to peter out the nearer they approach the actual village level. The pyramid of Indian bureaucracy, immensely efficient at the top, crumbles at the point of impact with the masses, particularly in the agricultural sector. Indian civil servants do not like the countryside, particularly in the backward areas where they are most needed; once removed from their desks, they often become bewildered and nervous. . . .[20]

I have quoted at some length from this thoughtful analysis not only because I believe it to be a true one, but because it makes some points which our press—as it lulls us into optimism with its assurance that "the humane Indian way will win in the end"—rarely makes. Especially important is the necessity of bringing the peasant population *into* the wealth-producing economy and not leaving him outside, and bringing him also into the *consumer market*. Anyone who has seen the village industrial workshops in China (there are hundreds of thousands of them in all), many producing comparatively sophisticated goods, or has compared the number of items that the Chinese peasants own and use in their homes with what they had before the revolution (or with the conditions of the Indian peasants), knows how successfully the Chinese have *brought their peasant population into the economy*.

As Mr. Paul Johnson pointed out, another essential is to get the city intellectuals and the "civil service" *involved with rural life* if rural advance is to take place. This, too, the Chinese have achieved, with students, teachers, and government officials from the city regularly participating in the work of the villages. But how they have been ridiculed and scorned for it by the press and the scholars in our country!

We have already seen that two of the inescapable conditions of progress in backward countries are the fullest attainable mobilization of the potential economic surplus, including that of the wealthier classes, and that the immense efforts that are required in the period of primary capital saving must be equitable.

In India neither of these conditions has been met.

[20] Ibid.

Several years ago Paul A. Baran, Professor of Economics at Stanford University, brilliantly summarized the reasons for India's failure to advance. Discussing the Congress Party, which still controls India's national policies, Professor Baran wrote:

> Yet this breadth of the national coalition which accounted for the enormous strength of the Congress Party in the days of its struggle for national independence at present nearly paralyzes the administration that it supports. . . . Setting out to promote the development of industrial capitalism it does not dare to offend the landed interests. Seeking to mitigate the most outrageous inequalities of incomes, it refrains from interfering with the merchants and moneylenders. Looking for an improvement of the wretched position of labor, it is afraid to antagonize business. Anti-imperialist by background, it is courting favors from foreign capital. Espousing the principles of private property, it promises the nation a "socialist pattern of society."
>
> . . . Anxious to reconcile irreconcilable needs, to compose radical differences, to find compromises where decisions are inevitable, losing much valuable time and energy in bridging recurrent conflicts within its fold, this government substitutes minor reforms for radical changes, revolutionary words for revolutionary deeds . . . the regime . . . is powerless to mobilize what is most important: the enthusiasms and the creative energies of the broad popular masses for a decisive assault on their country's backwardness, poverty, and lethargy.[21]

As long as a large share of India's agricultural proceeds is not used for the improvement of agricultural conditions but continues to be withdrawn by the landowners in the form of rent, India's farming will remain stagnant and the people will continue to be underfed. As long as a large share of the profits of India's industry are allowed to go abroad to foreign owners, and of what remains almost half continues to be distributed in the form of dividends, India's industry cannot find the necessary capital for its growth and development. But to take steps to correct these con-

[21] *The Political Economy of Growth* (New York: Monthly Review Press, 1957), p. 222.

ditions would require the government of India to *challenge the domestic and foreign moneyed interests*—and this the present government is neither able nor willing to do.

India's advance, like that of China's, in the end can come only under a government that is ready to meet this challenge. Conflict of some kind will probably be inevitable, for history (our own included) has shown that those in a position of power do not often give up without a fight. But conflict can be minimized, *if the issues are tackled in time.* Revolution is change that has been denied too long. By evading the real requirements for economic growth, by dodging its responsibility and postponing a genuine program of economic and social reform, the government of India is jeopardizing its historical opportunity—to transform in as peaceful a way as possible a great country from a state of unspeakable squalor and oppression to that of a rapidly advancing modern state.

As far as our press is concerned, very little space has been devoted to any basic analysis of India's predicament. Easy phrases such as "India's democratic way" have covered up a lot of nonthinking. Mr. Galbraith tells us that "Red China . . . is a failure" and that "India today is one of the success stories" of Asia; and Mr. Everett D. Hawkins, a Professor of Economics and Sociology at Mount Holyoke, produces a comparison equally startling:

> The "Big Leap Forward" in 1958, even discounting rosy Chinese reports, indicates real physical increases in production with an all-out regimentation of the work force and with wages rising less rapidly than productivity. India, on the other hand, is opposed to forced labor and expropiation. She has emphasized food and higher standard of living. . . .[22]

I wish that Ambassador Galbraith and Mr. Hawkins could walk through any village in India and then compare it with the life that today goes on in an equivalent village in China! And how, one must ask the professor, can *any* country attempt to raise itself from a state of backwardness without "wages rising less rap-

[22] *Current History*, December 1958, p. 335.

idly than productivity?" If he has invented a new economic theory he should announce it—I can assure him it will be wildly cheered by backward nations throughout the world.

India's border dispute with China affords a clear example of how some newspaper reports, far from being rooted in objective facts, fluctuate with the varying moods of official sentiment.

We have seen how in 1962 reports from India indicated a developing crisis in its economy. In July, India's Finance Minister was "chasing through the capitals of Europe" trying to raise $220,000,000; how assets had been "dropping inexorably to new all-time lows"; how India's foreign exchange reserves had practically disappeared; and how her industrial production was "far short of plans" and was "in some cases even declining." The over-all impression conveyed by these reports was that India was virtually bankrupt and that her production on all levels was faltering.

With the outbreak of the border fighting in October, these gloomy views vanished from the columns of the press. Overnight, it seemed, the Indian economy had moved forward—and so rapidly that within a few days we were being told that one of the chief reasons for the Chinese action along the border war was because India's economy was too successful!

Some quotations in chronological order from the press mark an upsurge in a country's economy so phenomenal that nothing like it has been seen in the world before!

> . . . They [the Chinese] have been trying to demonstrate to Asia that they have the answer to the salvation of mankind, but they have made such a ghastly mess of their revolution that they have now turned their guns on India to halt the more democratic development of that country.
> —James Reston, New York *Times*,
> October 21, 1962.

> . . . Peking may want to force India to divert resources that would otherwise go into building an economy that could outshine China's in Asia.
> —New York *Times*,
> October 28, 1962.

India, by a mixture of planning, incentive and free enterprise, has made undeniable strides out of poverty, in glaring contrast to Red China's inhuman regimentation which has brought nothing but hardship and near famine. The invasion may be aimed at disrupting India's political and economic life. In broadcast after broadcast, Peking hammered at India's "retrograde economic system" and U.S. aid.

—*Time*, November 2, 1962.

It is not a struggle for a few acres of land, it is a struggle for a way of life.

—Report of a speech by an
Indian author, San Francisco
Chronicle, November 3, 1962.

It is a terrible thing now to see war intervening. This dislocation of a very promising economic effort might be precisely what the Communist Chinese most want to achieve. . . .

—Editorial, *The Christian Science Monitor*,
November 3, 1962.

Our development through freedom was achieving a degree of success which, if it went on, would have convinced people that this was the way to develop.

—A report of a speech by the
Indian Ambassador. New York
Times, November 11, 1962.

With India surging ahead of Communist China in peaceful development, Communist China had to force India to divert her limited resources.

—UPI, from Washington,
November 20, 1962.

The whole uncommitted world was comparing India's economic advances as a democratic nation against the Peking Government's slips and stumbles. . . .

—Robert Trumbull from Hong Kong,
New York *Times*, November 25, 1962.

India has been making slow but orderly progress in building an industrial base for a better life for her people. China is in serious economic difficulties. The "Indian Way" with its reliance on democratic freedom is becoming a more attractive model in Asia.

The undermining of India's economic progress may, therefore, be one of Peking's principal objectives.

—Editorial, New York *Times*,
December 10, 1962.

India's democratic progress has obviously been too successful for China's own liking. . . .

—"The Cost of India's Defeat"
by Elizabeth Partridge, *The
Nation,* January 26, 1963.

For a few weeks—during the border fighting with China—the
remarkable "boom" in India's economy continued. It did not last
long. The success story was soon replaced by the tragically familiar
details of poverty and stagnation and a growing reliance on foreign
aid.

. . . an economy only imperceptibly inching forward . . .
one per cent of the Indian population . . . possesses 75 per
cent of its wealth, an imbalance which has been increasing
in recent years.

—*Liberation,* January 1963.
Report from New Delhi

One factor encouraging complacency . . . is the supply
of food grain free of foreign exchange under the American
plan. . . .

—*The Times* of London,
March 11, 1963.

[India] . . . is likely to ask for 6 billion rupees [$1,260,-
000,000] of economic assistance at the forthcoming meeting
in Washington.

—*The Christian Science Monitor,*
April 16, 1963.

. . . meanwhile vital steel targets are falling behind schedule.

—*The Christian Science Monitor,*
April 18, 1963.

Last year's growth rate of 2.1 per cent was slower than
the growth . . . of the population increase.

—*The Christian Science Monitor,*
April 18, 1963.

Agriculture production still shows no improvement over that of the last decade, which itself was only half of the rate envisaged for the third plan period.
—*The Christian Science Monitor*,
April 22, 1963.

Further indications of India's economic plight were contained in a report by Reuters from New Delhi on September 6, 1963. According to this report Dr. Lohia, a member of the Lok Sabakh, "maintained that 270 million Indians lived on less than four annas a day [about 4¢ U.S.] and between 100 and 150 million Indians had a daily income of less than two annas [about 2¢ U.S.]." Mr. Nehru claimed that average income per head in India is about 15 annas [about 17¢ U.S.] but a London *Times* dispatch from New Delhi pointed out that what the Prime Minister had overlooked was that about 1 percent of the population earns nearly half the total. "Whether or not statistics support Dr. Lohia's claim . . . it is plain already that Dr. Lohia was more nearly right than the Prime Minister."

(In striking contrast to India, by early 1963 reports from China indicated that after three years of recession the Chinese economy was again moving sharply upward—and this without any foreign aid.[23])

Stagnation in India is likely to continue until the Indian people and government are ready to come to grips with economic and social realities and are ready to pay the price that change demands. Whatever the mistakes the Chinese have made, and they have made many, they at least recognized the economic laws that govern a poor nation's advance, and acted on them. India, in avoiding these realities, has no alternative but to rely increasingly on foreign aid to keep its economy from total collapse.

In 1962 India received more U.S. aid than any other country,

[23] "New evidence digested by American officials has led them to a considerably more respectful and sobering view of the prospects of the Communist Chinese economy. . . . The administration is somewhat reluctant to publicize its changed view. The chief reason is the fear of putting India in an unfavorable light at a time of great Sino-Indian tension." *The Oregonian*, Portland, March 11, 1963—reprinted from the Washington *Post*.
See also "Postscript from Peking."

and her demands will not grow less. The main function of such aid should be to provide the Indian authorities with *time*; time to initiate some of the profoundly important changes that will enable the country to draw on its own resources and grow from its own strength. Tragic as it is, similar aid in the past has brought no such result, but has tended rather to allow those in power to postpone once again reforms that were already long overdue.

Though foreign aid can never be an answer to India's needs, while she can rely on it she is not likely to meet the supreme challenge, the mobilizing of the latent resources within the country itself: the potential savings in the hands of the few and the abundant energies of the people themselves. Nor can India ever do this while she maintains a system of economic privilege and gross social inequality.

These are some of the great issues of the world we live in, but the press has not helped us at all to understand them. In its reporting and by a kind of Alice-in-Wonderland interpretation, it is attempting to convince the American people that the remarkable progress in China has been a disaster for the Chinese people, and that India's stagnation is really "the better way."

Chapter 8

650 MILLION SLAVES

I. *Meanwhile, Back on the Communes, the Family Was Being Destroyed*

In the summer of 1957, when I was in China, almost 97 percent of all agricultural land was owned by what were known as "advanced co-operatives." Land and farm implements were held in common, and at harvest time, the profits were divided among families in proportion to the days of labor each family had contributed. These co-operatives on an average consisted of between one hundred and two hundred families.

Small units like this meant that no real modernization of agriculture (in other words no sizable increase in food output) was possible. Especially when it came to the building of dams and the development of irrigation canals, single co-operative farms were often found to be too small, and several co-operatives would need to pool their labor, machinery, and materials. Large-scale irrigation works often cut across land owned by several co-ops. Also, at a time when the government was pushing mechanization, farm machinery was usually too expensive for an individual co-operative to finance on its own, and several might then share in the purchase of a tractor or other machine. For these very practical reasons, during 1957 and early 1958 informal mergers of co-operative farms began to take place in various parts of the country—they were called *ta shê*, "enlarged co-operatives," or co-op federations.

These sporadic mergers of co-operative farms were the forerunners of the communes.

There was another, even more basic, reason why co-operative farms could never be the final step in the evolution of China's agriculture. Though they represented a vast improvement over anything that had come before, the co-operatives were incapable of solving the two fundamental problems that confront almost every undeveloped country in the world: namely, the chronic unemployment, or underemployment, of the peasant population; and secondly, their virtual exclusion from the nation's wealth-producing activities.

Contrary to the prevalent mythology here, the period 1949–56 found the average Chinese peasant's material betterment, limited as this was, on the upswing. For example, the elimination of landlordism had enabled the peasant to keep far more of· his crop than ever before. In addition, the vast flood control, irrigation, and reforestation projects that were immediately embarked upon by the new government served to help take up some of the peasant's slack season. Again, contrary to the myth, these projects did not rely on "slave labor" but, as was reported by an official Indian delegation visiting China in 1954, each worker was paid according to his work and was guaranteed a minimum wage.[1] Nevertheless, the fact remains that at this time China's peasant population generally remained outside the national monetary economy, and its time spent in agricultural production was not much more than that of the peasants of nations such as India.

While at peak periods—during harvest time, for instance—there was work for all, for most of the year there was always an acute shortage of work. A survey made in 1955 showed that the average number of days (or day equivalents) worked by Chinese peasants (men and women) was only 130 days a year—for men alone the figure would be somewhat higher. By 1957 (the last year before the communes) men and women in the advanced co-operatives

[1] New York *Times*, July 17, 1954.

were still only working the equivalent of 161 days a year.[2] (The figure for India was approximately 135 days a year.)

Thus, for more than half the year, five hundred million peasants in China were not engaged in farm work. And whatever the cumulative benefits of their labor on national projects, such as building dams and reservoirs, these were not immediately contributing to the gross national product of China. And this, it must be remembered, was in a country attempting to accumulate savings so as to be able to establish the base for a modern industrialized nation. This meant not only a slow pace in capital accumulation, it also represented a vast wastage of a valuable source of productive labor that was needed to go into large increases in agricultural production. The small, independent, co-operative farms with one or two hundred families in each, and with small financial resources, were in no position at all to provide a solution to this centuries-old problem. Therefore, in 1957 China's peasants were still basically subsistence farmers—as they still are in India and most other underdeveloped countries—cut off from the growing modernization and advancement of the nation as a whole.

If the five hundred million peasants in China were to be brought into the national wealth-producing economy and were in turn to reap the benefits of national progress as consumers, an altogether new and radical solution was required.

The informal association of co-operative farms taking place here and there in 1958 indicated that the time had come for a new advance. It is clear from his writings that Mao Tse-tung had long been aware that the small co-operative farms could not meet China's agricultural basic problems. In the summer of 1958, after visiting one of the "enlarged co-operatives" in Honan province, where members had extended their association into a more formal structure, Mao expressed his approval. Great publicity was then given to these new developments, and the amalgamation of co-

[2] An extensive prewar survey made in China by Professor J. R. Buck showed that on average the number of ten-hour work days (or day equivalents) of the Chinese peasant was then 133 per year. This and the other figures quoted are taken from a valuable report on the rural communes by Shigeru Ishikawa of the Institute of Economic Research, Hitotsubashi University, Japan, and printed in the *Far Eastern Economic Review*, September 29, 1960.

operatives into larger units spread very rapidly throughout China. These amalgamations now began to be known as "communes."

Before this movement began, China's agriculture was based on 740,000 small "advanced co-operative" farms; within a few months the whole of China's rural life was transformed, as these co-operatives were amalgamated into twenty-six thousand (later consolidated into twenty-four thousand) communes.

But the communes were much more than "co-operatives—only larger." Commune managements took over the direction not only of the agricultural work, but the organization of rural industries, banking, road-making, education, the establishment of communal dining halls, the enlargement of medical facilities—clinics and hospitals, and all public works.

The change-over was far too sudden, and far too swift. The enthusiasm and the muddle were vast. The fiscal details of the transfer of ownership of property rights from the co-operative to the commune must alone have been a nightmare of improvisation. Peasants were taken from urgent agricultural work to build schools and dining halls and medical clinics. In most communes basic food was given free as part of the wage system but some, in their initial enthusiasm (believing that "communism had arrived"), were supplying free clothes, free haircuts, free everything. Some communes declared that all personal possessions—even bicycles and pots and pans—should henceforth be considered communal property. Day nurseries sprang up everywhere so that women could be free to participate in the commune work force. Some communes even attempted to move in one leap into the final stages of communism—and gave "to each according to his need," expecting all to "give according to their abilities." Consumption as a result soared and stocks were soon exhausted.

All this was happening during a year when harvests (even when all allowances have been made for exaggeration) were the highest in China's history, even larger than the 1957 harvest—deluding many into the belief that it was the commune system, rather than good climatic conditions and other causes, that had created this bumper crop.

Vast plans were drawn up, and some were actually put into

effect, for rural re-housing to make the living conditions of the peasants more comparable to those in the cities—but plans were always based on the retention of the Chinese family unit of three generations. This was specifically laid down in a government directive (emphasis mine):

> Nurseries and kindergarten should be run well, so that every child can live better and receive a better education there than at home, so that the children are willing to stay there and the parents are willing to put them there. *The parents may decide whether their children need to board there, and may take them back at any time they wish.* The old existing houses must be reconstructed step by step; new, picturesque townships and village settlements must be built by stages and in groups; these will include residential quarters, community dining rooms, nurseries, kindergarten, the Homes to Honor the Aged . . . schools, hospitals, clubs, cinemas, sports grounds, baths and latrines. The construction plans of townships and village settlements should be thoroughly discussed by the masses. We stand for the abolition of the irrational, patriarchal system of family life inherited from the past and for the development of family life in which there is democracy and unity. . . . Therefore in building residential quarters, *attention must be paid to making the houses suited to the living together of men and women, the aged and the young of each family.* It is true that the Chinese people have broken the feudal patriarchal [family] system. It must be known that this patriarchal system has long since ceased to exist in capitalist society and this is a matter of capitalist progress.[3]

Under the direction of anyone who had ever had experience in construction work, industrial workshops were set up in all villages and small towns of rural China. Within a few months no fewer than six hundred thousand workshops had been constructed and were functioning. Many of these were at first very primitive; some were housed in reconstructed cowsheds or old barns. Larger, state-run industries would provide and set up the necessary machinery and would send engineers from the cities to train the

[3] "Party Resolution on Questions Concerning People's Communes." December 10, 1958, *New China News Agency* (English translation).

young peasants to make simple parts and components needed in the factories. The young Chinese peasants—who had until then never been exposed to machinery of any kind—took to these workshops with immense enthusiasm, and often more immediate agricultural work was neglected.

These young people, both girls and men, were astonishingly quick to master the necessary mechanical skills, and already by 1960, when I returned to China, some of these workshops were turning out sophisticated apparatus of high precision and good finish. It never ceased to astonish me to walk into a decrepit building in some remote village and find inside peasant girls working at fifteen or twenty modern precision lathes, or in special dust-free rooms assembling delicate electronic apparatus that had to meet the very closest tolerances.

With all these new developments in high gear through the summer and fall of 1958, a collective euphoria appears to have gripped the Chinese people—and even the leaders were not immune. While the communes were being established in the countryside, in the cities tremendous—and often highly successful—efforts were being made to increase industrial production. Hours of work were stepped up, production targets continually increased; one factory would compete with another and factory workers at the end of the week would wait for the production statistics to be announced as eagerly as we might wait for the baseball results. The "Great Leap Forward" was in full swing.

By the end of the year the general disarray in the countryside had become obvious. The agricultural production returns were found to have been grossly exaggerated. Discontent was being voiced by peasants who had been persuaded to give up their own possessions; many found that the work expected of them was too great.

As the initial élan gradually subsided, it was realized that stubborn agricultural problems cannot be solved overnight. Sober appraisals of 1958's great efforts were made, and decisions and instructions were formulated that brought the commune effort on to a far more realistic basis. Those who had given up their private possessions could reclaim them; homes were returned to private ownership; work hours were cut back to a maximum of forty-eight hours a week (except during harvest time). Many rural re-housing projects were postponed until more immediate agricultural needs were met.[4]

In the course of the next few years other changes in the commune system were found to be necessary. Greater initiative in the management of agricultural work was granted to the smaller village units; the authority of the party cadres, who often knew little about agricultural techniques, was very much restricted; a certain proportion of land was returned to the peasants for private production. All these corrections show that the communes had been introduced too rapidly. But though changes in the structure of the communes have been considerable, the commune has retained administrative control over such things as schools, medical services, the homes for the old people, the commune workshops as well as the public services such as road-making, irrigation development, banking, and the purchase of mechanical equipment such as tractors, harvesters, pumps, etc.

During the food shortages of 1960–62 a few Western observers felt that it was the existence of the new commune administrations which made possible effective rationing procedures and equitable distribution of food resources, thus preventing what might otherwise have been a vast national calamity, with perhaps millions dead from starvation and the diseases that come with malnutrition. This opinion, which was to be proved correct, was exactly opposite from that voiced by American experts who contended that China's "famine" was a *result* of the commune system.

The errors had been many, and the Chinese are the first to admit it. It is easy for us to scoff at what now can be seen to have been obvious, and often ludicrous, errors. The faults and the changes in administrative structure led to press reports and com-

[4] I would estimate that by 1962 only a comparatively few peasants, perhaps 2 percent, had been given new homes either in individual houses or in family apartments. Ninety-eight percent of the peasants were living in precisely the same small huts and houses that they have always lived in.

ment stating that the communes had been "abandoned" as "failures."

Thus, an AP report from Hong Kong in early 1961 declared:

> Communist China has abandoned its "big leap forward" and is breaking up the people's communes, both launched 2½ years ago with great fanfare.

The headline for this startling news in the San Francisco *Chronicle* on January 29, 1961, ran: RED CHINA DROPS FARM COMMUNES.

Some China experts in this country were insisting that the revisions had been so drastic that the communes "existed in name only." The truth of the matter is that the communes have continued to exist and have never been "abandoned." There was great emphasis in our press on the mistakes, the bungling, the overestimation of the 1958 grain figure, the return of initiative to the smaller village groups, while the achievements have been almost wholly ignored.

(Though the communes had been "dropped" in 1961, the *Chronicle* on April 22, 1963, reported: "Even through the depths of winter the largest cities, Peking and Shanghai, are reported to have been well supplied with vegetables and fruit grown in communes on the outskirts of the city.")

As a result of the commune movement China is the first major backward peasant country that has virtually solved the age-old problem of rural underemployment. With the establishment of village industries and workshops there is now no shortage of work, however the seasonal agricultural demands may fluctuate. The peasants of China, who as recently as 1957 were on the average only working productively for 161 days (or day equivalents) a year, today are working 300 days a year. An Indian trade-unionist whom I met in China in 1960 told me that the elimination of rural underemployment, in his view, was the single most impressive achievement of the Communist regime.

Hundreds of millions of peasants today are no longer merely subsistence farmers but are fully integrated into the wealth-producing activities of the nation as a whole. They are now within, and not outside, the national monetary economy; they are involved in it as wealth producers and as *consumers*.

Already in 1960 (to my astonishment) the communes were having to set up banks for the personal savings of the peasants—such *savings* would have been unthinkable before 1949. A detailed survey of banking in Asia by a Shanghai correspondent for the *Far Eastern Economic Review* appearing in the issue of April 11, 1963, shows how far the masses of the Chinese people are now included in the monetary economy. It reported that the branches of the People's Bank of China

> in any city and throughout the country are even more nu-
> merous than the postal and telegraph branches. . . . There
> are frequent nation-wide campaigns for promoting thrift and
> encouraging savings by all and sundry. Every branch and
> agency of the Bank handle savings accounts. . . . Ac-
> counts of public utility companies, house rent and taxes
> are usually paid by customers direct to the account of the
> enterprise with the Bank, through any branch or agency.
> . . . Since a bank agency is found in every locality and
> community, no matter how small, this arrangement is con-
> venient to the working people. . . .

In sharp contrast, the section of the report dealing with banking in India tells us: "Quite a large part of the economy is still non-monetised. . . . Bank offices are concentrated mostly in a few big towns."

As I have seen myself and as other travelers to China have also reported, the social amenities available to the Chinese peasants today are widespread. They now have education, medical services, community cultural activities, movies, old-age security. They no longer have to wait from harvest to harvest for payment but are given a regular wage. They enjoy opportunities to develop hobbies of all kinds. They can train as nurses, teachers, veterinarians, mechanics, electricians. There are schools to teach reading and writing to those who missed school in their childhood; and travel-ing libraries bring books to the remotest villages. For the first time, millions of peasants are able to read—and do! This would have been inconceivable even a few years ago.

And nearly all these advances were made possible by the establishment of the rural communes.

Now let us turn to see what was reported to us about the communes.

It was in the autumn of 1958 that this new word "commune," with its ominous undertones, began to appear in our press. Some new and tremendous upheaval was shaking China's society. Very few facts were at first available, but the press left us in no doubt that whatever the facts were, they were very sinister. Soon the news was out—the Chinese government was deliberately reducing the 650 million people of China into a condition of the most abject slavery.

> Under the communes, which merge collective farms and even urban districts into large groupings, individual homes are often eliminated and members live in communal houses and eat in mess halls.
>
> —Tillman Durdin, from Hong Kong,
> New York *Times*, October 16, 1958.

On November 14, Secretary of State John Foster Dulles gave his official endorsement to these stories. In a speech before the representatives of Colombo Plan, assembled in Seattle, he declared that the Chinese were "imposing mass slavery on 650 million people." They had "degraded the dignity of the human individual" and "had created a vast slave state."

This hint from high officialdom was all that was needed. For example, Marguerite Higgins reported:

> The United States now concludes that the drive to organize mainland China's 500,000,000 peasants into militarized barracks life based on communes is well on the way to being an accomplished fact. . . .

(To build enough barracks to have 500,000,000 peasants in barracks life "well on the way to being an accomplished fact" within a few weeks is an astonishing logistical feat! Especially in a country where lumber is scarce. China was apparently able to accomplish within a few weeks what the U.S., throwing in *all its national resources*, might have been hard-pressed to do in five years!)

Miss Higgins continued:

As one official put it, what Mao Tse-tung has done . . . makes Stalin look like a piker. . . .

It is not only Washington that is appalled by the regimentation, which finds women "liberated" from their homes and placed in barracks separated from their husbands and everyone from teen-age youth to oldster trained to put gun worship over ancestor worship.

—New York *Herald Tribune*,
November 25, 1958.

Mao Tse-tung has herded more than 90% of mainland China's 500 million peasants into vast human poultry yards. . . .

Even the old folks, for whom the commune has established "Happy Homes," are kept busy with scheduled chores, . . . when the inhabitants of the Happy Homes die, their bodies are dropped into a chemically treated pool and converted to fertilizer. . . .

Logical next step . . . is the "Saturday-night system," under which a married woman worker lives in a factory dormitory, is alone with her husband only on the odd Saturday night when she has the use of a dormitory room all to herself.

—*Time*, December 1, 1958.

[*Time's* memory erred. The family had already been destroyed 6½ years earlier. On June 18, 1951, *Time* had reported:

Chief among the traditions under all-out Red attack is China's revered institution, the family. . . . Marriage, except for the purely functional reason of procreation, is officially discouraged everywhere and permitted only after long investigation of the couple's political reliability. . . . Newlywed party members are permitted to live together for one week only, thereafter sleep each at his own place of work. . . . Party members' children usually are taken from the mother at the age of six to eight weeks and boarded by the state. . . .

But *Time* must share with the New York *Times* the honors for the early discovery of what the Chinese Communists were doing to the family. Five years before the communes, the *Times* was raising its editorial hands in horror on October 3, 1953:

> Of the countless crimes of the Red regime of Mao none has been as terrible as the crime against the minds and hearts of the good Chinese. . . .
> There is first of all the assault upon the mores and morals of the good Chinese family, . . .]

But seemingly with the arrival of the communes, the families had to be destroyed all over again.

> . . . In theory all mainland China is now in the process of being reorganized into communal living. The children are reared in nurseries. The men and women live in communal dormitories, eat in communal mess halls, and work in military-type organizations. . . .
> —Joseph C. Harsch, Special Correspondent of *The Christian Science Monitor*, December, 10, 1958.

Three days later, the same reporter wrote:

> Not all people in China are yet living in the communal dormitories, eating in the communal mess halls, handing over their children at birth to the communal nurseries. . . .

But he implied that it would not be long! And what appalling sacrifices the Chinese peasants were being forced to make:

> In the Chinese experiment there is, in theory, no room for personal luxury, and no future for personal savings. In most communes the individual is in theory provided by the commune with all his needs. "Needs" do not include spending money, cars, motorboats, private garden plots, private housing, or dachas in the country.
> —*The Christian Science Monitor*, December 13, 1958.

Having considered the dreadful implications of peasants denied their cars and motorboats, Mr. Harsch later in the month concluded that what was going on in China was

. . . the greatest mass sacrifice of human heritage, human comfort and human effort in all time.

—December 24, 1958.

For over a year the newspapers poured out vivid accounts of the horrors taking place in China. In December 1958 Mr. R. H. Shackford wrote a series of articles entitled "Chain Gang Empire" for the Scripps-Howard newspapers. The series began unequivocally: "Abolition of the family is an avowed, primary sociological objective of Red China's new commune system—the first serious effort in history to put a whole nation on what amounts to a prison chain gang." One of the drawings accompanying this series showed a row of skulls on a blood-spattered wall, upon which were written (in letters of blood) "Family destruction," "bestiality," "slave labor." Mr. Shackford found nothing but unmitigated evil in what was going on.

> Each commune has about 10,000 families, but can go as high as 20,000. Each member of these families capable of doing anything becomes, in fact, a slave of the commune which, in turn, is a slave of the central state regime in Peiping.
>
> —December 16.

> Husbands and wives are being separated. Children are being raised by the state in institutions run by Communist Party functionaries. Grandparents are being herded into "houses of happiness" for the aged if they can't work. . . .
>
> —December 17.

> Official policy on individualism is clear: there will be no more individuals in China if Mao has his way. Individualism is listed with parochialism and capitalism as a major sin against communism.
>
> —December 18.

Mr. Shackford's sources of information for this frightful description of developments in China are not cited. In the course of these articles, he referred to unnamed and undated Chinese publications, an anonymous "Communist writer," unidentified reports, and an undated copy of the Catholic publication *America*, from which he extracted this quotation (not giving the name of the author): "Here is a nightmare phantom of collectivism which for open horror, gross inhumanity, and sadistic ambition dwarfs any devil materialized within the Communist bloc in 41 years."

On December 17, 1958, *The Christian Science Monitor's* chief Far Eastern correspondent asked: "And finally, will the average Chinese accept the new social and economic strait jacket with docility? Will he relinquish his children, his home, his wife, and his independence?"

Two days later, the *Monitor's* regular Hong Kong correspondent, Takashi Oka, apparently had news that the Chinese building industry had after all met all quotas: ". . . almost all of mainland China's 500,000,000 peasants have been herded into 'people's communes.'"

Though the barrack construction program was apparently proceeding successfully, the enslaving of 650 million people was meeting some difficulties. In a long dispatch from its correspondent in Tokyo, the UPI on December 18 discussed the likelihood of revolt:

> Competent students of Chinese affairs in Manila, Singapore, Bangkok, Taipei, Macao and Hong Kong told me these troubles could even include open revolt—on a scale much larger than anything the Communists obviously are experiencing and putting down with force right now. . . .
>
> Since the communes destroy the family system, each man is more or less on his own. If he is separated from his family and made a mere unit in a machine, his family no longer is a "hostage" and he has nothing to lose if he revolts to throw off his chains.
>
> Since husband and wife are separated and can be together perhaps only once every two weeks, the commune system is not likely to be voted the most popular way of life, however much it may appeal to the political bosses of China.

Throughout 1959 and into 1960, the press continued to give accounts of the horrors of the commune system and the "nightmarish" life of the people in them. On October 1, 1959, in an editorial entitled: "Ten Years of Red China," the New York *Times* commiserated with the Chinese people:

. . . the peasant masses . . . found out too late the reality behind the initial attractive Communist promises of land reform. In the past decade they have been deprived of their land and dragooned first into collective farms and then into communes whose Draconian severity of regimentation has no analogue even in Soviet experience. . . .

. . . We may suspect that no people has ever been forced to work so hard and for so little as the Chinese people these last ten years. . . .

They have suffered much in these years and have been regimented as has no other people of modern times by the most totalitarian regime of the twentieth century.

In the liberal monthly *The Progressive*, an article by Hyman Kublin, a professor specializing in Far Eastern history at Brooklyn College, declared:

Never before in the long span of Chinese history has the power of the state and its manipulation impinged so heavily and directly upon the people in the myriad towns and villages. Gone are the days when the toiling peasant could express with surety his dictum of government. . . .

(And never before, I might add, in the long span of Western scholarship, has a China "specialist"—and a Fulbright scholar to boot—ever before talked about "the toiling peasant" of China expressing "with surety his dictum of government"!)

I have given only a small fraction of the literally hundreds of articles, editorials, learned reports, and foreign correspondents' dispatches that appeared in the press describing the development of the communes in this general manner. My selection, I think, is a fair sampling—and chosen chiefly from the more distinguished organs of American journalism. In looking through the files, I was struck by two things—first, the high degree of uniformity in all the accounts. There were variations, of course, but they all followed the central theme that the Chinese people were in the grip of a ruthless regime.

The second striking impression I obtained was the paucity—indeed, the virtual non-existence—of any thoughtful interpretation. Even if these dreadful things were happening, there was little to tell the reader *why* they were happening, except in the shallowest possible terms. A quarter of the human race was being "enslaved" by the most "ruthless dictatorship in history," but we were really told nothing more. And being told nothing could only reinforce the first conviction, that the Chinese leadership are men of almost limitless evil intent.

The commune movement began in 1958, between my two journeys to China. In 1957, I had already experienced the shock— the almost disorienting bewilderment—of coming to a country and finding it so very different from the country that I had been led to expect. I knew the extent to which the press had misled me once. I was on guard. So I read the accounts of the communes with a very great deal of skepticism—especially the reports about the breakup of the families. (I felt I knew the Chinese well enough to know that if any government attempted to break up the family, it could only end in being broken up itself.)

And yet—and this is testimony to the pervasive effect of any lie if it is reiterated sufficiently—I returned to China in 1960 expecting to see some very disturbing changes. Some reports, of course, I had dismissed. I could not conceive of *any* government, however much it desired to, being able to build enough barracks for five hundred million people within a few weeks. Those statements condemned themselves. But I must admit I expected to see *some* barracks, *some* ominous changes in the mood of the people, at least *some* indications of brutal treatment. In other words, I could not bring myself to believe, in spite of my skepticism, that these reports that I had been reading had no basis in reality.

While in China in 1960, I was able to talk to the ambassadors and staffs of most of the Western and neutral embassies about the communes; I had long discussions with well-informed Europeans, including technical experts, who had been in China several years; I traveled thousands of miles, spent days in communes of my own choosing; I walked to work with peasants and ate with them in their communal dining halls. I found nothing to justify the reports that I had been reading in our press. I also found that these reports were not credited—indeed were ridiculed—by the diplomatic representatives of Western countries in China.

It should be pointed out that all the while the stories and opinions quoted above were appearing in this country, some factual material on the communes was being published abroad. These reports were by Canadians, Europeans, and Asians who wrote from firsthand observation in China.

I would like to offer a few samples of some accounts of the communes in China which sharply conflicted with what we were being told in our daily papers (italics mine):

Renée Dumont, Professor of Comparative Agriculture at the Agronomic Institute, Paris, in an article entitled, "Chinese Agriculture":

> Without the *active* and *voluntary participation* of the *majority*, the mountains would not have been terraced nor would the terraces have been held in place by gravel, nor would the gravel have been humped, basket by basket, from the river beds. It is my impression that the Chinese Party has succeeded, after due deliberation, in marrying its authority to the peasant's consent, a consent obtained by protracted explanations.
>
> —*Le Monde*, Paris, October 12, 1958.

Edward B. Joliffe, lawyer, leader of the Co-operative Commonwealth Federation of Ontario:

> Having visited such communities this year—and having entered many a peasant home forty years ago—I am amused by the story, zealously spread by certain writers from their posts in Hong Kong and Formosa, that the peasants (five hundred million of them) are kept in the co-ops by coercion and terror.
>
> —*Maclean's Magazine*, Canada,
> November 22, 1958.

An article by Professor Charles Bettleheim of the Sorbonne, entitled "China's Economic Growth," states:

> I think that one must first of all recognize that the manner in which Chinese economy and society are developing presupposes an essentially energetic direction which can be neither of a bureaucratic nor of an administrative nature, nor, still less, come in the shape of pressure from the police (as some people imagine). Such growth implies great clear-

ness of thought, a lucid vision of all the possibilities of development, of the manner in which these possibilities are inter-connected, of the effort which each and every one is prepared to make in order to transform these possibilities into reality. This development also implies that this lucid vision does not remain the privilege of some people who keep aloof from the masses, but on the contrary, is shared by the masses.

. . . Once the masses understand that technique has nothing mysterious about it, one witnesses the extraordinary development of enterprises run by local authorities and co-operatives, one witnesses a real technical revolution coming from the masses themselves.

—*Economic Weekly*, Bombay,
November 22, 1958.

Sir Herbert Read, eminent British poet and art critic, was in China in 1959, Sir Herbert was President of the Institute of Contemporary Arts in London.

The nature of the revolution that has taken place in China is not yet known to the Western World. . . . It is difficult for anyone who has not been to China to realize that within the year 1958–59 an entirely new form of social organization came into existence in this country—a form that owes little to the Soviet pattern and that may for this reason be of great significance to other parts of the world. . . .

A commune is distinguished from a collective farm, or a state farm, in that it is not concerned solely or even primarily with agricultural products, but is a way of life for a region. It includes all the small industries on which agriculture is immediately dependent, as well as all questions of trading and supply, education, health, welfare, cultural amenities and military defence ("home guards"). . . .

I have mentioned autonomy as one of the distinguishing characteristics of the Chinese commune. . . . Such autonomy is economic, but in the case of the People's Commune of China, it is also political. I made a particular point of clarifying this question, because it is always assumed that communism must be bureaucratic. The communes do receive visits (about once every two months, and after ten days' notice) from agricultural and economic (accountancy) experts sent from Peking or the provincial capital; but the purpose of these visits is to aid and advise the communes. . . .

It does not matter what the system is called: it is a living reality and the Chinese Communist Party itself claims that it is an entirely new form of social organization . . . *what counts more than statistics is the happiness and contentment of the peasants.* Their standard of living is still far below that of Western European standards, but it is four times as high as it was ten years ago. . . .

—*Eastern Horizon*, Hong Kong,
September 1960.

"A Visit to China" by Sir Cyril Hinshelwood, President of the Royal Society (Britain's most eminent scientific body):

There is much that is tremendously impressive and admirable in the New China: there is, of course, no doubt that an upheaval of a far-reaching kind has taken place: there are some aspects of the socialist state which are uncongenial to a Westerner: but most of the things for which, at a distance, I had admired and loved the old China, seemed to me to be intact, and some indeed appeared to be fostered more sedulously than ever. China possesses, of course, a communist organization with what most of us here regard as the inevitable restrictions associated with it. But the Chinese people never had much personal liberty and *it is quite likely that many of them are now freer in some ways than they have ever been.* And certainly the constructive achievements are very impressive indeed. . . .

The total picture was warmer and more human than I had been led to expect. . . .

The commune I visited, I must confess, did not seem an unhappy sort of place.

—*The Oxford Magazine*, Oxford,
November 5, 1960.

Dr. Joseph Needham of Cambridge University, eminent historian of Chinese science and a Sinologist, who served during World War II as scientific attaché to the British Embassy in Chungking, writing of a trip made to China in 1958:

Current criticisms of the "communes" seems to rest often enough on limitations of outlook characteristic of highly industrialized Western societies. People here who dislike the idea of families eating in restaurants and canteens know only Western homes provided with gas stoves, electric washing machines, etc.—if they had had any experience of the slavery of the Chinese woman throughout the ages to the charcoal or brushwood stove and the primitive water supply, they would understand that the cooperative farm or works restaurant and the public bath today seem more like heaven on earth to millions. . . . Emancipation of women to follow careers, whether on the farm, railway or factory, or in intellectual work, is one of the most remarkable features of present-day China, as I know from personal contact with innumerable friends all over the country. Nor am I particularly shocked by the idea of restaurants where one does not have to pay, having enjoyed many a meal under such conditions in the kibbutzim of Israel as well as in the educational institutions of my own country. This is a matter of pride in China today, not of compulsion or regimentation. . . .

—New Statesman, London, December 20, 1958.

From these extracts we can gain an idea of the general impression that the communes made on an internationally known French agronomist, a Canadian lawyer and politician, a distinguished French economist, a British art critic, one of England's foremost scientists, and a Cambridge University scholar acknowledged throughout the world as in the forefront of living Sinologists. Each was aware of the complexity and scope of the changes that the Chinese were attempting to bring about in their society; each was able to examine these endeavors at firsthand; each clearly approached the commune movement with an open attitude and with an understanding of the historical circumstances in which the Chinese were attempting to solve their age-old problems of backwardness and poverty. These men are all acknowledged experts in their field. While critical of some aspects of the communes, they were unanimous in their judgment that the communes had achieved much. If there are features that characterize each of these accounts, it is fairmindedness and a balanced judgment.

Let us now turn from these examinations of a social phenomenon affecting half a billion people to a description of the communes presented by one of our own leading China experts, Mr.

A. Doak Barnett. Mr. Barnett is frequently cited as an authority on China; his contributions are sought by leading periodicals; his book *Communist China and Asia* is considered in America as a standard reference book.[5] Mr. Barnett has not been to China for more than fourteen years—through no fault of his own. He has not been able to examine the working of the communes as the others have, to learn about them at firsthand. Some of the men we have quoted—and a host of others equally well qualified—had provided firsthand reports of what they had seen in China by the time Mr. Barnett wrote his book.

This, in part, is how Mr. Barnett describes the communes he has never seen, and I invite the reader to compare what he says with the extracts that we quoted above:

> The communes have portentous implications for China's future. Economically, they represent an audacious attempt to organize and mobilize the entire rural population behind a regimented, intensive campaign to develop both agriculture and rural industry. They have greatly expanded the labor force that the regime can control. . . .
>
> Perhaps the most startling features of the communes have been the social innovations. If carried through to their logical conclusion, these will give Peking a degree of political control over the Chinese population which is almost Orwellian. . . . Meals are to be eaten in communal mess halls rather than in the home. Children are to be put into communal nurseries, which ultimately are to become full-time boarding institutions. Old people are to be put into special homes for the aged. The many functions which women have traditionally performed at home—sewing and weaving as well as child care and cooking—are to be taken over by the commune. . . . Where practicable, the rural population is to be rehoused either in new villages or in special barracks-like buildings. . . .
>
> . . . all of these measures are undermining the traditional role of the Chinese family.
>
> The decision to embark upon the communization program is perhaps the Chinese Communists' biggest gamble to date. In treating the Chinese people callously, imper-

[5] Published for the Council on Foreign Relations by Harper & Brothers, New York, 1960.

sonally, and ruthlessly, as raw material to be organized and manipulated by the state for its own purpose, they may be going too far, even for a totalitarian regime. . . .[6]

In my book *Awakened China*, I gave some detailed descriptions of communes I visited in 1960 and how the peasants could hardly believe what I was saying when I asked them about the "separation of the families." Edgar Snow had the same experience:

> Near the civic center I inspected several new brick homes. Most residents were in the fields, but before a two-room cottage I met a lady of sixty-five working in her tiny garden of sunflowers and cabbages. She invited me in for tea and I sat beside a fine old Chinese table, several chairs and a teak chest. . . . The furniture had been acquired during the division of land—and landlord's furniture.
>
> Rice simmered in a pot over a new brick cook stove in the tiny vestibule; water was available from a new well. Here the old lady lived with her son and daughter-in-law, both of them at work. . . .
>
> "You do the family cooking?"
>
> "A little breakfast for everyone, yes. The children eat where they work. We have supper together in our team dining room. It's great blessing, being able to take meals outside."
>
> "In what way?"
>
> "Ai-ya! In every way. No scrambling for fuel, preparing food, dish washing, pot washing, smoking up the house! Of course the cooking is not always the best. When we get tired of it we eat at home."
>
> "Was there ever any attempt to make your son and daughter-in-law live apart, in separate barracks—to divide men from women?"
>
> My question had to be repeated and explained by the interpreter. The old lady looked at me in astonishment. Of course not. Could that be "human"? She wanted to know if it was practiced in my country.[7]

These sources I have cited, reporting in such sharp contrast to what some of our own press and specialists were saying, only scratch the surface of reliable information that was published

[6] *Communist China and Asia*, pp. 24–25.
[7] *The Other Side of the River*, p. 449.

abroad in those early days of the communal system. Prominent visitors from many Western countries and in every conceivable field, who went to China at the time, returned home and wrote and spoke about what was taking place—scientists and industrialists, scholars and doctors, writers and painters, bankers and economists. And whatever their criticisms, they described China and the newly established communes in much the same manner as the men I have just quoted. Yet, with rare exception, daily newspapers in the U.S. did not avail themselves of the opportunity to use such reports.

The press in our country was right in recognizing the commune movement as something of profound importance, and that it created many fundamental changes in the life of the people concerned. It was undoubtedly right in assuming that not all the peasants of China supported these changes with enthusiasm; but it was wrong in concluding that the commune movement was imposed on the mass of the people against their will; it was proven wrong when it continually speculated that a "revolt" of the peasants was likely—for it didn't happen; it was wrong in reporting that the five hundred million peasants had been herded into barracks (I must repeat that I have yet to meet any reporter or observer who was in China who claims he has seen these barracks, or a foreign embassy official in Peking who gives this story any credence).

We must therefore conclude that on all essential questions concerning the communes, the general impression conveyed by our press and our experts was misleading. Rumors were reported as fact. Reports by refugees were far too heavily relied on. The conditions that gave rise to the communes and the basic agricultural problems that required solution were never adequately analyzed. Accounts of the communes were exaggerated, and the little interpretation that was attempted was meaningless because it was itself based on inadequate or erroneous information.

It was in this manner that the American people were informed about an event of extraordinary significance and complexity that affected a very large proportion of the people of our world.

II. The Exquisite China of the Past

A theme running through many of the press accounts about the communes is the "destruction" not only of the family, but "traditional society." Distress at the departure of ancient values was expressed by Mr. Tillman Durdin in an article contributed to the *Atlantic Monthly* in December 1959:

> Methods have been ruthless, devious, and destructive of traditional human values. . . .
> Overturning the old social order, based on Confucian precepts of family loyalties, filial piety, respect for age, supremacy of male over female; and veneration for ancestors and tradition, the Communists have reshaped China's millions. . . .

W. W. Rostow expressed the same misgivings about Communist designs on tradition four years before the communes were begun:

> . . . the major effort of the Communist regime has unquestionably been to strike at the foundations of traditional Chinese society. . . . The Legalist concept, which has been present, but generally muted, in Chinese society for almost two millenniums, is now again attempting to destroy the age-old, generous, humane moderate tradition.[8]

The image of the Chinese as a humane and generous people for many years was powerfully implanted in the American mind. Mr. Harold Isaacs, in a study of American attitudes toward the Chinese people, found that by a large majority of a representative panel, there was recurring mention of the Chinese as a "superior people," and of:

> China's ancient and great culture; a beautiful, wonderful, cohesive culture; its great civilization; a bond of ancient traditions; a culture devoted to the arts and sciences; . . . great respect for Chinese thought, Chinese architecture, cus-

[8] *The Prospects for Communist China* (published jointly by the Technology Press of the Massachusetts Institute of Technology and John Wiley and Sons, Inc., New York, 1954), pp. 118–19.

toms, mores . . . the wise old Chinese; a great and noble race; a people highly cultured for many centuries. . . .[9]

These deeply implanted images in the minds of Americans who had not been exposed to the realities of Chiang's China were profoundly shaken when the Communists took power, and they were finally shattered at the time of the Korean conflict when it was discovered that these humane, wise Chinese, whom we thought of in terms of philosophic calm and patience, as "unmechanical" and artistic, could fly jets and handle artillery and were able to fight our Army to a standstill. The old image vanished and in its place, as Isaacs reported in his book, there came a quite different one. The principal ingredient of this new image of the Chinese was the idea of their vast numbers; we began to think of them in terms of the "human sea," the "expendable hordes," "the faceless mass," "fanaticism," "cruelty," "treachery," and the picture of them as an urbane, humorous, likable people, deeply attached to ancient traditions, gradually vanished from our mind.

Neither of these oversimplified concepts of the Chinese, of course, has any validity, but the earlier, idealized, image was sufficiently ingrained in our consciousness and was there for so long, that many could only relinquish it with pain and remember it with nostalgia.

No people—and I do not apologize for repeating this so often—can be understood except in terms of their own history. If we are to understand the Chinese of today we must relate them to a past that is real and not to a past that is unreal. We should heed these words of Professor Keith M. Buchanan, of the University of Wellington, New Zealand, who was in China in 1958 when the communes were in their first stages of development and who reported afterward:

> . . . if we want to understand the almost feverish energy and the dedication with which the people of China are throwing themselves into this gigantic task of economic development, we must keep in our minds a picture of old China—not the China of exquisite jade carving and golden-

[9] Harold R. Isaacs, *Scratches on Our Minds*, p. 89.

roofed pagodas and elegant scholarship, but a country of poverty and exploitation. A country where children with swollen bellies died by the wayside, and the peasants ate roots and grass; a country where the collapse of the 1911 Revolution left the peasant and factory worker at the mercy of a rapacious ruling class; a country where the gap between the rulers and the ruled was so great that $6 billion of American aid failed to ensure the survival of a corrupt and despised regime.[10]

In the course of thousands of articles, hundreds of editorials, and so-called expert analyses, American readers rarely have been reminded of what China was really like. Newspaper experts like Mr. Durdin, scholars like Mr. Rostow, and their colleagues can write movingly about the "social order, based on Confucian precepts of family loyalties, filial piety, . . . and veneration for ancestors"; the "age-old, generous, humane moderate tradition," and so on; but they remain silent regarding the unspeakable conditions which the Chinese were attempting to eradicate—and of which Professor Buchanan from New Zealand reminds us.

They failed to relate the Chinese revolution and the commune development to the real China of the past—if they had done so they might have understood, and helped us to understand, what the Chinese revolution was about. They might then have spoken of these tremendous efforts objectively. And, of course, in not relating the present to China's past, I believe they missed the main point. Mr. Richard Walker, for instance, as long ago as 1955 (three years before the communes) was saying that the purpose of the 1950 distribution of land to the peasants was "all too clear. First, complete destruction of the traditional pattern of rural life. . . ."[11] Indeed it was! And anyone who knows what that "traditional pattern of rural life" was like would say: *And why not!*

As a newspaper and magazine writer, Mr. Jack Belden spent many years in China before 1949, traveling widely through the country areas. In his famous book, *China Shakes the World*,[12]

[10] "The Many Faces of China," *Monthly Review*, New York, (May 1959).
[11] *China Under Communism—The First Five Years*, p. 137.
[12] New York: Harper, 1949.

Mr. Belden gives us a vivid picture of the realities of life in China:

> Have you ever considered what it means to be a Chinese in the interior of North China? Almost completely outside the influences of modern science and twentieth-century culture, the peasant was a brutal, blundering backwoodsman. He had never seen a movie, never heard a radio, never ridden in a car. He had never owned a pair of leather shoes, nor a toothbrush and seldom a piece of soap. . . .
>
> A characteristic North China peasant proverb was the following: "Husks and vegetable peelings are foodstuffs for half a year." Truly startling revelation! It meant that the peasant could not even eat grain under the old rule, but only the grain shells or husks. . . .
>
> The average consumption of millet, from what peasants in the poorer areas of North China told me, used to be two and four-fifths bushels a year. In the richer grain-producing areas it was only four bushels a year.
>
> Rich area or poor area, the consumption of meat for the average farmer was only one and one-third pounds a year. Just about the weight of a good T-bone steak you might gobble down at one sitting.
>
> In the cotton-producing areas, farmers used to get two and two-thirds pounds of cotton cloth and the same amount of raw cotton a year per person. In the areas where cotton was not produced, a man got only one pound of cloth and a half a pound of cotton.
>
> Figures. But those figures spelled tragedy for the peasant. A man used to be lucky to have rags. Suits were often shared between two and three people. When a father went out, he would put on the family pair of pants and leave his daughter naked on the bed. A man and wife would split a pair of pants between them. No wonder in North Shansi women did not go out into the fields.
>
> . . . The Chiang regime could not reform as long as it dared not attack the landlords. And it dared not attack the landlords because in essence it represented feudalism itself.
>
> What do we mean by feudalism? Technically speaking, the name is incorrect. And certain learned philosophers, both Chinese and foreign, have taken great pains to point

out that feudalism does not exist in China because there is no serfdom; that is, men can sell their labor freely. It is true that China abolished this formal type of feudalism many years ago, just as it is true that the penetration of the West destroyed the self-sufficient natural economy of the centralized feudal society and placed much of Chinese life under the demands of a money economy, though with few progressive results, as we have seen. But this manner of looking at the problem of China is academic in the extreme and takes no cognizance of the feudal remnants that exercise such an important role in the lives, thoughts, customs, habits and emotions of the people. In abolishing serfdom, the Chinese did not entirely do away with the power of the landlord to conscript labor, to jail debtors and to control the life and even death of his tenants; it did not completely abolish child slavery, the custom of buying and selling girls nor the system of concubinage or forced marriage. All of these conditions are irrevocably bound up with the rule of the landlords and the gentry. . . .

The institutions of slave girls, concubinage and forced marriage were also irrevocably tied to the landlord system. All the fine Kuomintang laws on this subject were meaningless unless landlordism itself were abolished. Slave girls not only worked in landlord homes in the interior, but were bought by merchants and shipped to Shanghai where they were forced to become prostitutes or, if too ugly, factory girls. In this they had no choice, being bound over to the party who had contract to their bodies. Far from helping to end this system, the revolutionary army of Chiang Kai-shek helped to perpetuate it. In various Kuomintang army headquarters I have seen with my own eyes officers call in the local gentry and ask their aid in securing young girls for their use as long as they were in the territory. The girls, so obtained, were not prostitutes, but generally the virgin daughters of poor farmers. . . .

If the villages behind Chiang Kai-shek's lines remained comparatively peaceful, that was only because the peasant was awaiting leadership and an opportunity to rise. . . . For this simple man, born to tenant, feudal slavery, to an overworked and crowded plot of ground, stunned into obedience beneath the grasping landlord's hand, dispossessed from his land by crooked deals and savage violence, robbed of his wife's caresses and his children's laughter, suddenly rose with an impassioned thrill and, under the threat of death itself, began to demand land and revenge.[13]

In examining, as I have had to do for purposes of this work, the innumerable references to the communes in books, in the press, in speeches, in scholarly essays, I was struck by the very great contrast in the tone of voice customarily used when speaking about the communes—or the Chinese revolution generally—to the tone of voice adopted when discussing the conditions of China under Chiang Kai-shek. This is worth examining, for it tells us much.

Mr. Richard Walker, for example, in his book *China Under Communism—The First Five Years,* uses these charged words and phrases *in his introduction alone:* "masters" (three times); "fanatically"; "inhumanity"; "unbelievable cost in terms of human and cultural destruction"; "ruthless"; "people . . . eliminated"; "submit abjectly to total control"; "new Chinese despotism." On other pages of this book he suggests that the Chinese people were "kept in an almost perpetual state of mass hypnosis" (p. 77); in addition, "mass mobilization and mass hypnotism" (p. 99); "cost in terms of brutality and human suffering" (p. 127); "Under Mao's government fear has crept into every soul" (p. 214); "the floods of 1954 offered one more opportunity for instilling terror" (p. 231); "Machiavelli" (p. 241).

A scholar of Dr. Robert North's considerable reputation uses these words in one of his studies: "communist engine of frightful proportions"; "diabolically"; "high cost to freedom and dignity"; "Bolshevik supervisors"; "brutally clear"; "Machiavellian" (several times); "regimentation"; "slavish efficiency"; "totalitarian curtains."[14]

And John King Fairbank of Harvard employed such terminology as: "totalitarian monster," and quoted another writer's reference to the Chinese as "blue ants."[15]

[13] Ibid., pp. 129–58.
[14] *Moscow and Chinese Communists.*
[15] *The United States and China* (Cambridge, Mass.: Harvard University Press, 1958), p. 315.

This list could be continued, but enough has been quoted to indicate the intensity of moral and human indignation which even scholars felt when they addressed themselves to developments in Communist China. The point I wish to make is that scholars and apparently others, as far as I have found, felt no such moral outrage when considering conditions in pre-revolutionary China. It is extraordinary to me to see with what understanding and detachment they were able to view the China of Chiang Kai-shek.

Unlike Professor Fairbank, Mr. Richard Harris of *The Times* of London has been twice to Communist China. He lived and worked in China many years before 1949. He totally rejects the "ants" description of the Chinese. Speaking on the B.B.C. in February 1961, Mr. Harris begins a discussion with the author, Mr. Nicholas Wollaston, with these words: "People who, in writing or talking about China, refer to 'the ant-state' or 'the organization of ants' seem to me to have no feeling at all for what the Chinese are like. Whatever one's views are about organization, the people who are being organized are not, and never have been, ants." To this Mr. Wollaston, who has also been to Communist China, replied: "I absolutely agree. . . ."

Mr. Walker has a range of epithets to describe the Communist regime, yet when it comes to what I consider the unspeakable conditions of exploitation and misery of the Chinese peasants in Chiang's time he refers calmly to the "*malpractices* of some of the large landowners." Dr. North, who talks of the Communists with high moral indignation, is able to write with admirable restraint when on page 202 of his study he finds it necessary to criticize Chiang. "Unfortunately," says this China specialist, "the integrity and efficiency of Chiang Kai-shek's government were open to a *measure of legitimate criticism.*" And later, on page 240, North notes that Mao's victory in 1949 was accomplished "partly by virtue of China's wartime confusion, weakness, and disillusionment, partly through exploitation of Kuomintang *inadequacies.* . . ." (my emphases).

Professor Fairbank, who uses such words as "monster" and

"evil" about the government of Mao Tse-tung, uses far gentler words about a phony 1948 currency reform. By means of this "reform," Chiang and his officials—before retreating to Taiwan—all but squeezed the remaining savings of gold, jewelry, and foreign currency from the middle class, netting themselves the equivalent of about two hundred million American dollars. Without mentioning the corruption involved in this deal, or the cynicism with which it was executed, the professor describes it as a currency reform "which collapsed."

It is also interesting to note certain changes made in some of Professor Fairbank's earlier criticisms of Chiang's actions. For example, on pages 190–91 of the 1948 edition of his widely read book *The United States and China*, we read that

> . . . Chiang was able by military force and political manipulation to take over the leadership of the revolution and consolidate his position. He treacherously crushed the vigorous labor movement in Shanghai. . . . The new Nanking Government expelled the Chinese Communists from its ranks and instituted a nation-wide white terror to suppress the Communist revolution.

In the 1958 edition (p. 176), Chiang no longer *treacherously* crushed, but merely crushed what is now described as the *Communist-led* labor movement. Chiang no longer instituted a nation-wide *white terror* to suppress the Communist revolution but a nation-wide *effort*.

Though it is a well-recorded fact that Chiang did indeed institute an appalling slaughter of what had been his former associates (see for instance the description in the New York *Times* of the "ruthless slaughter" in Canton, quoted in Chapter 3), the 1958 edition of Professor Fairbank's book substitutes for another reference to the "white terror" (p. 192) the phrase (p. 177) "military campaigns."

And finally, the New Frontier's own Professor W. W. Rostow, in his *Prospects for Communist China*, who on page 27 finds the Communist land reform "often bloody" and "ruthlessly executed," four pages earlier described Chiang's wholesale massacres of his former Communist associates in 1927 in very restrained words. "Chiang," says Rostow, "completed the removal of the Communists from the KMT structure, killed many Communist leaders, and did what he could to destroy the Communist organization. . . ." Six pages prior to this, Rostow discussed the "chronic financial corruption in the KMT" which was "incontestable" with no discernible note of moral disapproval and he apparently saw it primarily in terms of placing Chiang in "*awkward circumstances.*" (emphasis mine).

"Awkward circumstances," "inadequacies," "open to a measure of legitimate criticism," "malpractices"—it is almost always in such restrained terms that our academic experts write about the corrupt and vicious regime of Chiang Kai-shek. This is as misleading to the public as the general press reporting. No one reading the later works of these experts would find an adequate picture of the regime which the great masses of the Chinese came to loathe and which they finally rejected—a regime supported by a narrow and selfish upper class whose main preoccupation was the retention of its position of power and privilege. No student could learn from the books of these scholars the depth of the animosities which Chiang had aroused, nor the level of degradation to which the ordinary Chinese had for so long been reduced.[16]

To remind ourselves of these realities we must turn to the words of Theodore H. White and Annalee Jacoby—written at a time of greater frankness about Chiang's China:

> . . . the civilization of China in our own times, rested on the effective enslavement of the common man. He was chained to his land and ensnared in a net of social convention that made him prey to superstition, pestilence, and the mercy of his overlords. He shivered in winter, hungered in famine, often died of the simple hardship of his daily

[16] I am here referring primarily to American scholars writing since 1949. Journalists, writers, and correspondents provided American readers with accounts of conditions under Chiang—e.g., Belden, Peck, White, Stowe. Since 1949 these accounts by American writers have been reduced to the merest trickle. The best and most comprehensive firsthand account of Communist China by an American is Edgar Snow's *The Other Side of the River*, published in 1962.

life before he reached maturity. On this base rested the thinnest conceivable superstructure of a leisure class that profited by the peasant's toil and preserved for posterity the learning and graces it had inherited from antiquity.[17]

[17] *Thunder Out of China*, p. 20.

Chapter 9

MR. ALSOP'S CHINA

To several million readers the thoughts, observations, and judgments of Mr. Joseph Alsop help to make up their picture of the world they live in. Three times each week from coast to coast go his columns entitled "Matter of Fact." Alsop is a columnist with a mission and a hope. His mission—to warn his countrymen of impending calamities; his hope—that he will be able to arouse us to our danger before it is too late.

To Mr. Alsop the Chinese Communists are an embodiment of all that is evil and brutal. Year after year his "Matter of Fact" columns have pointed out the monstrous catastrophe that has befallen the Chinese people.

I do not know Mr. Alsop and I have no reason at all to doubt that he writes his columns and articles with a very high sense of duty to the American public. For more than ten years he has been writing of the dangers that China has presented to our security and interests. As early as 1953 he was hinting at the most ominous possibilities.

> *Mr. Alsop's warning:* Southeast Asia has everything that China needs. The rice, the rubber, the minerals, timber and petroleum. . . .
>
> Southeast Asia will still be soft and virtually undefended two years from now. . . .
>
> Unchallengeable Chinese military power; an acutely painful problem in China; a wonderfully easy solution of

that problem across undefended borders . . . such is likely to be an explosive combination in Asia in the rather near future. . . .

—October 12, 1953.

As a matter of fact: China has not yet moved into Southeast Asia. The "explosive combination" of ten years ago has not yet exploded.

Mr. Alsop's warning: On June 6, 1954, Mr. Alsop, with his brother Stewart, was telling his readers that the Chinese Communist government "is preparing to pick up Indo-China"; and reported Chen Yi's "fall from power and favor."

As a matter of fact: China never "picked up" Indo-China; Chen Yi today is Foreign Minister.

Mr. Alsop's warning: . . . [There is] the clear possibility, almost verging on the likelihood, that the United States will end by having to fight an atomic war for Formosa's off-shore islands.

—March 3, 1955.

As a matter of fact: There was no war, atomic or otherwise.

Mr. Alsop's warning: The scheme of the communes is frankly intended to transform the whole countryside of China into a series of slave farms, of a character without any modern parallel.

The probable horrors of this new phase in China go beyond the bounds of normal imagination . . . it is a reasonable forecast that the Communist massacres will pass a hundred million human beings.

. . . One way to relieve China's internal pressures, diminish the need for massacres and ease the situation generally is to add the resources of China's rich neighbors to the southward to China's own inadequate resources. And in these circumstances it is unwise to ignore the possibility that the attack on the off-shore islands is the first, tentative, venture of a much more ambitious scheme of conquest.

—October 6, 1958.

As a matter of fact: Having (unlike Mr. Alsop) been to many communes in China I believe the description of them as "slave farms" has no basis in actuality.

There have been no "massacres" in the communes and

there are Western experts who believe that the existence of the communes' administrations made equitable
distribution of supplies possible during the food shortage
period and prevented famine conditions.

No attempt has been made to "add the resources of
China's rich neighbors to the southward."

Mr. Alsop's warning: . . . the present labor corvees com-
prise close to 100,000,000 people. In other words, the
number of Chinese currently engaged in forced labor
is a good deal more than half the population of the
United States. . . .

—January 4, 1959.

As a matter of fact: For this statement no sources are
quoted except nameless "official analysts." I do not
believe that anyone who has seriously studied developments in China at firsthand would support this view.

Mr. Alsop's warning: Among the tiny number of Americans who know the factors in the problem there is almost
breathless excitement about the rebellion in Tibet. It
can, they say, shake the Chinese Communist regime
vastly more profoundly than the rebellion in Hungary
shook the Soviet regime. . . . The strain of the Communes plus the strain of Tibet can just imaginably equal
a general explosion.

—April 10, 1959.

As a matter of fact: There were no indications that the regime was "shaken"; there has been no general explosion.

Mr. Alsop's warning: On this date he told his readers that
the Chinese were reduced to dining on afterbirths.

—May 12, 1961.

As a matter of fact: It is now generally acknowledged that
there was a serious food shortage in China but no famine.

Mr. Alsop's warning: [Will] China explode as a result of this
ruthless experiment?

When any government has embarked upon a course
that appears to require tens of millions of human sacrifices a year, one must surely consider the possibility of
failure. . . .

. . . in ten years the individual ration will be raised to
. . . 1,500 calories per day. . . .

To this blood-chilling resume, one must add . . . testimony from the Chinese mainland [pointing] to a serious breakdown . . . of the public discipline of the drilled, intimidated people.

—May 17, 1961.

As a matter of fact: The Chinese regime has not "failed." There have been no human sacrifices. The average ration is now far above 1,500 calories per day and rising. (See Chapter 6, "The Starving Chinese.") There has not, as far as we know, been any breakdown of public discipline.

Mr. Alsop's warning: The Chinese Communist government is now providing the Chinese people with a national diet averaging 600 calories per day. . . .

—September 13, 1961.

As a matter of fact: Medically this makes no sense.[1] The Chinese would all now be dead. There are still 700,000,000 of them left.

Mr. Alsop's warning: . . . the Chinese masses are now receiving a nationwide average of 1,300 to 1,600 calories per day. . . .

. . . this being the case, the figures raise the question whether Communist China is not caught in a remorselessly descending spiral from which a vast upheaval of some sort is the only likely way of escape.

—April 13, 1962.

. . . the evidence is clear that Communist China is now suffering from an acute generalized industrial breakdown. . . .

Once again . . . the question has to be asked whether Communist China is not caught in a remorselessly descending spiral.

—April 16, 1962.

As a matter of fact: Food production up; industrial production up; international trade up. No descending spiral, remorseless or otherwise.

[1] The Food and Nutrition Board of the U. S. National Research Council gives 709 calories as the minimum for the maintenance of a thirteen-pound (two- to six-month-old) *baby!* (Home and Garden Bulletin No. 72, U. S. Department of Agriculture, *World Almanac,* New York, 1962.)

Mr. Alsop's warning: THE COMING EXPLOSION IN RED CHINA, heading of his article in *The Saturday Evening Post.*
—August 11, 1962.

As a matter of fact: Still no explosion in sight.

This article in *The Saturday Evening Post*—"The Coming Explosion in Red China"—is worth examining in some detail. Virtually the same article, in an extended form, appeared under another title, "On China's Descending Spiral," in the July–September 1962 issue of the *China Quarterly*, a leading Western journal addressed principally to scholars and specialists in the China field. A number of passages in both articles were identical; others were identical except for a phrase or a few words; the theme was the same in both.

Mr. Alsop paints a very grisly picture of the conditions in China and what he believed lay in store for the Chinese people. Using mostly *The Saturday Evening Post* article, we can summarize Mr. Alsop's views as follows:

The serious plight of Communist China raises a basic political question: Are there any limits at all to the sufferings that a police state can inflict on the people they have in their grip? Remembering Stalin, some people might think there are no such limits, but Mr. Alsop believes that there is a point beyond which it would be dangerous to push the Chinese people. He points out that Mao could much more easily attain his ambition to make China into a military-industrial giant if there were fewer people in China. But suppose, he says, that an order went out to send half of China's six hundred million to the slaughter houses (in the *China Quarterly* the figure used was one-third) and that another order was given to "compost the 300,000,000 plus corpses for fertilizer, which the Chinese fields need very badly" could Mao, Mr. Alsop asks, really rely on his orders being carried out?

He thinks not, and this shows that there *is* a point beyond which it would become dangerous for Mao to inflict suffering on his people. The question then arises whether China may not already be moving toward the "explosion point."

It seemed clear to Mr. Alsop when he wrote his article that

China was caught in a "remorselessly descending spiral"; each year "growing hungrier and hungrier and producing less and less." He thought this downward spiral might even be "self-perpetuating." If the harvest in 1962 was good the spiral might be reversed, but he saw little hope of this. In fact, he rather suspected that the downward spiral itself "almost forbids a generous harvest."

The initial "down-twist" began with the "most megalomaniac proclamations" ever heard from the Chinese leaders. This was when the communes were organized—"vast, drilled rural slave-labor camps, each comprising 30,000 to 40,000 peasants, in which at the outset even love was supposed to be rationed, with husbands and wives sleeping in different communal dormitories." (He gave no such description of the communes for the more scholarly readers of the *China Quarterly*.)

The second phase of China's "plunge into misery" led the leaders to reverse many of their policies. All capital construction was stopped. Output from existing plants suffered a "vertiginous drop" without parallel in any other country since World War II. By the winter of 1962 industrial production in China "was expertly estimated" at no more than 30 percent capacity.

In the countryside there was a corresponding retreat, almost a rout, with the communes being "dismantled and dismembered." As far as food was concerned, Mr. Alsop thought that in the "late winter of 1962" the average diet level was from 1300 to 1600 calories a day. He didn't think the peasants could have been so "hideously undernourished" for three years on end so he says, "we may guess" that by the end of 1959 the average diet level was about 1800 calories a day and that it dropped after that.

Those, therefore, were the main features of the second down-twist in the spiral. It was "far more terrible" than the first. During the first down-twist the peasants had to "pay with misery" for industrial growth. On the second down-twist industry itself "fell into ruin." Unless China was rescued by a good harvest (which he had already said was unlikely) an even more terrible third down-twist was to be expected.

Discussing the exodus of refugees and the military buildup against Chiang Kai-shek's possible landing, Mr. Alsop thought these developments "much less ominous" than an order that 30 percent of the people of China's cities must be sent back to the countryside. To have between fifteen and thirty million people shifting for themselves in a countryside "already deep in misery" was like loose parts rattling about in machinery already dangerously out of order.

The reason for China's downward spiral, Mr. Alsop traces to the fact that Mao was attempting to follow a pattern of industrialization set by Stalin. Stalin got away with it because the standard of living in Russia was higher and could drop 50 percent and still have a safety margin. China had no safety margin at all. Mao as a result pushed his people "far below a bearable subsistence level" and the result was "catastrophic." We can infer that it was catastrophic because whereas Stalin never hesitated as he strode to his goal "through rivers of blood," Mao soon quailed and began desperately to try to repair the damage he had done— and this was not because he was "either more humane or less ruthless" than Stalin.

These attempts to correct a disastrous situation, Mr. Alsop says, have failed. The depression of the living standard of the Chinese in 1959 was "like stoving a huge hole in the bottom of a boat."

(The idea of a hole in the bottom of a boat was developed further in the *China Quarterly* version. Before mentioning the hole in the boat, Mr. Alsop said that the "plunge into misery" of the Chinese peasants in 1959 was "different *in character* from the plunge into misery" of the Russian peasants in 1929. "It had the same kind of difference as a benign and a malignant tumor. It went vastly further. It was very much more terrible, causing Mao to quail where Stalin had not quailed." It is at this point that Mr. Alsop suggested that the Chinese leaders were like people trying to lighten their boat by throwing just about everything overboard to lighten it—but the boat continued to sink lower in the water. It could now be lightened only by throwing the passengers overboard as well—in other words, by deliberately reducing China's population.)

Coming back to *The Saturday Evening Post* version, we next find Mr. Alsop showing how even the return of tiny plots of land to the peasants for their private use led to terrible results. According to Mr. Alsop, one-quarter of all available fertilizer in China is human excrement. As even the most rigorous police state "cannot control the individual's disposition of his own excrement," the peasants naturally used it on the privately owned plots of ground. Mr. Alsop asks us to imagine what happened when more than a quarter of the available fertilizer supply was used on only half of 1 percent of the usable land. He gave this private use of human excrement as one of the reasons for the bad harvests.

Mr. Alsop believed that the Chinese population had stopped growing and was possibly even declining, because of the desperately low level of nourishment.[2] In fact, he thought this population decline was Mao's best hope. His problems would be greatly simplified if the population was massively reduced. "If Mao can just hang on somehow while the people he leads are reduced by something like a quarter," he might yet win through, though at the cost of 150,000,000 lives. This is quite a possible solution but something would break "before a quarter of the Chinese are exterminated by their government's own acts."

Before a quarter of the population is exterminated, the regime itself might collapse—a palace revolution might bring in a new set of Communist leaders. But Mr. Alsop thinks this is unlikely. It is more probable that Mao will continue on, "battening down a hatch here and making a concession there and hoping for an upturn." (*China Quarterly*) But if this hope comes to nothing, a breakdown of the entire system might occur. No Western nation in modern times has experienced the "nadir of wretchedness" (*China Quarterly*) which is the present condition of China. The system might break down in China; and if the army rallied to the people the system *would* break down.

[2] In an interview with Edgar Snow, reported in the New York *Times* of February 3, 1964, Mr. Chou En-lai indicated that the very opposite might be the truth—that far from a *declining* population growth the Chinese government is faced with the problem of an increasing growth. After speaking with approval of the Japanese achievement in reducing their rate of population growth to 1 percent, Mr. Chou gave reasons as to why the Chinese are not likely to be able to equal this within the next few years: "For example, with improved living conditions over the past two years, our rate of increase again rose to 2.5 percent!"

"All, indeed, is uncertain except one thing: China's descending spiral cannot continue unendingly without causing at least one of the three kinds of breakdown" outlined in the article.

That, I believe, is a fair summary of Mr. Alsop's article, "The Coming Explosion in Red China."

The basic hypothesis on which Mr. Alsop's argument was grounded, the *raison d'être*, as it were, of the entire exercise, was soon disproved by events.

Shortly after the article appeared, the food shortage in China was generally acknowledged to have eased, industrial production was again moving upward, and foreign trade statistics showed that China's commerce was once more expanding. Within a short while a high British official reported after his visit to Peking that effective organization for the distribution of food had prevented starvation, that conditions were improving, that national economic development was going forward again; and this general assessment was confirmed by *The Times* of London. But if Mr. Alsop replies that this information was not available to him before he wrote his article, but only afterward, then let us point out some of the evidence which was available long before his piece appeared which might have suggested to him that perhaps his basic surmise was erroneous.

Three months before the Alsop article appeared in *The Saturday Evening Post*, the British government announced officially in the House of Commons that the refugees arriving in Hong Kong showed no signs of malnutrition (and this would hardly indicate they had reached a "nadir of wretchedness"). About the same time the authoritative *Far Eastern Economic Review*, which is published weekly in Hong Kong, included in its issue of May 24 an article by Colina MacDougall discussing the question of the refugees. She had written:

> Everyone who has seen the refugees has commented that they do not seem to be starving . . . their stories are roughly the same: they are people from the rural areas of Kwangtung, some of whom had worked in Canton and been sent back to the farms in the "aid agriculture" drive.

... They all give food shortage and the general discomfort of life as their reason for coming. None of the refugees has claimed political asylum, or said that he was escaping from the Communist regime as such. That many would welcome the opportunity to go to Taiwan ... is doubtful.

Food shortage and discomfort—that was indeed a reality; but surely a far cry from the "plunge into misery"—very much more terrible than the Russian, so terrible that it caused "Mao to quail where Stalin had not quailed"! There are other facts that might have given Mr. Alsop pause. The average nutritional level in China, even during the food shortage, was significantly higher than in India, but no one was suggesting that India was on the point of "exploding." Following a trip to Southeast Asia and Hong Kong, on July 31, 1962, a Scripps-Howard correspondent reported that "there is not one shred of evidence known to the West that famine threatens Communist China." In addition, the Reuters dispatches from China, while reporting food shortages, failed to make any mention of the coming explosion Mr. Alsop was predicting with such certainty. There was also Professor Gilbert Etienne's very careful and sober analysis of conditions in China (see page 115), based on his own direct observations.

These reports and others might have suggested to Mr. Alsop that things in China were not as desperate as he believed.

In the subsequent issue of the *China Quarterly* there appeared ten "commentaries" on Alsop's essay by China "specialists." They took up thirty-four pages. They were full of the normal academic solemnities. Seven of the ten were scholars working in the United States or Britain; two were British correspondents; one was a European "news analyst" working out of Hong Kong. Of the ten, to the best of my knowledge, only one had ever set foot in China since 1949. Michael Lindsay of American University in Washington had worked with the Communists in North China during World War II and returned there—his most recent visit—for a brief period in 1954. Several of the ten gave general support to Alsop's thesis; some hedged, partly agreeing and partly not; some voiced serious reservations; but—and this is to me the really astonishing fact—all but one treated this Alsop article as a contribution worthy of scholarly discussion. Only Mr. Kenneth Walker of the London School of Oriental Studies differed. I quote part of his comment:

> I found it difficult to decide whether or not to accept the Editor's invitation to comment on Mr. Alsop's article. To accept was to indicate a willingness to treat it seriously, even to imply that I recognized it as an authoritative contribution with scholarly claims. I do not, however, regard the article in this way at all, but an essay in wishful thinking. In commenting, then, I am giving the article more publicity than it deserves. On the other hand, it has been put to me that as Mr. Alsop is a famous journalist, some readers of *The China Quarterly* will accept his views on China as gospel. In spite of the arrogant and categorical tone of the article, I find it hard to accept that many readers of the journal will believe that Mr. Alsop's views are current doctrine among all those who try to study China's economic development, but in case there are some, perhaps one or two comments will make it clear that it is not so. . . .

After subjecting Mr. Alsop's use of the comments of refugees to a devastating analysis, Mr. Walker concluded:

> Meanwhile, it is important that the few shreds of evidence available on China's economic position should be used with care. We must not try to answer questions which cannot be answered. Our conclusions and claims must be fully documented; our assumptions clearly stated. . . . On all these points I consider Mr. Alsop's article to be deplorable. It will hardly convince the Chinese Government that to let scholars and journalists into China for lengthy periods would necessarily give rise to more responsible comment.[3]

Why did the editors of the *China Quarterly* run this piece in the first place? Did they really consider it worthy of scholarly debate? Why did they select these particular specialists to comment on it? Why choose men who had never been to Communist China but who could only attempt to understand it from

[3] *China Quarterly*, October–December 1962.

the outside?—with the exception of Michael Lindsay, who *had* been to Communist China, who had formerly worked with the Communists there, and (judging from his books and writing) is now one of the sharpest critics of the regime. Why were at least *some* of the very fine scholars who have seen China recently not chosen?

Is it any wonder that we remain tragically ignorant of the facts about China?

Part III

CHINA WANTS WAR

Chapter 10

THE CONDITIONING OF AMERICA

Deeply implanted in the minds of Americans is the belief, the certainty almost, that of all the nations in the world today, China is the most belligerent. If she is less dangerous today than Russia it is only because she is not yet as powerful. *But give her time.*[1]

The questions that I am most frequently asked at my lectures are those that revolve around China's "aggressiveness," her "wish to expand," her "disregard for human life," and "what will happen when China has the nuclear bomb?"

THE CHINA DANGER

A regime that manifests the desperate xenophobia now being displayed by the Chinese Communist Government cannot but be a constant, unpredictable threat to neighboring territories. . . .

Editorial, New York *Times*
(Western Edition), August 3, 1963.

PEKING'S GRAND DESIGN

Communist China has made no secret recently of its resolve to enter upon a Napoleonic phase of expansionism . . . with the leverage of 700,000,000 people and a vast territory

[1] According to a Gallup Poll of March 24, 1963, 47 percent of those asked believed that China will be a greater threat to world peace than Russia in 1970; 34 percent thought that Russia will be the greater threat.

virtually immune to conquest, its rulers feel bold enough to blueprint their ambitions. . . .

> Editorial, New York *Times*,
> September 14, 1963.

. . . we find a great powerful force in China organized and directed by the Government along Stalinist lines surrounded by weaker countries. So this we regard as a menacing situation.

In addition, as I said, that Government is not only Stalinist in internal actions but also has called for war, international war, in order to advance the final success of the Communist cause. . . .

I would regard that combination, if it is still in existence in the nineteen seventies . . . potentially a more dangerous situation than any we've faced since the end of the second war.

> President Kennedy at his news
> conference on August 1, 1963,
> as reported in the New York
> *Times*.

Influenced by statements such as these, it is no wonder that the vision of China in the minds of most Americans is dominated by a sense of danger. China represents a threat that we cannot clearly define and presents a future menace against which we hardly know how to prepare. One human being out of four is a Chinese—we have a picture in our minds of vast hordes and limitless manpower. We know that if it comes to war we could *defeat* China, but we sense instinctively that we could never conquer her.

The enormous confidence of the Chinese leadership disturbs us—they don't behave as leaders of a poor and backward nation; they don't seem to *need* us.

For fourteen years we have been told by our press that the Communist leadership was nearing collapse—but it remains today in full and confident control. We debate among ourselves as to whether we should "recognize" China, but we suspect that she would quickly reject recognition unless we offered it to her on her own terms. Year after year we have stubbornly opposed her being accepted in the United Nations, and are now beginning to wonder whether the ostracism we have imposed on her has not, after all, been to her advantage. Our support of Chiang Kai-shek is costly and gives us no compensating advantages; and no moral support, for we know he is a poor representative of the principles we claim to be defending. Thus we have reached an impasse and can see no way through it, unable to visualize how our problems with China will eventually be resolved.

These are some of the components that make up an image of China that gives us a deep sense of foreboding when we consider our future relations with her.

Above all, it was our experience with the Chinese in the Korean conflict that set this pattern of thinking. This costly armed collision, far more than the collapse of the Nationalist government, opened up a wholly new chapter in our relations with the Chinese people. In our memory had remained the Chinese soldier under Chiang Kai-shek—ill-disciplined, underpaid, good humored, dishonest, slovenly, unable to make good use of modern weapons; the despair of his American military advisers. When in the autumn of 1950 a new kind of Chinese army swept down upon the American troops and forced them to retreat, a host of images were swept away as well. It was Korea that finally expunged the picture of the Chinese as a kindly, urbane, likable people. The men whom we thought "couldn't handle machines" were now flying jets and were found to be better artillerymen than the Germans.[2] In our anger and bewilderment old images revived. We began to think of the Chinese (as we did in the Boxer War half a century earlier) as savage and brutal, a people with no regard for human life. We once more saw them in terms of the "faceless mass," "aggressiveness," "the Yellow Peril." The Mogul hordes had returned.

To suffer defeats at the hands of the Chinese was a staggering

[2] Harold Isaacs, in *Scratches on Our Minds* (p. 226), quotes a member of his panel, "one of the country's best-known newsmen," as saying: "The Chinese were better artillerymen than the Germans ever were." *Life*, November 20, 1950, described the new Chinese armies as "a menacingly Russianized fighting force." On April 5, 1954, Secretary of State Dulles read to a congressional committee what he called an "ominous account" of Chinese technical military help being given to the Vietminh army. A few years earlier, a suggestion that any "technical aid" provided by the Chinese could be considered "ominous" would have been laughable.

national humiliation. To be fought to a standstill and sign an armistice which brought us no victory was an experience that ate into our national consciousness more deeply perhaps than we realize. It is this humiliation, and the bitterness that arose from it, that has above all made it so difficult for us ever since to view China and her actions with dispassion.

We are told by the press so often that China's intentions are aggressive that we tend to see "proof" of this in all her actions—though these could sometimes bear quite different interpretations. We are sometimes puzzled and hurt when other nations, even some of our closest allies, do not view China in the same dark light as we do. Nor are we sufficiently detached to see that some of China's "belligerence" is a very natural response to our own hostility.

The picture of the Chinese as belligerent, aggressive, warlike, expansionist, ruthless, and ready to plunge the world into war has been frequently presented by the press. This general description of China is well summarized in an editorial in the New York *Times*:

> Communist China is and will remain indefinitely a big, overpopulated, economically stricken nation whose present rulers have unsatisfied ambitions that impel them into a belligerent, revolutionary attitude. They see United States power and influence as the chief barrier to these ambitions and regard hostility, even war, between the Soviet Union and the United States as a way toward removal of the American obstacle to their aspirations.[3]

A wholly different tone was taken by Mr. Richard Harris, the China expert of *The Times* of London, a paper even more conservative in outlook than the New York *Times*. He has known China since his youth. His last visit to China was in 1960.

> Whatever their revolutionary fervor or however much the propaganda churned out in Peking, any careful examination of Chinese policy towards south-east Asia shows conclusively, in my view, that China wants neutralist governments with which she can be friendly—and no more. Burma, Indonesia,

[3] January 24, 1963.

and Cambodia are all evidence of this. I think Laos, if it is ever allowed to settle down, will prove the same. What the Chinese want is the removal of American power which they believe is a threat to them.

After reviewing the whole mosaic of events in Southeast Asia, Mr. Harris concludes that ". . . China has no expansionist ambitions."[4]

This sober assessment by a highly informed and responsible writer of China's non-expansionist intentions is apparently shared by the best intelligence of the U.S. government. On August 1, 1963, the New York *Times* (Western Edition) reported from Washington that a high-level review conducted by the administration had concluded that it was "unlikely that Peking will depart from its policy of 'minimum risk' in foreign affairs" and that the "United States suspects that China plans no major adventures."

But only *two days later*, on August 3, the *Times* (Western Editon) printed the editorial THE CHINA DANGER which we have already quoted, in which China is pictured as "a constant, unpredictable threat to neighboring territories. Red China now displays an implacable hatred . . . to all other countries and peoples that do not accept its grim philosophy of hate and violence. . . ."

And this was followed, as we have seen, by the other fear-inspiring editorial on September 14, in which the *Times* warned its readers of China's "resolve to enter upon a Napoleonic phase of expansionism."

What are we to think of editorials such as these in America's most influential newspaper?

In reading over innumerable press reports, the columnists, and the weekly magazines of the past few years, I was struck by the extraordinary paucity of any solid analysis of China's foreign policies. There was plenty of denunciation but mighty little explanation. Here are a few of the words used when discussing China's foreign policies, not taken as one might think from the

[4] *The Listener*, London, September 6, 1962.

sensational press but from some of our more respected journals: "war-mongers," "threatening," "terrifying," "implacable," "psychotic," "fanatical," "rigid," "smoldering belligerency," "obsessive hatred," "impervious to rational argument," "intransigent," "dread apparition," "evil portent."

The Chinese, we have been told over and over again, "reject peaceful co-existence"; they "support wars of national revolution even if it means risking nuclear war"; they would "welcome a war between the United States and the Soviet Union as that would leave them the strongest power"; they don't mind "losing half their population because there would still be 300,000,000 left"; they have "absolutely no regard at all for human suffering"; they "blamed Russia for weakly withdrawing the missiles from Cuba"; their attack on India was "unabashed aggression"; they are "infiltrating" wherever they can into Southeast Asia; "to feed their hungry millions they are almost certain to move either into the 'rice bowl' of Southeast Asia or into the Soviet Union"; they are uncompromising in their dispute with the Soviets because they feel "the Russians are taking too soft a line with the United States"; they are attempting to "grab the leadership of the Communist world" and they have the "ultimate ambition to rule the entire world."

I do not believe it is exaggerating to say that these words and statements in a broad way represent what most Americans believe to be the nature of the Chinese Communists and the foreign policy they are pursuing.

It conjures up the nightmare dreams of Hitler. It is a picture of paranoia and madness.

Some experts, indeed, have warned us in so many words that the Chinese leaders are indeed near madness. Michael Lindsay, a China specialist originally from England, now in Washington, believes that the Chinese have fallen "under the control of people near the borderline of actual insanity." He regrets there are still people "who are unwilling to face the unpleasant realities of political fanaticism." These people, Lindsay continues:

> assume that the Chinese Communist leaders must really be normal people who, if rightly approached, would join

in reasoned discussion and negotiation for the peaceful settlement of disagreements, and whose obsessive hatred of
America would disappear if rational grounds of suspicion
were removed.[5]

    . . . appropriate Western policies would have to be
based on a realization that relations with the Chinese People's Republic are not a problem that can be handled
within the categories of traditional diplomacy but only within
new categories of applied international psychiatry.[6]

(So we need to train special diplomatic psychiatrists to deal
with the Chinese!)

Lindsay, who during the war against Japan served for three
years with the Chinese Communist guerrillas—when presumably
they were less "on the borderline of actual insanity"—is one of
the most vocal of those who believe the Chinese are fanatics. But
he is not alone.

Mr. Stewart Alsop, in *The Saturday Evening Post*, October
26, 1963, wrote an article entitled:

THE MADNESS OF MAO TSE-TUNG

In this article, Mr. Alsop tells us that the Russians "have
made no secret at all about their conviction that Mao is
mad. . . ." While warning us that allowances should be made
for Soviet distortions and exaggerations, Mr. Alsop nevertheless
says that the "American experts" (he doesn't name them) agree
that what the Soviets have revealed "is true in substance." He
goes on to warn us that: "The madness in Peking is a fact—and a
fact of world significance. . . ." He ends his article by telling us
that one conclusion can certainly be drawn from all the evidence
"that the Chinese leaders have 'gone crazy.' To permit these men
to get their hands on even a limited nuclear capacity would be an
act of supreme folly. . . ."

I suggest that Mr. Alsop and Mr. Lindsay, before telling us that
the Chinese leaders are madmen, would do well to read some of
the accounts of Westerners and others who have met and talked
and negotiated with them. In none of these accounts have I

---

[5] *The China Quarterly*, No. 10 (1962), p. 57.
[6] Ibid., p. 59.

seen even the remotest hint that Mao and the other leaders are mentally disturbed or irrational men. The very opposite, indeed, is the truth. From Mr. Malcolm MacDonald's remarks on his return from China (see page 105), one gains the impression that the Chinese are tackling their problems in a very realistic manner. M. François Mitterand, a former French Minister of State, gives a very vivid account of his meeting with Mao Tse-tung in the *New Republic*, October 23, 1961. He writes of Mao's "extreme courtesy, a quiet straightforwardness." (For contrast one need only recall the many descriptions of Hitler's rantings and shouting or of the cold craftiness of Stalin in his later years.)

Mr. Lindsay and Mr. Alsop might also have done well to read M. Edgar Faure's account of his meeting with Mao described in his book *The Serpent and the Tortoise*.[7] As a former Prime Minister of France, one must suppose he has *some* ability to size up other men of importance. Mao's manners, he says, "are of extreme and pleasing simplicity." He relates how Mao Tse-tung spoke with candor and realism about the backwardness of his country and the immensity of the task that faces them. Mao, at the close of the interview, accompanied his visitor to his car. "From this last picture of him through the car windows—the well-known face above the close shut collar of the beige tunic—that hand raised in a gesture of sympathy—I retain an impression of force, of naturalness and of 'presence.'"

Hardly a description of a paranoic!

Mr. Alsop's article reached me while I was in China. I discussed it with several members of the Western embassies—men who have personally met and had dealings with Mao and Chou En-lai. I think it is absolutely true to say that not one would share Mr. Alsop's or Mr. Lindsay's views that these leaders are "near the borderline of insanity" or anywhere near it! I, also, have met several of the Chinese leaders and saw not the slightest indication that they were mentally disturbed or "fanatical" men.

I think that all talk of this kind is dangerous. Because the

[7] New York: St. Martin's Press (1958), pp. 27–33.

Chinese leaders, far from being mad or wild, are probably among the most intellectually disciplined, best-informed, most coolly reasoning leaders in the world today. As long as we consider them "fanatics," "paranoics who don't mind risking a nuclear war," and suggest that they are men who act "wildly" and so on, we are deluding no one but ourselves.

Scholars have sometimes been quite ready to use newspaper speculations about Chinese expansionism. For example, Dr. Robert North of Stanford University provided an alarming list of places into which China was "infiltrating" as early as 1951 and 1952. Quoting three issues of the New York *Times* as his source, this scholar wrote (interpolations mine):

> ". . . there were reports of Chinese Communist infiltration of Nepal from Tibet [*never happened*], of rapid growth on the part of the Nepalese Communist Party [*never grew to be of any political consequence*], and local estimates of a Chinese Communist take-over within a matter of a few years [*twelve years later, hasn't happened*] . . . in August Robert Trumbull, quoting "unimpeachable sources" in the area, reported systematic Chinese Communist infiltration of Afghanistan, Nepal, Bhutan, and Sikkim . . . [*the sources may have been unimpeachable but they were wrong. There has been no Chinese Communist infiltration of these countries, all of which are in friendly relations with China*].[8]

From the day that China "was lost" or opted out of the Free World fold, some of the scholars have been warning us of Peking's "expansionist" aims. Under the heading "External Expansion," Professor W. W. Rostow wrote:

> The effort to exploit possibilities for external expansion has evidently colored all aspects of China's domestic policy since 1949. Although we have no direct evidence, the only hypothesis which fits into known facts is that the broad strategy for expansion was settled between Stalin and Mao at the meeting in Moscow from December 1949 to February 1950 . . . it was almost certainly agreed that, under Soviet

[8] *Moscow and Chinese Communists*, p. 273.

guidance, the North Koreans would attempt their adventure of June 1950, while Communist China would seek to conquer Formosa, support Communist military efforts in Indo-China, and encourage and lead Communist efforts at subversion elsewhere in Southeast Asia.[9]

There is no evidence for these sweeping generalizations, and there has been no attempt by China to recapture Formosa; and it is unlikely that she would, even if she could, if she felt that by using force she would risk a general war. But Rostow's is a fair example of the hypothesis of Chinese aggressiveness that has come to be generally accepted. In the preface to his volume, Rostow advanced his ideas as to how we should meet "Peking's pretensions to power in Asia":

> . . . we are deeply persuaded that . . . a vigorous Free World policy—political, economic, and military—can contain the military threat of Chinese Communism, defeat its pretensions to political and ideological leadership in Asia, and, in time, diminish or even remove the danger we now confront.[10]

Rostow is a scholar. For the newspaper-reading public the theme of China's expansionism has been expressed in simpler and more vivid language. In the same year that Rostow's book appeared, the veteran columnist Robert S. Allen opened one of his widely syndicated columns with these words: "Blood-drenched history is being repeated among the Red moguls of Peiping."[11] Many writers in the press have used similar charged expressions— the "Red Peril," the "Yellow Peril," "Oriental cunning," "the inscrutable Asiatic," "hordes," etc.

The specialists have presented essentially the same image in rather more "scholarly" language. In their works one can find

[9] *The Prospects for Communist China*, p. 67.
[10] Ibid.
  Several years later, in his capacity as foreign policy planner in the Kennedy administration, Rostow accompanied General Maxwell Taylor to South Vietnam. Not long after his visit over 10,000 American "advisers" and technicians were taking an active role in upholding the Diem regime, which some critics have compared to that of Chiang Kai-shek in its despotism, nepotism, corruption, and its ability to attract the hatred of the people.
[11] New York *Post*, October 11, 1954.

constant assertions of "xenophenia" and "chauvinism." For example, Allen Whiting, in his book *China Crosses the Yalu*,[12] devotes several pages to Chinese "xenophobia." And Mr. R. G. Boyd writes:

> Chauvinism has long been recognized as a dominant factor in the psychological make-up of the Han Chinese.[13]

The Chinese unquestionably have intense national pride and (perhaps with good reason) a suspicion of foreigners. But China's pride and her sense of ethnocentrism should not, as it often is, be confused with expansionism.

The extent of Chinese "expansion" often depends on which authority you read. The eminent barrister and statesman, Arthur H. Dean, as early as 1957 noted a large increase of Chinese-controlled real estate:

> Having regained control of Manchuria and taken over North Korea, the Chinese Communists, in cooperation with their ally, Ho Chi Minh, have taken over North Vietnam, are infiltrating Laos and Cambodia, are threatening South Vietnam, Thailand and Burma, and have made serious inroads into the political life of Indonesia, where rumors of an impending coup have been frequent.[14]

The impact of such cumulative statements of China's sinister advances is frightening. Let's examine them:

"regained control of Manchuria": Manchuria was always Chinese except during its occupation by the Japanese. This is as sinister as France's regaining control of Paris in World War II.

"taken over North Korea": North Korean government still in control.

"taken over North Vietnam": North Vietnam government still in control.

[12] New York: Macmillan, 1960, pp. 4–6.
[13] *Communist China's Foreign Policy* (New York: Praeger, 1962), p. 47. No substantiation is offered for these assertions of Chinese chauvinism.
[14] Howard L. Boorman, Alexander Eckstein, Philip E. Mosely, and Benjamin Schwartz, *Moscow-Peking Axis: Strengths and Strains*, with an introduction by Arthur H. Dean, (New York: Harper, 1957. Published for the Council on Foreign Relations), p. ix.

"are infiltrating Laos": disproved by UN commission—it was Russia, not China, that gave military aid to the Laotian rebels.

"are infiltrating Cambodia": Cambodia was at this time a strongly neutralist nation.

"are threatening Thailand": What evidence is there for this?

"are threatening Burma": Burma is on peaceful and friendly terms with China and in 1962 signed a border agreement in which China gave up some territory to Burma.

"have made serious inroads into the political life of Indonesia, where rumors of an impending coup have been frequent." The repatriation of Chinese to the mainland in 1959–60 was accompanied by some friction, but friendly relations have been maintained since. In 1963 Liu Shao-chi, Chinese Head of State, paid a formal visit to Indonesia. There has been no coup.

This broadside was launched by a U.S. statesman, who was later to be entrusted with some of the most delicate negotiations with the Soviet Union.

A frequent practice employed by both scholars and the press is the interchange of the word "China" with "Communist," and by this sleight-of-word linking revolutionary movements in Asia with the Chinese whether there is any evidence for such an association or not. For example, Professor Howard L. Boorman, in the same volume as Mr. Arthur Dean, writes:

> . . . The protracted war in Korea and the *Communist* conquest of northern Vietnam have confirmed . . . the recrudescence of *Chinese* power in Asia.[15] (emphasis mine)

It was not, as one would infer from this statement, the Chinese but the Vietnamese themselves who "conquered" North Vietnam!

One could present literally hundreds of examples of such generalized statements about Chinese aggressiveness.

One example is worth some examination because it backfired painfully.

In September 1959 we were told in dramatic headlines that the North Vietnamese (it was suggested with Chinese support) had launched an invasion of Laos. Large-scale fighting was said

[15] *Moscow-Peking Axis: Strengths and Strains*, p. 1.

to be taking place. For days the "invasion of Laos" dominated the news. The State Department announced that the situation was "grave." Units of the Seventh Fleet were moved as close as possible to the danger zone. As the crisis grew there was talk in Congress of bombing the invaders with U. S. Navy and Air Force planes. Millions of dollars were spent in airlifting military supplies to Laos—and announcements were made that we might send troops as well as supplies if they were needed to "halt aggression." The press outdid itself in printing "communiqués" from the "invasion front." This was not subversion, we were told, but a military attack on a large scale. The American people were led to believe that our country was moving toward a crisis of great magnitude, and in those early September days the dread, but unspoken, fear of "another Korea" was abroad in the land.

By 1959, when all this was taking place, the press and the "experts" had so conditioned the American people to *assume* that China (and Southeast Asian Communists generally) were "expansionist" and "aggressive" that these shrill reports of the invasion of Laos were accepted without question. But when Secretary of State Christian Herter hurriedly called an emergency meeting of the UN Security Council, we received a shock. Other UN members were not at all ready to accept the validity of our reports of "invasion," and they insisted that a team of neutral observers go to Laos to get the facts at firsthand.

I was in Laos just before the UN team made its report. I was flown by army plane to Samneua, near where the fighting was supposed to have taken place. I had an all-afternoon interview with General Amkha, who was in command of the forces that were "repelling the invasion." I pressed him hard. He could produce no captured equipment for me to examine, no prisoners, no evidence at all (except some very fancy three-dimensional maps prepared in Washington) to prove that any invasion had taken place. On my return to Vientiane, I prepared a broadcast in which I forecast with a sense of confidence what the gist of the UN report would be.

And I was right. The UN investigators reported (as I knew they must) *that there had been no invasion at all*; and that such fighting as had taken place was of a trivial nature involving a handful of troops.

The truth was humiliatingly obvious. So anxious was the American press to report Communist "aggression" that for weeks it had misled the public. It had apparently accepted without adequate verification the propaganda, the communiqués, the "refugee reports" handed out by the Laotian government. Rumor had been passed on as fact. If the correspondents in Laos were not in a position to send much hard news, the papers at home compensated by providing exciting headlines.

So firmly was this story of the "invasion" of Laos implanted in the mind of the American public, and so closely had writers associated "China" with "Communism in Southeast Asia," that more than four years later, I am still repeatedly asked whether the "Chinese invasion of Laos is not proof of Peking's aggressiveness?"[16]

Between 1947 and 1949, when Mao Tse-tung's troops were defeating the armies of Chiang Kai-shek, equipped with American arms, there were rumors that Mao's success must be due to large-scale Russian military aid. We know now that this was not the case. The arms used by the Chinese Communists were *American arms*—either captured or sold to them by Chiang's officials—and equipment left behind by the Japanese.

Today, in South Vietnam and Laos, history is repeating itself.

On April 24, 1963 (in striking similarity to military events in China during the last years of Chiang), an American correspondent who had served in Vietnam for a year and a half, wrote:

Q. How does the Vietcong get its weapons?
A. Most Vietcong weapons are new U.S. weapons, captured in ambushes on government units and attacks on outposts. Often a Vietcong unit is organized initially with no weapons. The political organizer tells his men and women they must fight at first with handmade arms—spears, daggers, swords, and crude shotguns. To get better weapons, they must capture them from the enemy. The system evidently

16 For a more complete account of what he calls "The Laos Fraud," see William J. Lederer's A *Nation of Sheep*, pp. 11–31.

works. Vietcong arms now include modern recoilless cannon, heavy mortars, good machine guns and very large supplies of submachine guns.[17]

With millions of dollars worth of U.S. equipment, and thousands of U.S. military advisers, the regimes we are supporting in these countries are making little headway. We are told, without a shred of evidence, that the poor military performance of the Diem and the Laotian governments is partly due to the arms the opposition forces are receiving from the Chinese Communists. On May 4, 1962, a UPI dispatch from Vientiane reported:

> U.S. military sources said today the rebel forces which captured the town of Muong Sing Thursday in a renewal of the Laotian civil war apparently came from Communist China.

This story died down almost as quickly as it flared up, but the result was once again to hammer home the image of Chinese involvement in Laos—though it should have died when the UN investigating team made its report.

With South Vietnam the same is true.

In making a detailed study of reports regarding South Vietnam during the first four months of 1962, in a period when great military activity was taking place there, I could hardly find any mention at all, in countless articles, dispatches, and editorials, of Chinese involvement. Tad Szulc, reporting to the New York *Times* on February 26, after the Kennedy administration had turned down a Communist Chinese suggestion for consultation, wrote

> there was no belief in the Administration that Communist Chinese would seek to intervene directly in the Vietnamese conflict.

Five days earlier the New York *Times* quoted a Pentagon spokesman as saying:

> The United States Government has committed itself to support the Government of President Ngo Dinh Diem to

[17] Malcolm Brown, AP, April 24, 1963.

victory against the guerrillas which are backed by North Vietnam and the Soviet Union.

No mention at all was made of Communist China.

So constant and emphatic have been the reports of Communist fighting in Laos and Vietnam and so quickly is this associated in readers' minds with *Chinese* aggression, that refutations from the most unimpeachable non-Communist sources make little impression and are soon forgotten.

On March 6, 1963, the Washington *Post* reported a press conference given in Saigon by General Paul D. Harkins, chief of American forces in South Vietnam. According to the report by the Washington *Post* (my italics):

> Harkins said the guerrillas *obviously are not being reinforced or supplied systematically from North Vietnam, China, or any other place else.*

Whatever the chief of American forces in Vietnam might say, reports of Chinese "aggression" continued. Within a few weeks William R. Frye, writing from Bangkok, had the Chinese on the move ready to strike all over Southeast Asia.

> Communist China is penetrating Southeast Asia or actively preparing to penetrate it on five identifiable military and diplomatic fronts. . . .
> . . . the supply line to South Vietnam through Laos has never been choked off. . . .[18]

The standard rule appears to be that whenever China is involved in a dispute China *is always the aggressor*. Occasionally— very occasionally—a courageous and refreshing voice is heard warning us that the facts if they were fully known might bear a different interpretation. We are so accustomed to hearing China's actions discussed in terms of stale banalities, that to hear a vigorous and untimid expression by an expert of quite another viewpoint is a very heartening experience.

In a speech before the United World Federalists, Urban Whitaker, Professor of International Relations at San Francisco State

[18] "Thailand Fears China on the Move," San Francisco *Chronicle*, April 29, 1963.

College, dealt forthrightly with the question of "Chinese aggression." Professor Whitaker's talk was broadcast February 9, 1963, by the non-commercial station KPFA in Berkeley:[19]

> I want to make a more specific response to some of the nonsense which we often hear about China the aggressive state. Examples are usually cited about Korea, Formosa, India, subversion in Indo-China, Tibet, etc. At the risk of speaking too long let me say a word about each of three or four of these. It is awfully hard to dispel the notion in the United States that China was the aggressor in Korea. And yet I think when we take an objective look at what happened in 1950 and 1951 on the Korean peninsula we have to agree that it would be natural behavior for any state bordering on the Yalu River to engage in some activity helpful to the friend to the south when that friend seemed about to be overwhelmed by a foreign and hostile power.
>
> Now I have not said that anybody is right or wrong. I am just saying that it is quite easy to explain how anybody with his territory bounded by the Yalu River would be concerned when an enemy approached that river. I suppose many Americans actually believe that the Chinese Communists were fighting in the Korean war from the very beginning. It is hard to convince people nowadays, as they look back thinking that it was the United States versus the Chinese Communists, that the Chinese Communists actually did not come into the war until November, after it started in June. The Chinese Communists did not come into the Korean war until after we had pushed back across the 38th Parallel and General MacArthur had announced his intention of going on to the Yalu River, the border of China. . . .
>
> . . . I do not think the Korean war is sufficient evidence to prove that the Chinese Communists are inherently aggressive or that we might expect them to be aggressive some place else. What it proves is that if the United States approaches the Chinese border from any direction the Chinese

[19] This station is one of three listener-supported stations run by Pacifica Foundation. These three stations in Berkeley, Los Angeles, and New York have consistently given opportunities for all sides of the China question and other controversial issues to be heard and discussed. In my criticism of the press and radio reports, I am glad to make an exception in the case of these excellent stations.

Communists are going to want to fight to move us back. It does not prove that the Chinese Communists are going to approach somebody else's border. Certainly it does not prove that they have designs of the Rocky Mountains.[20]

It is also hard to get Americans to look at Formosa objectively; and yet the Chinese desire, and clearly there is Chinese desire, to take Formosa is again hardly proof of inherent aggressiveness among the Chinese Communist leaders. Formosa has always been a part of China in their view; it has been a part of China from our view (except from 1895 to 1945 when the Japanese had taken it by military force). Chiang Kai-shek, our friend and ally on Formosa, agrees with the Communists that Formosa is a part of China, though he puts it that China is a part of Formosa. It is most difficult to cite this Chinese Communist desire to re-unite island and mainland as having anything whatever to do with an aggressive intent.

The Indian border question is also very difficult to talk about objectively, and make sense about with American people and with many others, including Indians. In the first place, the question who is right and who is wrong in setting the line at one place and another between India and China is a question to which we don't have a very good answer. And I suppose most Americans would say, if they were asked who's right and who's wrong in the border dispute, "the Chinese are wrong, they are the aggressive Chinese Communists, and the Indians are right."

But I wonder how many Americans who are firmly convinced of this know anything at all about the border dispute. So far as I can see, and I've read quite a few things about this dispute, there isn't any clear evidence on either side that the border ought to be drawn where it is drawn. Again, however, we can bring Chiang Kai-shek in to clarify the picture for us. Chiang Kai-shek's government drew the line that the Chinese Communists are now willing to fight to defend, and again Chiang Kai-shek and Mao Tse-tung agree that the line is where they think it is—they are both against the Indians. And, in fact, there is substantial evidence that the United

[20] Almost ten years after the Korean conflict started a China specialist, Allen S. Whiting, in a study made for the Air Force by the Rand Corporation, came to some similar conclusions about Chinese "aggression" in Korea. This report was later published under the title *China Crosses the Yalu: The Decision to Enter the Korean War*, (New York: Macmillan, 1960).

States has assumed in drawing its own maps and making its own conclusions in the past that the Chinese were right and the Indians wrong in the placement of that border. . . .

It is clear that the Chinese, not the Indians, took it upon themselves to resolve this dispute by resort to military force. And I think that's wrong. It doesn't prove that the Chinese are aggressive, it doesn't prove that they are bent on military expansion. I don't think, and I didn't think, when they were roaring down on the plains of Assam, that they had any intention of taking over India. . . .

So the Chinese have used force in resolving their border dispute with India, and I think that was wrong. But I think that it was also wrong for the Indians to use force in resolving their dispute with Goa, and it was clearly illegal for the United States to use force as we did in blockading Cuba in order to win the argument with the Soviet Union and Castro.

In any case, do all these things prove that the Chinese are inherently aggressive and that they are bent on military expansion? I think not. I haven't seen any convincing evidence that the Chinese believe that military expansion is possible, or that it is a good idea for them.

Such statements are rare and their impact small. The generally accepted view is that the Chinese leaders and their foreign policy are "aggressive." It would be quite impossible, in my opinion, to come to any other view if one were to rely on our newspapers and many of our syndicated columnists and weekly newsmagazines. It certainly is not the purpose of this book to examine China's foreign policies and pass judgment on them. The point I am making here is that I believe we have been given too little objective information. Tibet, Laos, Vietnam, India . . . the image of "aggression" is deeply implanted in our minds. Whenever these "acts of aggression" take place, the invariable epithets are trotted out, the cartoonists get busy with their drawings of the rapacious dragon, the usual outraged editorials are written—but the *facts?*

I shall examine in later chapters two cases of Chinese "aggression" which remain vividly in our minds—the Chinese-Indian border dispute and Tibet.

When each of these events is examined in detail, not in terms of cold war assumptions, but based on historical background and documented evidence, the issues that at the time seemed so gloriously certain are seen to be not nearly so unambiguous as they had been made to appear. We have already seen how the press and public officials referred to the "invasion of Laos" in 1959; and how stubbornly the belief persists—though repeatedly denied by our military men—that the Chinese are infiltrating into South Vietnam. The facts, I think, will show a similar situation with regard to our information about both the Indian border dispute and Tibet.

During the same week that the New York *Times* was telling its readers that the rulers of Communist China had resolved to enter upon "a Napoleonic phase of expansionism" and that "their first major objective" was to "establish their control" over the whole continent of Asia, Prince Norodom Sihanouk, the head of state of Cambodia, published a signed article in the September 17 issue of the *Weekly Nationalist*. Cambodia, with whom the United States had retained good relations, was strongly determined to maintain its neutrality. In this article Prince Sihanouk takes a candid look at America's fears about Communist China. It is worth quoting at some length:

> I want to remind our readers that this article is not intended to speak in defence of People's China because it has no need whatever for others to do so on its behalf. My purpose in writing this article is simply to answer those questions which prominent personages and journalists in the West have so often put to me . . . the naïveté of these questions stupefies and baffles me, but at the same time it permits me to gauge the depth of misunderstanding in the West of the greatest nation in the world . . . with all the consequences this will bring to our common future.

Sihanouk then describes his interviews with the late John Foster Dulles who told him, in 1958, that "according to reliable information I have obtained, the suffering of the Chinese people under the oppression of the Communist regime will soon reach its breaking point." Prince Sihanouk goes on:

. . . this is a classic and tragic example of the errors of judgment on the part of the West towards China.

. . . the political thinkers of the free world doubtless think they are very clever in flattering me, my government, and our "way of life" and in putting me in a dilemma: either to disown my own policy or recognize with them, the evil character of the Chinese government! . . .

The Chinese people know far better than the Western politicians what Mao Tse-tung's government has brought them because now they have land to cultivate and an income fairly distributed according to productive work; because even if they do not have feasts, their daily meals are assured and for the first time they have been eating their fill; (it is sufficient to look at the Chinese children to be convinced) because they are now decently dressed . . . because they know that they enjoy free medical care, that their children have the right to public education, and that they will not be abandoned in case of natural calamities; and because they are assured that there will be no more plundering by bureaucrats, soldiers, and pirates. . . .

. . . it is necessary to understand that for the first time in its modern history, China has become forever and completely free from foreign control . . . the Chinese people know that credit for this must be given to Mao Tse-tung and the Communist Party of China. . . .

. . . another grave psychological error of the West when dealing with China warrants attention. The West fears the emergence among the peoples of Asia of a People's China which is bent on conquests and ready to absorb all other Asian countries. . . .

This image . . . used widely since the commencement of the Sino-Indian border conflict, has no effect whatever on the minds of the Asians (with the possible exception of the Indians). On the contrary, and all the more remarkable, it is Westerners, including the elite, who are in a panic towards China!

. . . my feeling towards China is not mixed with any fear. I must say that neither I nor our people are afraid of China.

Our confidence in China is by no means naïve, nor is it without reason; quite the contrary!

The question is raised, on what grounds do the defenders of the "free" world say that China wants to conquer all Asia and particularly southeast Asia? . . .

After dealing with the way that Laos, the Sino-Indian dispute, and the use of overseas Chinese have been taken by the West as examples of China's aggressiveness, Prince Sihanouk says:

> . . . It is impossible for us to follow the Westerners in their judgement of China. They have conjured up the image by auto-suggestion, whereas we judge by facts.

The head of state of Cambodia is not the only leader of Southeast Asia who appears unafraid of China. Souvanna Phouma, the neutralist Prime Minister of Laos, said on his arrival in Paris on September 25, 1963, (Algeria France Presse dispatch) that

> "People's China was exerting no influence on the situation in Laos. . . . Up until now China has not shown itself. The influence we note, politically speaking, is that of the Soviet Union.

As far as I have observed, reports such as this or the article by the head of state of Cambodia are given little or no attention in America, and our people remain convinced that "China wants war!"

Chapter 11

"THERE WILL BE
THREE HUNDRED MILLION LEFT"

Without mentioning names or places Marshal Tito said the Chinese liked to boast that their population of 600,000,-000 was a guarantee of victory in war. According to President Tito, Peiping calculated that "if 300,000,000 were killed there would still remain 300,000,000 Chinese."

—New York *Times*,
June 16, 1958.

With these words by Tito, a major and perhaps immortal myth was born. (It was reported later that a somewhat similar statement was made in 1956 by Marshal Peng Teh-huai to a group of Japanese military officers visiting China. But the U.S. press did not take it up at that time. The "ready to sacrifice 300 million" story went into circulation only after Tito's speech quoted above.)

Ask any group of Americans, and nine out of ten will have heard (in one form or another) that China "wouldn't mind a war because even if half of them were killed there would still be three hundred million of them left."

No one today even knows that the remark originated with Tito, or if they do, that Tito and the Chinese at the time he made it were engaged in any angry exchange of polemics.

It was *said*, and that was enough. Here was further "proof" of the unspeakably callous nature of the Chinese leaders. The remark was eagerly seized upon, disseminated, editorialized, analyzed by learned scholars, embroidered, enlarged, broadcast, discussed on

TV, written about by a score of columnists—until today it is a central and ineradicable component of our picture of the Chinese.

Tito's words were part of a long speech. A number of American correspondents were there; they all reported the speech, but only the *Times*' correspondent thought the remark about the Chinese worth mentioning. (The AP's long account of Tito's speech contained only one reference to China on the international level, saying that "China was against relaxation of tensions in the world.")[1]

The day following the report from its correspondent in Belgrade, the *Times* ran an editorial in which the editors drew their ominous conclusions:

TITO DARES THE LIGHTNING

In terms of drama, of course, the highlight of Tito's address was his exposure of the peaceful professions of the Chinese Communists. We knew from the past bloody history of the establishment and consolidation of Chinese communism—a process which cost countless lives—that the present Peiping rulers regarded human life cheaply; but even the most bitter Western opponent of the Peiping regime would have hesitated to believe Tito's revelation that they regarded 300,000,000 lives as of little import.

The story was soon in orbit.

From then on it was difficult to find anyone writing about China who would not contrive to include some reference to the Chinese being ready to sacrifice half their population. Thus on July 28, Joseph P. Lash, who was writing about the United Nations for the New York *Post*, reported the following awesome facts about developments in China (my numerals and my comments):[2]

1. Chinese Communist leader Mao Tse-tung has been pushed aside in Peking, and a reactionary "China Lobby" in Moscow is gunning for Soviet Premier Khrushchev, according to reports reaching the U.N. [He is still, five years later, the acknowledged leader.]

[1] New York *Herald Tribune*, June 16, 1958.
[2] The New York *Post*, July 28, 1958.

2. Chinese communism is described as having in the last 18 months taken an almost "catastrophic" turn toward the slave state. Stalinist Russia and George Orwell's nightmarish vision of "1984" are called benevolent compared to what is taking place in Red China. [I was in China during this period and judging by what I saw, I believe this description is untrue. See also Chapter 8, "650 Million Slaves."]

3. The man in the driver's seat in Peking is said to be Premier Chou En-lai. [Mao Tse-tung is still the leader, Liu Shao-chi is Head of State, Chou En-lai is Premier.]

4. At the Communist "summit" meeting in Moscow Mao is said to have remarked that another world war might well mean the death of 1,500,000,000 people; but of the 600,000-000 who would survive half would be Chinese and they would rule the world. [So it is now Mao who said it; and the Chinese would not merely "win a war," but would "rule the world." And a billion and a half deaths in the next war is now on the record!]

The *Herald Tribune*, relying on the AP report from Belgrade which didn't mention it, carried nothing about the Chinese readiness to sacrifice three hundred million of their population. Not, that is, until three months later, on September 23, 1958, when the editors rather tardily discovered what they proceeded to call "Red China's New Weapon," and they wrote an editorial:

> Months ago, Marshal Tito reported that Red China's Communist leaders were talking more and more ominously of risking war if necessary to obtain their expansionist aims. That these aims are a new form of imperialism is now being made apparent by an equally ominous switch in Red China's population policies. . . .
>
> . . . Population increase is now being regarded as an asset, since it will provide all the more man power for the ambitious industrial projects, as well as for cannon fodder.
>
> This new view of population as a military asset has led the Chinese to boast (as Tito has revealed) that they can win a war even if atomic weapons are used: "Even if 300,-000,000 Chinese were killed in an atomic war, there would still remain 300,000,000."

Quoting another correspondent, the *Herald Tribune* editorial continued:

> "The Chinese program is almost terrifying in its audacity.
> . . . Its success could soon make of China the greatest power
> the world has ever seen."
>
> . . . Communist China is the first nation to adopt a pop-
> ulation explosion as an instrument of state policy. It is a
> mark of the implacability of leaders who have turned a face
> of unrelenting hatred toward the West and all its ways.

This editorial is a masterpiece of imaginative development. On
a foundation of a few words of Tito's which its own news columns
had not reported at the time, the editorial staff of the *Herald
Tribune* found it possible to construct a whole edifice of meanings
and implications and motives and intentions. "War" becomes
"atomic war." Though Tito didn't mention it, the Chinese are
now "talking more and more ominously of risking war" and they
have "expansionist aims." China's large population is now seen to
be much more than what it appears—a lot of people—but has become "an instrument of state policy" to be used "for cannon fodder." And all this—risking war, expansionist aims, large population,
cannon fodder—is associated with China's "unrelenting hatred
toward the West and all its ways."

Tito's words in the course of time have appeared in almost
every newspaper, every magazine dealing with China, hundreds
of syndicated columns and editorials. Tito himself was soon forgotten. It is sometimes Mao who is said to have made the remark,
sometimes Chou En-lai, sometimes the Chinese Foreign Minister,
Chen Yi; once it was an unnamed general in Tokyo.

The story continues. Drew Pearson said (on October 28, 1959)
that Mao "doesn't worry about atomic war because [China] could
lose half its population"; and it's only a little step from not worrying about war to *approving* war.

> The Chinese government approves war, agitates for war,
> and predicates its entire existence on war. . . .
> —Lucius Beebe, San Francisco *Chronicle*,
> January 28, 1963.

The authorship of the famous remark remains forgotten, and
the number of his people that Mao is ready to sacrifice varies, too;
but never China's eventual doom.

Referring to an official Department of Agriculture report, the New York *Herald Tribune,* in a front-page feature, wrote on October 17, 1962:

> A vast and grisly wasteland, offering only a future of non-existence to a massive but starving population, is Red China's bleak prospect for 1980. . . .[3]
>
> The plight of people never bothered Mao. He said that in case of nuclear war, Red China would emerge best off in the world. Why? Even if 200 million lives were lost on the mainland, there'd be more people left in China than perhaps the rest of the world combined.

The arithmetic may be confused but the purport is clear. For whoever is reported as the author of the statement and whatever the number of Chinese to be sacrificed, it is always dutifully presented to show what monsters the Chinese leaders are, how callously indifferent to the wholesale sacrifice of human lives.

Tito, himself, must be amazed. Rarely has so much mileage been wrung from so brief a remark by any leader. And who really knows whether the Chinese ever said what he said they said!

During the height of the Quemoy crisis in 1958, some of our commentators went far beyond anything Mao was alleged to have said. Mr. Holmes Alexander, the columnist, writing on July 23, said (my italics):

> We have ingested the Communist-concocted idea that it is wicked to kill our enemies with A-bombs or H-bombs. You can read it in editorials. You can hear it in speeches. "Spare civilization by swearing off Nuclearonics. . . ."
>
> Are we afraid to throw this punch? Are we ashamed to possess it? Are we sorry we knocked out two Japanese cities in 1945 with atomic bombs instead of fire bombs? Are we in a mood to *blow up the world, destroy every vestige of life upon the planet,* rather than lose a war?[4]

[3] Not much more than six months after this official report was issued, and long before 1980, it was apparent from all reports that China's food supplies were improved and agricultural production was once more moving upward.
[4] McNaught Syndicate.

Afterwards, I searched for some editorial reproach, some protest from readers . . . I found none.

It has always struck me as rather strange that Mao's remark (if he ever made it) that half the population of China would survive a war caused such a furor in our press. That the Chinese, like other civilized people, have had to take into account the possible effects of nuclear war is not startling. We accept estimates of how many of *us* might have to be sacrificed to win a war calmly enough—in fact I don't know of any country in the world that so openly calculates and debates and discusses the number of people who might be left alive after the bombing is over. Mr. Joseph Alsop has long been preparing us for the number of "megadeaths" that we must expect to suffer. Mr. Herman Kahn's macabre book,[5] in which he spoke of sixty million deaths or more as "acceptable," was read and considered soberly by thousands. For what we do, the press violently castigates the Chinese, and from it draws all kinds of absurd and frightening conclusions.

And in doing so, it conditions us further to accept the image of the Chinese as inhuman monsters.

While Tito's "disclosure" of Chinese readiness to sacrifice three hundred million people is the stuff that columnists' dreams are made of, scholars and specialists tend to seek something a little less crude—all the while following the same general line.

In the writings of Mao Tse-tung they found what they were looking for. And like the columnists with the three hundred million casualties, they have squeezed out of it every ounce of juice.

Over a quarter of a century ago, while Mao and his group of guerrilla forces were busy fighting both the Kuomintang and the invading Japanese armies, Mao delivered a long speech (in English it runs to fourteen pages) on "Problems of War and Strategy."[6] Much of this five-thousand-word address was historical and

[5] *On Thermonuclear War* (Princeton, N.J.: Princeton University Press, 1960).
[6] Mao Tse-tung, *Selected Works*, Vol. II (New York: International Publishers, 1954–1956), pp. 267–81.

theoretical, and in the course of it Mao said: "Every Communist must grasp the truth: 'Political power grows out of the barrel of a gun.' "[7]

One would not have imagined that in a country which won its own political independence by using guns, this rather mild and obvious phrase would appear very startling. But nevertheless, torn out of context and with no reference to the conditions under which it was made, it has been often used at the highest levels of scholarship as conclusive proof of the wicked and warlike nature of Mao Tse-tung. The phrase, or part of it, was also used as a title of a book *Out of the Gun* by an Australian journalist, Denis Warner, who reports on China from Southeast Asia.

Reviewing this book in *The Christian Science Monitor*, a correspondent who covered China by being there in a bygone era, extended the quotation:

> Mao Tse-tung, Communist China's leader wrote in his book "Problems of War and Peace" [the reviewer confused Mao and Tolstoy at this point]: "Every Communist must grasp the truth. Political power grows out of the gun. . . . Anything can grow out of the barrel of the gun. . . ."[8]

Two years later, A. Doak Barnett, a leading China specialist and Ford Foundation staff member, devoted several pages of his latest volume to the "Philosophy of Power," and used the same quotation as a springboard for launching his own version of what Mao Tse-tung thinks:

> Communist China's leaders also attach very great importance to the intimate relationship between military and political power. As Mao Tse-tung stated bluntly in 1938, "Political power grows out of the barrel of a gun. . . . Anything can grow out of a gun." The Chinese Communists have no moral scruples or inhibitions about the use of force . . . they regard force as a perfectly legitimate instrument of policy. As Mao wrote in 1936,
> "War is one of the highest forms of struggle for the settlement of contradictions between classes, nations, states, or

[7] Ibid., p. 272.
[8] Ronald Stead, January 17, 1958.

political groups in a certain stage of development since the beginning of class society . . . There are two kinds of war in history: revolutionary and counter-revolutionary. We support the former and oppose the latter. Only a revolutionary war is holy. We support holy national revolutionary wars and holy class revolutionary wars."[9]

In this quotation Mr. Barnett availed himself of two parts from Mao Tse-tung's work and is guilty of what I would consider some very misleading quoting. No one reading his selection would suppose that the three ellipses after the words "since the beginning of class society" represent a jump of *three pages* into another section of Mao's essay; and a study of what Mr. Barnett omitted discloses that what is omitted, far from showing that the "Chinese Communists have no moral scruples" about the use of force, is instead part of a closely reasoned argument as to how wars can finally be eliminated.[10] Indeed, the heading of the section from which Mr. Barnett selects the latter part of his quotation reads: "The Aim of War Lies in Eliminating War." The sentence immediately following this (not quoted by Barnett) reads: "War, this monster of mutual slaughter, will be finally eliminated through the progress of human society, and in no distant future too."[11]

A reading of Mao's long analysis of what constitute just and unjust wars would, I think, give readers almost the opposite impression as to the Chinese leader's feelings about war than they would arrive at from reading Mr. Barnett's quotations. What is more, because his quotation stops where it does (to continue after a gap of three pages) readers were unable to see the very next sentence. This missing sentence contains, I think, a central point in Mao Tse-tung's thinking—the absolute necessity to examine carefully the laws and anatomy of war: "Without understanding the circumstances of war, its characteristics, and its relations to other things, we cannot know the laws of war, cannot know how to direct it, and cannot win victory."[12]

[9] A. Doak Barnett, *Communist China and Asia*, p. 75.
[10] Mao Tse-tung, *Selected Works*, Vol. I (1954), see pp. 176–79.
[11] Ibid., p. 179.
[12] Ibid., p. 179.

When one considers that all this was written several years before the outbreak of the Second World War and before the Japanese invaded and overran much of China's territory, an analysis of the laws of war can no more be considered "proof" of Mao's warlike nature than discussion of military tactics before Pearl Harbor by officers in the Pentagon proves that they were devoid of any "moral scruples."

The phrase about "political" power and the gun barrel is catchy. Mr. Barnett used it once before in the course of contributing to the *Atlantic Monthly's* special China issue in December 1959. Alice Langley Hsieh, of the Rand Corporation, and other scholarly specialists in the field have also cited Mao's few words as evidence of his hunger for power.

That those who wish to prove how "belligerent" the present-day leaders in China are, still rely on a part of a single sentence extracted from a speech made a quarter of a century ago—a speech made to a band of soldiers who had only recently survived a six-thousand-mile retreat—is in itself, I think, significant.

Nor have the China specialists been alone.

On December 1, 1961, Adlai Stevenson used this twenty-five-year-old quotation in the UN to show how belligerent the Communist regime is, how unworthy to be admitted to the UN; and in 1962 the former U. S. Air Force Chief of Staff, General Thomas D. White, assessing the weaknesses and strength of China's military position, was still relying on this tired old quotation:

> Her enormous population is now backward, her industries are not technically oriented, her natural resources undeveloped, and her vast area without adequate communications. But the political philosophy of this massive land is violently militant both at home and abroad. Mao Tse-tung has said, "Political power comes from the barrel of a gun."[13]

It would appear a legitimate request that our scholars, statesmen, and soldiers, attempting to convey to us some knowledge of Mao's thoughts about war and the use of force, should give us

[13] *Newsweek,* September 3, 1962.

more than a few selected quotations, with this phrase about the "barrel of a gun" thrown in. Mao Tse-tung, after all, is one of the great, and probably the most prolific, of military theoreticians of our day.

Chapter 12

"CHINESE AGGRESSION"—
THE SINO-INDIAN BORDER DISPUTE

So solidly built into our consciousness is the concept that China is conducting a rapacious and belligerent foreign policy that whenever a dispute arises in which China is involved, she is instantly assumed to have provoked it. All commentaries, "news reports," and scholarly interpretations are written on the basis of this assumption. The cumulative effect of this only further reinforces the original hypothesis so that it is used again next time with even greater effect.

This certainty of Chinese aggressive and expansionist aims is not shared by our allies who have been in far closer and more continuous contact with the Chinese government. In the United States it is absolute and unvarying.

Thus it was entirely predictable that when on October 20, 1962, fighting broke out along the Sino-Indian border, the unanimous response, like a conditioned reflex, was that this was a "naked and unprovoked attack" by China against her southern neighbor.

Neutral countries, one should mention in passing, took a much more cautious and judicious view.

It would probably come as a surprise to most Americans that most of the neutral governments do not subscribe to the Indian-American-British interpretation of what actually took place. The staunchly conservative *Daily Telegraph* of London reported from its correspondent in New Delhi, on October 29, 1962:

But what really hurt in New Delhi was the discovery that the rest of the neutral block deserted India to a man. Most seemed to prefer the Chinese version of the events leading up to the final collision.

It may be valuable, therefore, to take this border conflict as a "case history," and to examine the anatomy of the dispute in detail. My purpose is not to prove that the Chinese were blameless, or that they were not guilty of provocative acts. Rather it is an exercise in laying out as far as one can the facts of a complicated issue *as they really happened*, and only then to draw conclusions from these facts.

The chronological story of the dispute as I outline it in this chapter is, I think, accurate. The meaning I draw from it readers must accept or reject as they will. But if I am right, this dispute provides another example (almost as clear-cut as the "invasion of Laos" story of 1959) of how our press and officials, speaking in what appears to be impressive harmony, by deceiving themselves misled a whole nation.

It would be hard to find any part of the world with a longer or more checkered history than the vast mountainous region which separates China from Burma, Nepal, Pakistan, and India. These borders, undefined and often previously disputed, are a legacy of history. Almost all conflicting claims along this border can find some support in history, ethnography, or in common justice. The history of this area supplies enough material for any party to support any claim. Under these circumstances it is obvious that the only way to a peaceful resolution of the various claims is through a process of compromise. And this was in fact exactly the way the borders between China on the one hand and Burma, Nepal, and —later—Pakistan on the other were settled. In none of these cases were there armed clashes. In all cases the status quo was taken as the basis of negotiations and adjustments were then made, one way or the other, taking into account historical and geographical factors and the interests of the parties involved. All three borders were demarcated and recognized in formal international treaties.

On balance in the process of give and take, it has been generally acknowledged China gave considerably more than she took.

Between China and India matters took a very different course. No basis of negotiations could be agreed upon. Numerous armed clashes continued, culminating in large-scale warfare. Why did this happen? Has China's attitude been more "aggressive" toward India than it was toward Burma, Nepal, and Pakistan? Or has India, unlike these other countries, been unwilling to compromise?

On this question the record is absolutely clear. China unquestionably was seeking an amicable settlement through discussion and mutual accommodation, suggesting that pending a settlement both parties should maintain the status quo as it existed in 1959 when the border clashes began. India has at all times insisted that all her principal claims must be conceded before the discussions could begin. There can be no doubt in the mind of anyone who studies the record that it has been India and not China that has stood in the way of a settlement through mutual compromise.

So, we must ask, was this because the status quo of 1959 was specially disadvantageous for India? Were there reasons why the choice of this particular moment was unacceptable to her? Before we can answer this question we must examine the border situation as it was in 1959.

The Sino-Indian border is divided into three sectors. The western sector separates the Ladakh area of Kashmir from China's Sinkiang province and Tibet. The middle sector separates three Indian states from Tibet (the disputed areas in this middle sector were quite minor and need not be discussed here). The eastern sector separates the Indian state of Assam from Tibet.

In the eastern sector the Indians controlled the disputed area, claiming what is known as the McMahon Line to be the legal boundary, a line drawn up unilaterally by the British. The McMahon Line was named after the British delegate at a conference held at Simla in 1914 which was attended by representatives of Britain, China, and Tibet. The Chinese government refused to sign the draft Convention and no Chinese government since has ever accepted the McMahon Line. The Chinese today still claim, as they did then, that the traditional boundary included the southern slope of the Himalayas and was never based on the watershed which was the basis used for drawing the McMahon Line.[1] They point out that the people who have lived here are Tibetans or of Tibetan origin and the place names are also Tibetan and not Indian.

The Chinese say that some of the area between the traditional border and the McMahon Line (about thirty-five thousand square miles, including much good farming land and valuable forests) had been taken by the British from China at a time when China was too weak to resist. This area was organized by the British and was known as the Northeast Frontier Agency (NEFA), and it retains that status today under Indian rule, together with additional territory occupied by India in 1951. The Indians reject the Chinese claim and state that the McMahon Line merely confirmed the natural, traditional, ethnic and administrative boundary in this area.

This Indian interpretation of the McMahon Line is greatly weakened by the fact that the official *Survey of India* map published by the Indian government in 1917; the map attached to the 1929 edition of the Encyclopædia Britannica; the 1940 edition of the Oxford Advanced Atlas (Bartholemew); and the 1942 edition of Philips' Atlas all show the border as claimed by China and not the McMahon Line as claimed by India. In the course of a long note addressed to the Indian government on December 26, 1959, the Chinese Foreign Office pointed out that the Mc-Mahon Line

> was not adopted on the official map 'Tibet and Adjacent Countries' published by the *Survey of India* in 1938. . . . Neither was the so-called McMahon Line followed in drawing the eastern sector of the Sino-Indian boundary on the map 'India 1945' attached to the 1951 third edition in English of the *Discovery of India* written by Prime Minister Nehru himself. . . .[2]

[1] The former Acting Governor of Assam, Sir Henry Twynam, wrote in *The Times* of London on September 2, 1959, that "The McMahon Line, which sought to secure the main crest of the Himalayas as the frontier, does not exist and never has existed."

[2] *Documents of the Sino-Indian Boundary Question* (Peking: Foreign Language Press, 1960).

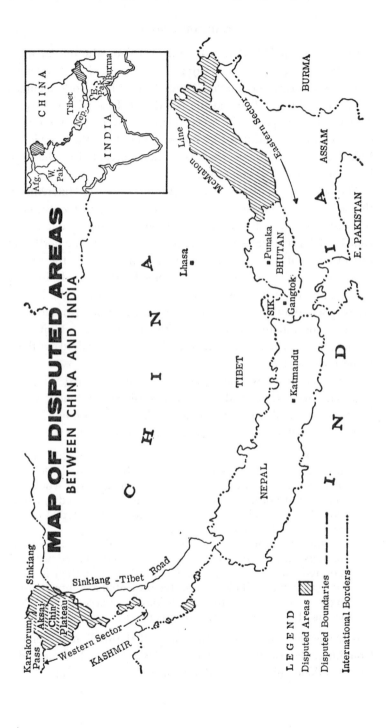

MAP OF DISPUTED AREAS
BETWEEN CHINA AND INDIA

Even when the McMahon Line appeared on the official maps ´ of India in 1950, 1951, and 1952, it was marked as "undemarcated." Up to 1958 the London Times Atlas of the World included both the traditional line and the McMahon Line with the words "Disputed Area" printed between them. The weight of these facts overwhelmingly indicates the Indian claim that the McMahon Line merely "reaffirmed" what was always accepted as the legal boundary cannot be supported.

The situation in the western sector in 1959 was different. In this sector, the Chinese and not the Indians were in possession of the disputed area—about thirteen thousand square miles. The Indians claim that the legal border is considerably to the north and east of where it is at present. But here again, in 1950 the official Indian maps show this area as "undefined." It was only in 1954 that the *Survey of India* map for the first time showed the boundary precisely drawn. What had happened between 1950 and 1954 to justify the Indian government (without reference to China) in claiming an area that had until then been acknowledged by them to be undefined?

The explanation is that after the Chinese entered Tibet in 1950–51, what Britain and India had considered a "buffer state" between India and China was removed. As Mr. Nehru, in a speech to the Lok Sabha on February 21, 1961, expressed it:

> When the Chinese first entered Tibet . . . frankly we did not expect any trouble on our border, but, naturally, looking at things in historical perspective, we thought the whole nature of our border had changed. It was a dead border, it was now becoming alive, and we began to think in terms of the protection of that border. . . .
>
> Our attention was first directed, naturally or not, to these borders, and a high level, high power committee was appointed, the Border Defense Committee, right then in 1951 or 1952, I forget. This Committee presented a comprehensive report, and many of the suggestions were accepted by Government, some were not. This was ten years ago.

It seems clear that one of the things that this Border Defense Committee did was to decide what border it proposed to "defend." This was done unilaterally without consultation with China. From then on a border which had never been defined became in the Indian view precisely determined.

But now—still considering this western sector—we enter a phase of the dispute which even the Indians find it embarrassingly difficult to explain. Across territory in the Aksai Chin area (which India had now unilaterally defined as being hers) the Chinese had been constructing a highway. This road, which follows an ancient caravan route across the high Aksai Chin plateau, provides the Chinese with the only practical communication between Sinkiang and central Tibet. This was the route by which Chinese troops entered western Tibet from Sinkiang in 1950 without any complaint from New Delhi. The transformation of this old caravan route into a modern highway was (in Chou En-lai's words) a "gigantic task." Thousands of Chinese must have been engaged in the work. The survey work for the road was started in 1954, and the road itself was not completed until 1957. But though this road was crossing land that India was claiming as hers *no protest was made until* 1958—a year after the road was completed and four years after it was begun. Why, we must ask, did the Indian government wait so long before complaining of these Chinese "incursions" into Indian territory? The answer is simple: *the Indian government had no idea what was going on in this area.* This is how Mr. Nehru explained it to the Lok Sabha on February 23, 1961:

> It was not clear to us whether this proposed motor way crossed our territory. The first suspicion that this might be so came to us in 1957, from a map published in Peking. We did not even then know definitely whether this transgressed our territory. The map was a small map, but half a magazine page. We did not know, but we began to suspect it . . . as we did not have proof, we did not protest then.

But even with their suspicions aroused, the Indian government made no effort apparently to confirm the presence of this road or its location, for no protest was made until 1958.

How is it possible that a government does not know what is going on in part of what it claims to be its territory? The answer again is an obvious one. India had never actually exercised jurisdiction over the territory it was now claiming. Though readily accessible from the Chinese side, the Aksai Chin plateau can only be reached from India after weeks of difficult travel across barren and unpopulated mountain ranges.

With these facts in mind we can now get an over-all picture of the situation as it existed in 1959—the situation which China wished to take as the basis for negotiations and which India rejected. In the east the Indians were in possession of the disputed area—thirty-five thousand square miles. In the west the Chinese were in possession of the disputed area—thirteen thousand square miles. It was in 1959—in August and October—that the first serious armed clashes occurred. Reacting to these encounters, the Chinese government on November 7 (a date that was to figure frequently in subsequent correspondence) proposed that both sides should withdraw at once twenty kilometers from the actual line of control to avoid further incidents and that negotiations to settle the location of the boundary should be begun. The implications of this proposal were quite clear. The Chinese were in effect offering to accept the McMahon Line in the east provided the Indians would accept a line in the west which would secure for China the important highway which they had built. This proposal was rejected by the Indian government. No negotiations could take place, they said, until the Chinese accepted not only the McMahon Line but India's definition of the boundary in the west, which she had unilaterally defined on her maps without discussion with China.

The rejection of this sensible compromise put forward by China was, we can now realize, the real turning point in the dispute. It is very hard to see how any rational person could regard the Chinese suggestion as arising from anything but a sober sense of realism and a desire for a peaceful settlement. India would be getting legal recognition of thirty-five thousand square miles in the east, including much farm land and forests, in exchange for giving up her claim to thirteen thousand square miles which she had never occupied, which by no stretch of the imagination could be considered to have value to her, and which (on the Indian side) could only be reached with the greatest difficulty.

The Chinese were offering to swallow a bitter pill by accepting the McMahon Line—the very name of which denotes its imperialist origin and a reminder of past humiliation at the hands of the Western powers. The Indians were in control of the area up to the McMahon Line and the Chinese knew they could not be dislodged without military conflict. Though subsequent events showed they had ample power to throw the Indians back, *the Chinese did not want a war with India and proved it by being willing to make very considerable concessions to avoid one.*

All the tragic events that have happened since were the inevitable result of India's rejection of the only compromise that could have led to a peaceful settlement of the border dispute. What in fact followed? Having defined the Chinese occupation of the Aksai Chin plateau as "aggression," the Indians began, logically enough, to apply military pressure to oust the Chinese. During the next two years the Indians pressed forward, clashing increasingly with the Chinese, and they were successful in advancing against relatively light Chinese resistance. As Mr. Nehru put it in addressing the Lok Sabha on June 20, 1962:

> India had opened some new patrol posts endangering the Chinese posts and it was largely due to movements on our side that the Chinese had also to make movements. It is well known in knowledgeable circles in the world that the position in this area has been changing to our advantage and the Chinese are concerned about it.

Throughout the summer of 1962 there were indications of Indian preparations for military action, which undoubtedly were watched carefully by the Chinese. Addressing Parliament on August 13 and 14, Mr. Nehru described the government's preparation:

> We have concentrated on increasing our strength, military strength, strength in communications, roads, etc. We have a special border roads committee which has done very well —I do not know exactly—thousands of miles in very difficult terrain. We built up our air supply position by getting aircraft—big aircraft—from various countries; we have got some helicopters too; but in the main it consisted of big transport aircraft; there were some from the United States and some from the Soviet Union. . . . We improved our military

position, our supply position, and we have got our troops in various areas there with forward posts. If they [the Chinese] have got nine posts, we have got 22 or 23 or 24.

With India openly improving its military position along the frontier areas, the Chinese must undoubtedly have been making their preparations also. With India consistently refusing to negotiate on reasonable terms and pursuing her "nibbling" tactics from 1959 on, the Chinese must have been convinced that they would sooner or later have to administer a severe defeat to the Indians before any negotiations were possible. It is hard to see what alternatives they had. They were certainly not ready to accept the prospect of a border in perpetual conflict.

This, then, was the general background to the large-scale fighting that broke out all along the border on October 20, 1962. The events which immediately preceded these hostilities (with our present knowledge of what was about to happen) are interesting to recall and can be summarized below. China had already repeatedly put forward proposals for negotiations which India had rejected. India's rigid attitude had by this time caused some adverse comment.

(*July 26*) India offered to negotiate the boundary dispute on the basis of the study undertaken jointly in 1960.

(*August 4*) The Chinese responded and proposed that discussions begin as soon as possible.

(*August 22*) An Indian note said that before discussions could take place the border in the western sector must be restored to its status quo (the border as defined by India).

(*September 13*) The Chinese said there could be no preconditions. They again proposed that each side withdraw twenty kilometers to avoid further incidents and suggested that the representatives of the two countries meet on October 15 in Peking and then in New Delhi, alternately.

(*September 19*) The Indians agreed to the proposed date and place but insisted that the talks should have the specific object of "defining measures to restore the status quo in the western sector."

(*October 3*) A Chinese note reiterated the proposal that both sides should enter speedily into discussion and that neither side should refuse to discuss any question that might be raised by the other side.

(*October 6*) The Indian government rejected the Chinese proposal and called off the talks scheduled to begin in Peking on October 15.

(*October 12*) Nehru announced that he had instructed the Indian army to "throw the Chinese" out of the disputed areas. (The New York *Herald Tribune* main editorial headline on October 15 was: NEHRU DECLARES WAR ON CHINA, and the editorial went on to say that Nehru's orders to his troops were "tantamount to a formal declaration of war." *The Guardian*—England—described Nehru's order as an "ultimatum.")

(*October 14*) China called upon Nehru to "pull back from the brink of the precipice." China was "absolutely unwilling to cross swords with India."

(*October 14*) Krishna Menon (still Minister of Defense) declared: "We will fight to the last man, to the last gun."

(*October 15*) Nehru called upon his people for discipline and sacrifice.

(*October 16*) The Indian Defense Ministry instructed ordnance factories to start maximum production even if it meant having three shifts on a round-the-clock schedule.

(*October 17*) China charged India with repeatedly violating China's air space and invited India to shoot down any Chinese planes if they flew over Indian territory. (New York *Times*, October 19.)

(*October 20*) Large-scale hostilities began along the entire front.

And we are asked to believe—by the Indian government and by numberless Western editorial writers, politicians, and radio reporters—that this fighting came as a "tremendous shock and surprise" to the Indians!

Contrary to the general assumption in this country that the Chinese opened the attack on October 20, some British reports indicated the opposite. The *Sunday Telegraph*, on October 21, reported: "India made a secret high level approach to the West for support *shortly before launching her offensive against the Chinese* on the Himalayan border, it is now learned . . ." (my italics).

The general assumption in the American press was that the Chinese had initiated the fighting. Further light was thrown on this matter, however, by a report in the New York *Times* of April 19, 1963, based on a UPI dispatch from Washington:

TAYLOR INDICATES INDIANS
STARTED CLASH WITH CHINESE

General Maxwell D. Taylor, Chairman of the Joint Chiefs of Staff, indicated in secret Congressional testimony made public today that India might have started the border fight with Communist China.

The previously accepted version of the border fighting that flared last fall was that Communist China had attacked Indian troops. . . .

[Asked by one Congressman] "Did the Indians actually start this military operation?"

"They were edging forward in the disputed area," replied General Taylor. "Yes, sir."

At this point the testimony was censored out of the public transcript.

To return to the events on the border in October 1962:

By October 24, military operations on all fronts were decisively in China's favor. On this day Chou En-lai made one more attempt to bring the hostilities to an end and to settle the dispute peacefully. He sent Mr. Nehru a three-point proposal:

1. Both parties affirm that the Sino-Indian boundary question must be settled peacefully through negotiations. Pending a peaceful settlement the Chinese Government hopes that the Indian Government will agree that both parties respect the line of actual control along the entire Sino-Indian

border, and the armed forces of each side withdraw 20 kilometers from this line and disengage.

2. Provided that the Indian Government agrees to the above proposal, the Chinese Government is willing, through consultation between the two parties, to withdraw its frontier guards in the eastern sector of the border north of the line of actual control; at the same time, both China and India undertake not to cross the line of actual control. . . .

3. The Chinese Government considers that, in order to seek a friendly statement of the Sino-Indian boundary question, talks should be held once again by the Prime Ministers of China and India. At a time considered to be appropriate by both parties, the Chinese Government would welcome the Indian Prime Minister to Peking; if this should be inconvenient to the Indian Government, the Chinese Premier would be ready to go to Delhi for talks.[3]

India's response to these practical suggestions was swift. On the same day (October 24) they were rejected. Three days later, Mr. Nehru wrote: "My colleagues and I are not able to understand the niceties of the Chinese three-point proposal, which talk about 'lines of actual control,' etc."[4] (One cannot help but wonder whether Mr. Nehru would have adopted this supercilious tone if he could have foreseen the resounding defeat that was in store for his armies!)

On November 15, the Indian Ministry of Defense announced a large-scale attack in the eastern sector, and the next day the Chinese counterattacked and resumed their advance. By now the Chinese armies were looking down toward the plain of Assam and were in a position to threaten India's main oil field. Sela, nearly fourteen thousand feet high, the main Indian position south of Tawang, was stormed and outflanked. Tezpur was evacuated in panic. The heartland of India now lay virtually defenseless before the Chinese armies. Wild speculations appeared in the press as to how far the Chinese would advance. The Chinese "hordes," so we were told, were hell-bent for the oil fields of India; they were driving to Calcutta on the sea; India was only the first step in the conquest of Asia—then Europe, and tomorrow the world.

[3] *Far Eastern Economic Review*, Feburary 28, 1963.
[4] Ibid.

. . . the entire Northeast Frontier region may eventually succumb to Peking's domination, opening the Bengali gate and menacing the Governments of India and Pakistan, if not all Southeast Asia.

. . . the long-range goal is that discussed decades ago by Sir Halford MacKinder, the geo-politician: conquest of Asia and then Europe, starting from the central Asian plateau that borders immense population masses. That is the long-range goal. (C. L. Sulzberger, New York *Times*, November 10, 1962.)

Just one day before the Chinese made their cease-fire offer, which put an end to the border warfare, some of this country's most respected newspapers were making these forecasts:

Red China needs a port, Shanghai is too far inland, and the Whangpoo River is too cramped. . . . But Calcutta is virtually undefended, and it is one of the great ports of the world. (Royce Brier, San Francisco *Chronicle*, November 20, 1962.)

The Chinese Communist attack on India is assuming massive dimensions. . . .

In this war the long-neglected Indian forces are being outfought, outmaneuvered, outgunned and are forced to fall back before the human waves of Chinese Communist warriors. These warriors have already jumped across the Himalayan barrier and are now streaming down mountain passes toward the Indian plains, oil fields and strategic airports. (New York *Times* editorial, November 20, 1962.)

The Chinese intention seems clear. It is to break through to the Assam plains and seize its main oil and coal regions.

Should this happen, the whole of eastern Asia with its heavy concentration of industries, including new steel, power, and fertilizer plants is in grave danger. (*The Christian Science Monitor*, November 20, 1962.)

With total victory over the Indian armies assured, the Chinese government on November 21 made their dramatic announcement—that they had ordered a unilateral cease-fire along the entire line to start the following day; and that from December 1 the Chinese armies would withdraw in the eastern sector to a line twenty kilometers behind the McMahon Line and elsewhere to a line twenty kilometers behind the line of actual control on November 7, 1959. On November 22 all fighting stopped; in December the withdrawals of the Chinese armies were completed; and later all Indian prisoners, and even captured weapons, were returned to India.[5]

Caught totally unprepared for such a move, many writers remained distrustful.

> Set no store by the Red Chinese ceasefire. . . . Mao and Chou haven't a live-and-let-live bone in their bodies. They will not stop this warfare . . . until they are stopped. . . .
>
> If the Red Chinese debouche to the Upper Ganges plain, which seems to be their target, they should be met by a thousand tanks, fleets of bombers, reconnaissance planes to seek out their formations and destroy them. India lacks this gear. Yet if we send it, it is no good lying on the docks of Calcutta and Madras. It needs crews to service and fight it.[6]

With the cease-fire the Chinese were at last able to impose *precisely those arrangements which she had so repeatedly offered as a basis of negotiation*—including her acceptance of the McMahon Line—and which India had so consistently and stubbornly refused.

The crucial question must now be asked: Why was the Indian government so reluctant, while there was still time, to reach a peaceful agreement with China—like Burma, Nepal, and Pakistan have done?[7] What were the pressures which prevented

[5] While the border fighting was taking place *The Christian Science Monitor* on October 29 carried an AP report with ominous implications: "The Chinese are said to be taking no prisoners."

As things turned out it was the Indians who never captured a single Chinese soldier involved in the "massive invasion."

On May 25, 1963, an AP dispatch from New Delhi in the San Francisco *Chronicle* reported that the last batch of a total of 3211 Indian prisoners was returned by the Chinese.

[6] Royce Brier, San Francisco *Chronicle*, November 26, 1962.

[7] In an interview with *U.S. News & World Report* (May 13, 1963), Pakistan's President Ayub Khan said: "Here, we are next-door neighbors to a great country having a very difficult border . . . we have agreed to have this border of 300 to 400 miles with China demarcated. If India had done that I have no doubt in my mind there would not have been any conflict between India and China."

such a settlement? The answer to this riddle will not I think be found in any further examination of the legal rights and wrongs of the border dispute itself, but rather by examining the extraordinarily difficult problems that were at this time facing the ruling groups in India.

Although India's economy is part "socialized," part "capitalist," the nation's ruling class (the big industrialists, the bankers, the upper ranks of the civil service, the army; in short, the "power elite" which makes the major decisions and sets the nation's direction) is by origin and mental habit deeply committed to a capitalist future for India. But in the conditions prevailing in the world today capitalism cannot solve the pressing problems of the backward countries. Where some development does occur—such as in Mexico, for example, or some of the Latin-American countries—the benefits go almost entirely to the few who are already privileged and the gap between them and the poor grows wider. In India, as we have shown in Chapter 7, "The Mathematics of Suffering," the circumstances are especially unfavorable for any rapid capital accumulation under the present system. But at the same time there are signs that the great masses in India will not indefinitely endure without protest their present condition of appalling poverty.

Nor can India's ruling groups ever allow themselves to forget that her northern neighbor and the country most like their own in population and stage of economic development, only fourteen years ago overthrew its own ruling class and since then has far outstripped India's advance. The Indian ruling classes are well aware that India's rate of progress must at all costs be speeded up if the Indian people are not, sooner or later, to follow China's example and attempt to seek a better life through social and economic revolution. The large Communist gains in the Indian elections in 1957 were the first warning signals.

Nehru, it is true, remains an immensely popular leader, and while he is in control he provides some reassurance to the ruling circles that India will not move decisively to the left. But his popularity tends to conceal, except to those most sensitive to it, the growing political restiveness of the Indian masses. But when

Nehru goes, as eventually he must, what then? Who will provide the unifying force? How can the ruling elite ensure that Nehru's successor will keep India moving to the right rather than to the revolutionary left?

Far from expanding rapidly, India's economy is stagnant. By 1960 it was clear that something was seriously wrong.[8]

Thus, there were complex and interlocking problems that confronted the leaders of India. A seriously faltering economy, an aging leader, a population living always on the very edge of subsistence and showing signs of looking to other means to solve their wretched poverty, and northward a China moving forward far more quickly than their own country. And above all (the most immediate need) the absolute necessity of getting yet more assistance from the only country that could provide it.

The connection between official Indian policy on the border dispute and pressing need for foreign aid was revealed in an astonishing report from New Delhi by one of Britain's top reporters. Nine months before the outbreak of hostilities, Stephen Barber reported (my italics):

> Reports during the past week say that preparations are now well advanced for strictly limited "probing action" against Chinese outposts established within Indian-claimed territory in the Ladakh and Karakoram Pass region. . . . Throughout the winter, military build-up has been detected in Leh, the principal town near the disputed Kashmir line. Apparently the Indian plan is to move highly trained mountain troops in behind the Chinese posts. . . . From well-placed Indian sources I understand that New Delhi's defense planners, with the agreement of experts in the External Affairs Ministry, have urged this move for three reasons:
>
> It should serve as a test of Chinese long-range intentions regarding India;
>
> It would test the validity of the underlying feature of India's foreign policy, which is that in the event of a Sino-Indian clash Moscow would bring pressure to bear on Peking to withdraw;

[8] See Chapter 7, "The Mathematics of Suffering," which gives further details of India's faltering economy.

> It would create a sympathetic mood towards India in
> Washington at a time when foreign aid appropriations, in
> which India's share predominates, will be under Congres-
> sional consideration.[9]

And even before October 1962 the United States had not concealed the fact that one purpose of aid was to keep India out of
the Socialist bloc. "The Administration is defending its request
for a boost in economic assistance to India on grounds that India
is a bulwark against Red Chinese encroachments in the Far East."
(*Wall Street Journal*, July 9, 1962.) "We know right now," said
Senator John Sparkman, Acting Chairman of the Senate Foreign
Relations Committee, in a television appearance on June 9, 1962,
"that India is pressing very hard against Communist China on
her northern boundary line . . . we ought not to be discouraging
India at the very time she is moving in the direction we have been
wanting her to move for a long time."

It has been said that just as the U.S. economy "needs the
cold war," so India needed the border dispute with China. These
propositions are of course oversimplified, but their meaning is
clear. Was it, in fact, ever possible, *within the terms of India's
present economic and social system* which the ruling elite are so
determined to maintain, for the Indian government to come to
a settlement with China and move once more toward friendship
with her? I think it is doubtful, for a friendly settlement with
China would probably have abruptly ended the foreign aid which
alone was keeping the system going.[10]

The results of *not* coming to a peaceful settlement with China
were apparent almost immediately after the large-scale fighting
broke out in October. Additional foreign aid on a very massive
scale was swiftly made available to India; a nation that was politically divided found a new and almost hysterical national unity
in the drive to "resist Chinese aggression" (and a unity it should

[9] *Daily Telegraph*, London, January 10, 1962.
[10] U.S. aid to India for 1962 totaled almost a billion dollars, lifting the Nehru
government to first place in the world picture. An AP dispatch from Washington on March 21, 1963, citing figures provided by the Agency for International
Development, reported: "In 1962, India was the biggest recipient of United
States aid, with $838,000,000."

be noticed directed at precisely the country whose revolutionary experience might under other circumstances have held a dangerous attraction for the Indian masses); and the Indian Communist Party was in disarray. Under the stress of the emergency, the government had already passed laws that curbed freedom of speech and which severely restricted left-wing political activity (it is not generally known in the West that from May 1961 it has been a criminal offense in India to question the rights and wrongs of the border dispute).

To sum it up, the immediate result of the rejection of any peaceful settlement with China was to move India decisively to the right politically, and decisively into the Western camp internationally.

This, I believe, is the real significance and meaning of India's dispute with China. It was a conflict which India was able to provoke by refusing any compromises and by making demands on China which were certain to be rejected. One thing is clear: if the ruling groups in India had felt that a settlement was in their interests they could have reached one with as little fuss as Burma, Nepal, and Pakistan did; and with not the slightest loss of national honor.

To the U.S., of course, the Indian move into the Western camp was a source of satisfaction. Dr. Oliver E. Clubb, Jr., a foreign policy expert at Syracuse University, wrote in the *National Observer* (November 12, 1962):

> For the United States in one sense the Sino-Indian conflict has been a windfall. Soviet influence in India has been weakened; leftist Indian Defense Minister, Krishna Menon, until recently a possible successor to Mr. Nehru, has been toppled from power; and America's ties with India have been strengthened as a result of prompt American military assistance. . . . Neutralist India, not pro-Western Pakistan or Thailand, clearly has become the strategic key to southern Asia and the principal balance to Communist China. . . .

Fears that a neutral India—the largest and most influential neutral nation—would one day move into the Socialist bloc could now be laid aside. The Indian economy will be increasingly militarized (already in 1963 vast increases in taxation have been announced to pay for its largest military budget ever)[11] and India's future dependence on U.S. military and economic aid will undoubtedly make her more responsive to suggestions from Washington.[12]

But the price of all this will be paid by the Indian people. Already the increased taxation for military purposes has doomed any hope of real economic improvement for a long time to come. No amount of U.S. aid can compensate for the damage that has already been done. A deteriorating economy will inevitably shift the government yet further to the right. Political democracy— India's greatest experiment—will be abandoned, except perhaps in name.

The significance of the dispute with China does not lie in the demarcation of boundaries high in the Himalayan mountains, but rather in India's rejection of a settlement with China in favor of involvement in the cold war. The benefits—and there will be benefits—that this decision will bring will be enjoyed by the few who are already among the privileged. The cost in suffering and continued poverty will have to be borne by the great masses of the Indian people.

[11] India's defense spending for 1963–64 of Rs. 8670 million ($1,820,700,000) represents 47 percent of her estimated revenue budget and is more than her entire revenue budget three years ago.

[12] In an editorial on May 28, 1963, *The Christian Science Monitor* studied Indian demands for military and economic aid calling for more than two and a half billion dollars.

Chapter 13

"CHINESE AGGRESSION"—TIBET

One of the charges of Chinese "aggression" that has occurred in the last few years, the suppression of the Tibetan rebellion has remained vividly in our imagination. I am not an apologist for the Chinese and I have no doubt that some Chinese soldiers were guilty of cruelty and caused suffering in Tibet; but I have learned to accept with the greatest possible caution accounts of an event which derive from one side only. Much reliance, for instance, was placed on the "International Commission of Jurists" which declared, in an interim report after a two-month study, that China had been guilty of genocide in Tibet.

> . . . Red China had engaged in a campaign of killing, torture, rape, abduction and forced sterilization in Tibet in the last 10 years.
> The commission published a 340-page report based mostly on accounts by refugees who fled to India after the futile Tibet revolution of March 1959.
> The report also included testimony by Tibet's exiled spiritual and political leader the Dalai Lama. . . .[1]

The title of the commission is imposing and, as the New York *Times* said on June 7, 1959, the body "under the chairmanship of a distinguished Indian lawyer, can hardly be called a propaganda organ. Its findings should be accurate and impartial."

Yes, they should have been; but were they?

[1] AP, Geneva, August 7, 1959.

I have read the commission's report. It struck me as a curious hodgepodge of "evidence," hearsay, and downright trivia. Though tragic events were recorded in it, any impartial court of law in either America or Britain would require a great deal more solidly backed evidence before declaring the Chinese guilty of "genocide."

We have on record one account by a Western correspondent who was actually present at a so-called "legal enquiry" conducted by the International Commission of Jurists. He is George Gale, correspondent for the London *Daily Express*, one of the most strongly anti-Communist newspapers in Britain. As the report of the International Commission of Jurists formed the basis of countless editorials thundering against Chinese "genocide" in Tibet, it is worth quoting Mr. Gale's dispatch in full (the paragraphs in parentheses are Mr. Gale's and form part of the dispatch):

UP IN CLOUD CUCKOOLAND WITH THE LAMA

I have just come down from hill station Mussoorie, seat of the Dalai Lama's exile Government.

I have also just come down from Cloud Cuckooland.

At an international legal enquiry in Mussoorie I heard the Dalai Lama reel off a list of fantastic allegations against Red China.

But he made no attempt to prove his allegations. Not a single document was produced. Not a shred of evidence was provided.

This was no way for the Tibetans to present their case to an official enquiry.

The case, as put by the Dalai Lama was that China was seeking to destroy the Tibetan race by:—

ONE: Mass sterilization;

TWO: The mass deportation of children; and

THREE: The mass settlement of 5,000,000 Chinese in Tibet.

The Dalai Lama was asked for details first about sterilization. He said: "My statement is true."

Pressed further he referred to one place where these acts "have been committed for so-called experimental efforts and under the pretext of counteracting certain epidemic diseases."

Figure 7 When fighting broke out along the Sino-Indian border, cartoons such as this helped to create the impression that the fighting was another example of "Chinese aggression."

'YOU'RE BRINGING ME BAD LUCK!'

Figure 8 This cartoon was printed in an American magazine for children. We often complain that the Chinese teach their children to "hate America."

WHEN A FELLER NEEDS A FRIEND

Figures 9 & 10 Cartoons reflect our changing national attitudes. The cartoon above was drawn in 1922 when the Chinese were our friends, the one below in 1955 when Japan had become our friend, China the enemy.

The Great Oriental Disappearing Act

Figures 11 & 12 Chiang Kai-shek has very rarely been shown in cartoons as a brutal character. Here he is depicted as a smiling magician. The cartoon below was published during the Quemoy crisis of 1958, when many people thought that Chiang was attempting to involve the U. S. in war with the mainland as his one chance of returning there.

No. 1 Boy

He said that 10 victims of these acts had gone to India as refugees. But seven of them had since died.

Pressed again, he said that he might be able to let the enquiry have the names of one or two such men—but he did not know about any women.

(I note in passing that in India—under the Government's family planning policy to reduce the rising birthrate—22,515 sterilization operations were performed last year.)

The Dalai Lama was tackled on the statement that 5,000,-000 Chinese settlers had arrived in Tibet.

His explanation of how this vast multitude—four times greater than Tibet's total population—was supported was: "Our country is not short of foodstuffs. Due to high altitude we can keep food for 25 years. There are many fish in our lakes."

He was asked: "How many children were deported to China?"

The interpreter said: "His Holiness cannot give you the right number. These children came from various parts of Tibet. Approximately, he thinks 10,000 were taken out.

"Some are resisting against the Chinese, and some who have studied in Peking are working for China."

(Again, I note in passing that Britain has much experience of educating selected children from Colonial countries, not all of whom return to their homeland.)

The eight members of the enquiry—set up by the International Commission of Jurists—sat through most of the day without complaining.

But at one point an English secretary of the enquiry burst out: "I would like to make it clear that as far as lawyers are concerned there is a difference between believing a thing to be true and proving it."

And an Indian professor of law, exasperated at having to listen to hours of allegation and not seeing a single document produced, exclaimed: "Have you no documents, decrees, laws? Where are the laws of Tibet to be found? I have looked all over India and haven't been able to find a single law of Tibet passed in the last 150 years!"

The members of the enquiry—three from India and one each from Ghana, Ceylon, Malaya, the Philippines, and Siam —are expected to publish their findings within two months.

Lord Shawcross was originally a member of the enquiry

committee. He resigned "due to unforeseen professional and personal commitments."

I am not surprised.[2]

And it was about this committee's report that the New York *Times* said: "Its findings should be accurate and impartial"!

In December 1962 I had lunch in London with Mr. Stuart Gelder, an able and experienced correspondent, who had only recently returned from Tibet. He went there commissioned by the London *Daily Mail* to write a series of articles. Several correspondents resident in Peking had been to Tibet in 1959 (among them the American Anna Louise Strong), but Stuart Gelder and his wife Roma were the first non-resident Westerners to travel to Tibet since the Chinese entered the country in 1951. Mr. Gelder told me that the Peking government agreed to their conditions that they could travel wherever they wished without restriction, and photograph and film whatever they pleased. They made a film which was shown on British television. All their negatives, both movie and still, were developed in England.

In reply to some blunt questioning by me, Mr. Gelder said that they had found no evidence of genocide or suppression of religion in Tibet. Their general impression was that the accounts of Chinese behavior published in the Western press were (his exact words) "fantastic exaggerations and distortions." The *Daily Mail* (though they paid for them) did not print his articles. Thus, as far as newspaper readers are concerned, this rare eyewitness report on Tibet was never seen.

It will be remembered that even before the flight of the Dalai Lama in 1959, a good deal of discussion had taken place in our press as to whether Tibet was a part of China as the Chinese claimed.

As in the case of Taiwan, while China was ruled by Chiang Kai-shek, there was no official (or editorial) doubt in the United States that Tibet was part of China. It was only after the collapse of the Nationalists in 1949 that the United States government began to convey the idea that Tibet was a "sovereign state" and there was even talk of supporting a Tibetan application for mem-

[2] *Daily Express*, London, November 16, 1959.

bership in the United Nations. By the time the Dalai Lama left Tibet there was widespread belief in America that it had been "invaded" by the Chinese—and this, of course, was then cited as yet another example of Communist Chinese "aggression."

Edgar Snow has directed attention to some facts about all this:

> During the Second World War China's suzerainty over Tibet was a subject of discussion between Britain, China and the United States. In an aide-memoire in 1943, the British Embassy in Washington conceded "formal Chinese suzerainty" but also wished to secure the Llasa government "the full enjoyment of local autonomy," and the right to "exchange diplomatic representatives with other powers." In reply the State Department unequivocally declined support for the latter aim when it declared: "The Government of the United States has borne in mind the fact that the Chinese Government has long claimed suzerainty over Tibet and that the Chinese constitution lists Tibet among areas constituting the territory of the Republic of China. This Government has at no time raised a question regarding either of these claims."[3]

This may strike many as being very legalistic and remote; and having little to do with the million and a half peasants trying to live their lives on the high windy plains of Tibet. What do they know of "suzerainty" and "aide-memoires" and decisions made in far-off capitals? But their lives nevertheless were profoundly affected. Peking, in 1959, after nearly nine years of gradual reforms, was beginning to alter some of the Tibetans' ancient ways.

Changes are nearly always painful, but let us not assume that all the changes the Chinese made in Tibet were bad. The Tibetan way of life may have sounded tranquil and romantic to many of us; but except for the few, it was appalling. Peasants and herdsmen were born into serfdom; they were bound all their lives in a feudalism as absolute as any during our Middle Ages. Only inaccessibility preserved it. One of the first "ways of life" the Chinese

[3] *The Other Side of the River*, pp. 588–89. Mr. Snow's quotations come from: *Foreign Relations of the United States, 1943, China* (Washington: 1957), pp. 630, 728.

attacked was to put an end to the barbaric punishments that were still meted out—the gouging out of eyes, the pulling out of tongues, and other revolting mutilations. The only secular schools in Tibet are those started by the Chinese; the only hospitals are those which the Chinese established after 1951. Land, most of it held by the monasteries, was divided among the serfs.

Almost a year before the "revolt in Tibet" there appeared in *The Times* of London a remarkable article on conditions in that area. I use the word *remarkable* only in the sense that it would be difficult to find an organ of public opinion in this country that would deal with the subject as did the eminently conservative *Times*.

> . . . The Chinese have considerably changed the pattern of Tibetan economy. For instance, within two years of their arrival they had totally abolished the system of unpaid labour. People living in the vast areas owned by monasteries and landlords could be drafted to work without pay by their landowners. The Chinese exerted their influence to end this system. . . .
> . . . Several thousand Chinese and a few Tibetans are busy conducting research on growing more food and improving sheep herds.
> The monasteries no longer retain their monopoly over education. Several schools have been opened under Chinese guidance; unlike the monasteries, they teach other subjects besides the scriptures. . . . Once the majority of the population was unfamiliar with coins; now they use Chinese currency for the smallest transactions. . . . In open spaces basketball poles and nets have blossomed. . . . People still look up when they hear the drone of aircraft engines, but they have become familiar with them. . . .
> . . . employment in Tibet has increased considerably, and the economic conditions of the Tibetans has been improved. This has given the Chinese the opportunity to fraternize and influence Tibetans, especially the lay masses. But the politically conscious and educated Tibetans were greatly offended by these reforms, and stayed on their guard against all Chinese moves. . . .[4]

For the upper classes—the theocracy and the landlords—the

[4] *The Times* of London, June 28, 1958.

coming of the Chinese was a calamity, the end of centuries of privilege. Some of them found they were even expected to *work!* It was their outraged cries that we heard in the West. That this minority suffered is not to be denied. But who is to say, here as elsewhere in the world, where the ultimate balance lies?

In 1956, in the richest and most populous region of Tibet, Peking introduced a system of taxation by which the hitherto untapped "vast revenues of the monasteries" would be affected. To quote again from *The Times* of London:

> The leading monks, already greatly offended by the Chinese and knowing that one day they would be totally powerless, thought the time had come to strike. They began spreading the story that the Chinese had levied taxes on the images of the Buddha to eliminate monasteries, and ultimately Buddhism, in Tibet. This rallied the militant inhabitants of Kham against the Chinese.
>
> When the monasteries declared that they would not pay the tax, the Chinese began to confiscate their properties. The monasteries resisted, and a minor war started in Kham. All those who were nursing grudges against the Chinese, the landlords, the big traders, and those whose arms the Chinese had confiscated, joined the monasteries (which always had their own arsenal of primitive arms) in an armed rebellion. . . .[5]

And as for genocide (in 1959) as charged by the "international jurists," Edgar Snow gives us all a sobering reminder:

> . . . current talk of genocide . . . falls wryly from the lips of American officials whose ancestors seized a continent from native Indians and wiped out nations of them scarcely more than a century ago. The march of civilization? No doubt. But let us leave claims to moral superiority in the vestibule. . . .[6]

Perhaps because of our painful Korean experience, perhaps for other reasons, we have convinced ourselves that the Chinese are conducting a highly aggressive foreign policy. The Chinese have certainly played their part in confirming this assumption by their

[5] Ibid. The 1958 fighting in Tibet was pictured in the American press as some sort of "Hungarian uprising" by the downtrodden and freedom-loving Tibetans.
[6] *The Other Side of the River,* p. 596.

pugnacious language. But students of military affairs, who pay less attention to words than they do to actions, well know that this popular image of the Chinese as reckless and belligerent is totally erroneous.

Some commentators have concluded that Peking's angry words are proof enough that we are dealing with rapacious, perhaps even paranoic, men. But these words may seem rational enough when some of the provocations that have evoked them are remembered. For years official U.S. policy was based on the determination to destroy the Chinese government: ". . . there are strong elements within the State Department and the Pentagon which believe that the Communist regime must be snuffed out sooner or later," reported *The Christian Science Monitor*.[7] There is "the clear possibility, almost verging on the likelihood, that the United States will end by having to fight an atomic war for Formosa's off-shore islands," wrote Mr. Joseph Alsop.[8]

We do not have to look to the Chinese press for details. In our own *Saturday Evening Post* we read:

> For nearly ten years, with every offensive weapon they could command, the Nationalist Chinese have carried on their own small, gnawing war against the Reds. . . . Protected from Red retaliation by the planes and guns of the United States 7th Fleet, they seek to harass and bedevil the Communists on the mainland. . . . Chinese Nationalist Air Force planes fly over the mainland mapping future targets. . . .[9]

"The U.S. also has experimental reconnaissance satellites whirling over China," reported *Newsweek*, on September 3, 1962.

And on September 20, 1958, Madame Chiang Kai-shek, on a U.S. nationwide television program, advocated the dropping of nuclear bombs on her own countrymen on the mainland!

Would we speak in quiet and measured tones if we were subjected to the same provocations, and by an infinitely superior military power?

[7] April 5, 1954.
[8] New York *Herald Tribune*, March 18, 1955.
[9] September 6, 1958.

The Chinese *words* are indeed violent and angry; their *actions* have been marked by an extraordinary prudence. Except where they have felt that their national security is at stake—as in Korea— they have been careful not to provoke a military clash with the armed forces of the United States. In India their action was an effective, limited-risk action called off promptly when their objective had been reached. Contrary to popular belief they have not been engaged in either Laos or Vietnam. Since 1958 they have not even attempted to retake the island of Quemoy, though it lies less than five miles from their shores; and even at the fierce height of the Quemoy crisis in 1958 they very carefully refrained from firing on any foreign vessel. They have made no attempt to take the island of Taiwan.

The distribution of the Chinese military budget indicates concern for self-protection—expenditure is largely on defensive personnel and weaponry: a relatively large fighter force (almost no bombers); a mobile land army and a large civilian militia; virtually no navy except for coastal defense vessels. The proportion of the national budget devoted to military expenditure has been *reduced annually* until in 1960 it represented less than 10 percent of the national budget.[10]

This is the country that is so often described as "expansionist," "reckless," and aiming "to conquer the world"!

As Allen S. Whiting of the Rand Corporation concluded after several years of study, Chinese foreign policy is much more rational, calculating, and cautious than we have been disposed to believe.[11]

---

[10] In 1959 expenditure on national defense was 5800 million *yuan* out of a total national expenditure of 52,770 million *yuan*, or almost 11 percent. In 1960, the total national budget was 70,020 million *yuan*, with military expenditure remaining the same, at 5800 million *yuan*, which represents 8.3 percent of this total. These figures were presented to the National People's Congress on March 30, 1960, by Li Hsien-nien, Vice-Premier of the State Council and Minister of Finance, and are reported in the *Peking Review* of April 5, 1960. (U.S. military expenditures in 1963 accounted for approximately 56 percent of the national budget.)

[11] "Communist China," *The Liberal Papers* (New York: Doubleday Anchor Books, 1962), pp. 283–302.

In this section of the book I believe I have shown with a few representative examples how the image of China as an aggressive and expansionist power has taken root in the minds of the American people. It is true that the Soviet Union, in the intensity of their dispute with China, has used many of the same charges about China's belligerence, her readiness to use nuclear war to gain her ends, and so on—and this in turn fortifies our own conceptions. But an erroneous image remains erroneous, however many may appear to share it.

My suggestion is not that we should approve of what the Chinese are doing or saying, but that we should stop deluding ourselves. We should know in far greater detail *what in fact is going on.* When this happens we will, I think, discover that for far too long a time we have been employing the vocabulary of self-deception.

Part IV

SOME MINOR MYTHS

Chapter 14

THE GIMO RETURNS

All this comes of founding a policy on untruths: on the untruth that the Red Chinese are planning the military conquest of Formosa, on the untruth that the offshore islands are related to Formosa, not to speak of the still bigger untruth that the real government of China is in Formosa and that some day it will move back to the mainland.

—Walter Lippmann, New York *Herald Tribune*, during the Quemoy crisis, September 9, 1958.

Like old generalissimos, some myths never die.

For fourteen years, like a religious rite performed by the emperors of old, Chiang Kai-shek stands up at least once a year to pledge his word that he will soon return to the mainland and there conquer his enemies.

And, like the perennial appearance of the groundhog, the newspapers dutifully print these pronouncements as "news."

Does Chiang himself really believe these annual proclamations?

To cling to hope is natural enough; and for a man of Chiang's temperament, and for a man who once held personal power of life and death over a quarter of mankind, to be impotent, to be confined to an island, must be an almost unbearably humiliating experience.

He has his memories and his minor glories. Eight hundred admirals and generals provide an admiring and dependent court.[1]

[1] "The Formosa Impasse," *Foreign Affairs* (April 1958), p. 443.

And plans for what will happen when they "return" have been endlessly discussed. But does he believe all this? Do any of them? He has an army on his hands—what has he to offer them but visions? Even if they are visions in which he no longer can believe himself?

Overweening conceit, of course, creates its own delusions; but there are times when even conceit is not invulnerable. Chiang must have his dark moments when he comes face to face with the tormenting reality that he no longer counts; that for all his strutting and his boasting, he has been swept aside.

Across on the mainland, but 110 miles away, his people are moving forward unbelievably, forging China's future; and in this he has no part to play. To 700 million of his countrymen he is now (when they think of him at all, which is not often) not much more than a hated name in history, a symbol of all that was rotten in their past, a reminder of a period of inconceivable sufferings and humiliations. If he ever attempted to inject himself in their lives again they would rise in unity and enormous anger and wipe him out for good.

Chiang knows this, he must; and his lieutenants know it.

As early as October 5, 1958, a Taiwan military spokesman reported to the London *Observer*:

> We haven't seriously considered invading the mainland for at least five years now. We have to keep up the pretense, of course, largely for domestic consumption—a matter of morale and discipline.

The myth of Chiang's "return to the mainland" requires another myth to give it plausibility—that terror, starvation, oppression, the destruction of family life and so on, have wrought such hideous suffering that millions of Chinese who had no use for Chiang before are now waiting for him with open arms as their "savior."

There are, in China, unhappy people. I met and spoke with a number of them. They are usually from among those who had personally suffered as a consequence of the revolution; the former wealthy or those among the intellectuals who found it impossible to identify themselves with the revolutionary world around them.

They talked—some of them—frankly enough, and sometimes bitterly. I would always ask them if they would throw their lot in with Chiang if he led an invasion and mounted a counterrevolution. They invariably would look at me with utter and blank astonishment, as if I were out of my mind even to conceive of such an idea. I came to think that any opposition movement would be doomed if Chiang's name was in any way associated with it.

The Canadian correspondent, Gerald Clark, reported the same view. Speaking to the World Affairs Council of Northern California on May 2, 1959, he said:

> The Chinese have not forgotten the corruption or inefficiency associated with Chiang Kai-shek and the Nationalists. I was in Peking when the Dulles-Chiang Kai-shek communiqué came out, after their meeting in Formosa and Chiang promised he would not attempt to regain the mainland by force. People in Peking laughed. To them it was almost as ludicrous a kind of statement as it would be for us if Khrushchev suddenly announced that he had decided after all, not to run for the presidency of the United States.

In terms of history, Chiang and his defeated army mean no more than the emigrés of the French Revolution, the seventy thousand Empire Royalists who fled to Canada during the American Revolution, or the White Russians who fled from the Russian Revolution. They all, in their day, clung to dreams of a triumphant "return." History has all but forgotten them. As far as military capability goes, Chiang and his forces have never had any more chance of successfully landing on the mainland than the forces of Fidel Castro have of capturing the Fontainebleau Hotel in Miami Beach.

I have collected the annual pronouncements of the Generalissimo and his lieutenants. They are pathetic, and oddly embarrassing to read. Here are men who once held high positions repeating resounding words that they know are hollow. Reading them now one can see how every year they would devise ways to make them, if possible, sound more convincing. "A new major strategy plan has been drawn up . . ."[2]—1949. In 1950: "We promised the people of Shanghai today that a Nationalist counteroffensive against the mainland would be under way this time next year."[3] In 1951, "all available manpower, material and revenue" were to be mobilized for the recovery of the mainland.[4] In 1952 Chiang predicted that an all-out bombing "might touch off a powder-keg of rebellion."[5] "My energy today," he declared that year, "is as powerful as it was 28 years ago."[6] In 1953 he said, "We are ready to launch a counteroffensive."[7] Again in 1953, "The moment of our counterattack is drawing nearer and nearer . . . hundreds of millions of our compatriots . . . are eagerly looking to us to deliver them at an early date."[8]

So, year after year, the brave, hopeless pretense went on.

In 1955 John Foster Dulles at last threw in the sponge. Even he couldn't keep up the myth.

On January 26 the Washington *Post* reported:

> Secretary of State John Foster Dulles has written off any idea of Chiang Kai-shek returning to the China mainland by force of arms.
>
> He did so in his Monday appearance before the joint Senate Foreign Relations and Armed Services Committee closed-door hearing. . . .
>
> One Senator said Dulles "absolutely" wrote off the return-to-the-mainland idea, so long nourished by Chiang's backers in the United States as well as by the Formosa government itself.

Mr. Dulles' China policy was long based on the assumption that the Communist government must be removed. When even he was persuaded that an attack by Chiang would be futile one might have imagined that other less stubborn supporters of Chiang Kai-shek might have given up too—or even Chiang himself.

[2] Minneapolis *Star*, July 7.
[3] New York *Times*, May 27.
[4] San Francisco *Chronicle*, December 3.
[5] AP, Washington, June 30.
[6] San Francisco *Chronicle*, June 17.
[7] UP, reporting a Chiang interview with a Japanese newspaper.
[8] New York *Times*, March 1.

But no; the myth lived on.

In 1958 Madame Chiang, according to a report in the New York *Herald Tribune* of June 28, was interviewed in New York:

> We are (and she emphasized the word) going to regain the mainland and don't let any one tell you different," she said, leaning forward tensely in her chair. "And we are going to do our own fighting."

We find the Oakland *Tribune* on October 10, 1959, giving great prominence to an AP story from Formosa:

> Chiang Kai-shek predicted today his Chinese Nationalist forces would be fighting the Chinese communists on the mainland next year.
>
> He declared the Nationalists would wipe out the Peiping regime and restore China's position as "a free, independent country."

In 1961 we find *The Christian Science Monitor*, on November 24, devoting a large spread to an interview by their correspondent, Takashi Oka. The introduction to this featured article stated:

> Despite skepticism among many free-world observers Generalissimo Chiang Kai-shek sturdily maintains that his Chinese Nationalist regime . . . will some day return to mainland China and liberate it from communism.

Newsweek, on April 9, 1962, looked to Joseph Alsop to give their report a note of conviction:

> Chiang Kai-shek declared that a "holy expedition from Taiwan to save our people may come at any time." This was more than routine trumpeting, according to columnist Joseph Alsop, who reported that Chiang "has been strongly pressing the U. S. Government to approve invasion of the Communist mainland . . . this summer or autumn."

A month later, on May 9, the same magazine, under the headline, INVASION FEVER, had Chiang all but on the high seas speeding to the mainland:

> The official and unofficial talk in Taipei was almost as striking as the sight of the four-week-old assault boats. "Back-to-the-mainland fever," says one Western diplomat, "is al-

ways endemic here. But it has never reached the proportions it has now."

On October 10, 1962, Chiang himself, according to a UPI dispatch in the San Francisco *Examiner*, declared:

> "I personally shall lead our anti-Communist people and our armed forces in Taiwan, the Pescadores and Matsu in a united movement against the Chinese Communists."
> "Time is auspicious for our national movement," he said.

And on October 14 the New York *Times*, in an editorial entitled: BACK TO THE CHINA MAINLAND? was carefully weighing Chiang's "important new initiative" in calling for a "revolt by military forces and civilians in Communist China." Chiang, said the editorial:

> accompanied this appeal with a specific new commitment to provide supplies, radio facilities and air support to regular military and to guerrilla insurgents. He promised to give formal recognition to revolting officers and units and to appoint insurrectionary leaders as "political and military chiefs" in their areas.

Do the *Times'* writers really take all this seriously? Don't they know that often Chiang's pronouncements about which they write so ponderously have been printed in mainland Chinese newspapers for comic relief?

The meaning of these solemn absurdities is clear enough.

By giving prominence and credence to empty pronouncements *issued for its own purposes by the Chiang regime*, the press wittingly or unwittingly allows itself to become the agent for misleading the public. The experts, the columnists, the editorial writers employed by the press were still in 1963 earnestly speculating about the possibilities of Chiang's "return." And this, eight years after the U. S. Secretary of State had evidently written off the idea that Chiang could ever regain the mainland by force of arms. It is true that these writers sometimes conclude, after a long balance of arguments, that perhaps the time is not yet quite propitious for Chiang's return. But even to take the question seriously at all is to mislead. It has about as much validity as an earnest discussion on Albania's ability to send a man into space.

> To suppose that a Chinese party which could not retain power when all was in its hand could now regain it with limited foreign support is to fly in the face of all history and indeed of common sense. It is certain that nothing could so well please the Chinese Communist leaders as to see Chiang's forces landed on the coast of China. In Formosa they can neither surrender nor be destroyed; on the mainland both surrender and rapid destruction would end the Nationalist Party forever.[9]

Those words of sanity were written by Professor C. P. Fitzgerald, a British Sinologist now living in Australia.

Where Chiang Kai-shek is concerned, our press has helped to create a *national climate of self-delusion*, reaching into the highest branches of our government.

Mr. Walter S. Robertson, Assistant Secretary of State for Far Eastern Affairs from 1953–59, was one of those who helped to mold our China policy during the 1951–61 decade.

> Robertson had made no secret of his conviction that Mao Tse-tung was a passing phenomenon and Chiang Kai-shek remained China's "real" symbol. Indeed, in 1957 the affable Assistant Secretary assured me at a Washington party: "Mao has no more real influence than the first taxi driver who goes by outside." To call such a statement meaningless, is to flatter it.[10]

Postscript

While I was drafting this chapter, Mr. Joseph Alsop devoted his column on May 10, 1963, to the question of Chiang's "return."

> The "return to the mainland," so long and so often proclaimed, may really be attempted this year by Generalissimo Chiang Kai-shek. . . .
> There are no boastful, empty proclamations now. Instead there are serious preparations. . . .

[9] *Revolution in China*, p. 213, Frederick A. Praeger, Inc., New York, 1952.
[10] C. L. Sulzberger, *What's Wrong with U. S. Foreign Policy* (New York: Harcourt, Brace, 1959), p. 198.

There is, in fact, no doubt at all that Chiang and his government at present intend to make the landing attempt early this summer, or perhaps in the next favorable season in the autumn. . . .[11]

And on May 28, Mr. William H. Stringer, Chief of the Washington Bureau of *The Christian Science Monitor*, wrote an article, CHIANG AND LURE OF MAINLAND, which began with the sentence: "Is Generalissimo Chiang Kai-shek likely to attempt an invasion of the Chinese mainland this year?"

Mr. Alsop, Mr. Stringer—would either of you care to take a bet?

[11] Washington *Post.*

Chapter 15

WHERE'S MAO?

At the time of this writing Mao Tse-tung, at the age of sixty-nine, is apparently in good health and exercising unimpaired authority. Edgar Snow, who spent many hours with him in 1960, said that for a man close to seventy, often reported dead, Mao was holding his own, and had had no serious illness for many years. Pictures of him, apparently as flourishing as ever, appear in the Chinese press and in the English-language magazines from China.

Almost from the day when he became head of the Chinese government, an extraordinary concern for Mao's health—even his safety—has been shown by Western correspondents and China "experts." Literally hundreds of news stories have been written that have had Mao in broken health, dying, purged, demoted, or just plain "disappeared." It is well known that Mao spends several months every year traveling through China, visiting towns and villages to keep in touch with the people. (He expects other cabinet members to do so, too.) This should have alerted correspondents to the possibility that when his name is not listed among those present at some function in Peking, it does not necessarily mean that something dire has happened to him.

On December 16, 1950, scarcely giving Mao time to set up shop in Peking after beating Chiang, Robert S. Allen, a widely syndicated columnist, asked: WHERE IS MAO? This, it will be remembered, was the period the Russians were much in the news (see Chapter 5, "When the Russians Took Over China"), so Mr. Allen, writing in the New York *Post* and noting an absence of reports of Mao's doings or whereabouts, concluded that the Russians had completely taken over the Peking government, and guessed that Mao was probably being held as a prisoner.

Mr. Allen did not believe that Mao had been liquidated for he thought such a "sensational development" would be bound to "leak out." He thought the best surmise was that he was being held as a prisoner of his own regime.

Later, on October 11, 1954, Mr. Allen was writing that Mao had cancer and might die before long.

K. M. Panikkar, Indian Ambassador to China, writing about the celebration of the anniversary of the Indian Republic in Peking on January 26, 1951, said:

> For weeks foreign papers had been publishing news of Mao's illness, asserting that he had been deposed by Liu Shao-chi. Many other canards of a similar character had found currency in foreign papers. The Hong Kong journals, which under Taipeh inspiration excelled in this kind of propaganda, had persuaded most Western diplomats that something was wrong with Mao. So when Mao arrived at any party, it created something of a sensation among them. . . .[1]

One of the Alsop brothers, this time Stewart, in his thrice-weekly column in the New York *Herald Tribune*, was still wondering about WHAT HAS HAPPENED TO MAO? on March 18, 1951.

Speculating on Chinese failure in Korea as having disastrous consequences at home, Alsop wrote that two apparently "solid facts" stood out. One was that something had happened to Mao Tse-tung, though no one really knew what; and the other was that the authority of the Communist government was "quite genuinely threatened" throughout large areas of the country.

Alsop continued:

> On the other hand, it is considered just as possible that Mao is either actually very ill, or that he has been marked for

[1] *In Two Chinas: Memoirs of a Diplomat*, Chapter X, p. 125 (London: George Allen & Unwin, 1955).

liquidation. Mao has tuberculosis, and he has also had several severe heart attacks. His death of natural causes would therefore not be surprising. But neither would it be surprising if he suffered the kind of convenient "heart attack" which has ended the careers of numerous European Communists.

Whatever Mao's fate, Mr. Alsop held out little hope for the future of Peking. ". . . the Chinese Communist apparatus is already being strained almost to the breaking point, according to reports which no longer leave room for doubt."

In the spring of 1954, *Time* Magazine showed an extraordinary solicitude for Mao's health and whereabouts:

WHERE'S MAO?

Persistent rumors have described the Chinese dictator as seriously ill with heart disease. Whatever the rumor, Mao did not appear at a New Year's meeting of high Communist officials, and he failed to show at a committee meeting on January 21 on the anniversary of Lenin's death. His birthday last November 17th went entirely unnoticed in China, though Russia and the satellites whooped it up in his name. (March 1)

STILL MISSING

Red China's rubric event of the week: a massive "memorial ceremony" in Peking on the first anniversary of Joseph Stalin's death. Notably missing from the ranks of the bigwigs: China's Dictator Mao Tse-tung, 60, who has not been seen in public this year. (March 15)

Last December Mao mysteriously vanished from the public eye, and rumors cropped up that Peking was concealing news of his death. There was even one report that Mao, 63, had died following an operation for cancer. . . .

Last week Peking papers arriving in Hong Kong carried seemingly genuine likenesses of Mao—looking thinner than usual—posing with 25 other members of the constitutional committee. While this made it almost certain that Mao is alive, his strange and unprecedented absence from important party meetings over a 14-week period remain unexplained. So in Hong Kong, Tokyo and Formosa rumors persist that he is sick.

The Chinese Communist press, naturally, ignores such rumors. . . . (April 12)

Two old China hands were also concerned about Mao in 1954. Preston Schoyer filed a story from Hong Kong for the New York *Herald Tribune* on March 14, which began:

> There is mounting speculation here on the whereabouts of Mao Tse-tung, the boss of Red China. . . . Two reasons are suggested by those studying Red China from this observation post for Mao's failure to appear at official Peking functions.

The reasons, Mr. Schoyer told his readers, were either politics or health. Of the two, he seemed to lean toward health which, he reported, "is the one most commonly given."

> . . . he is dangerously ill. Though as a young man he is rumored to have suffered from a tubercular condition, he has not shown signs of it for many years.
>
> Pictures today show him to be flabby and unhealthily fat. It is not improbable, as rumors attest, that he has high blood pressure and a bad heart. If so, he may have suffered a serious stroke. . . .
>
> Speculation on Mao developed two months ago because, so far as is known here, he had not appeared at any function since Dec. 24th, when he was reported to have attended a meeting of the Peking Politburo. . . .

Two weeks later, Henry Lieberman of the New York *Times* was writing:

> Mao's absence, along with his previous spotty health record and the current references to "collective leadership" in the party press, led to widespread speculation about his physical condition. Rumors spread that he was seriously ill and that a "triumvirate," consisting of Party Secretary-Premier-Foreign Minister Chou En-lai had taken over.

Not only Mao's physical well-being, but his political health also gave our writers much concern.

I was in China in the early fall of 1957. I did not notice that people there were much concerned about Mao's political position. I saw him—apparently in genial form—take his usual place as leader to watch the October 1 procession. I heard not the faintest whisper of a rumor that some great shakeup was afoot—not from the senior civil servants I spoke to nor from any of the many Western embassy officials I met. But, apparently, writers in Hong Kong knew something that was not yet known in Peking.

On November 22, 1957, *The Christian Science Monitor* ran a story from their chief Far Eastern correspondent: "Has Mao Tse-tung been replaced as China's Communist Party leader? Most informed Western intelligence groups here do not believe such is the case," read the next sentence; however, the correspondent himself must have thought there was more to the question than did the "intelligence groups," for he devoted much of his story to presenting the other side:

> . . . There have been, however, recurring reports here recently that . . . within the past two months the top leadership of Peking has shifted into other hands.
> The acting director of the Union Research Institute—a professional analysis group with at least indirect support from the United States State Department—gave a public speech in which he alleged Mr. Mao had lost his post in favor of Liu Shao-chi. . . .
> This claim, which was made by William Hsu, lacked any firm confirmation. . . .
> Mr. Hsu claims Peking is at present divided into two power cliques led by Messrs. Mao and Liu. . . .

For most of the following year, judging from the absence of news, Mao's health and leadership seemed to be fairly solid. But, by the end of 1958 and the beginning of 1959, predictions about Mao's fall were again being warmed over.

TOUGH SOLDIER LIKELY SUCCESSOR TO MAO read a headline over a Hong Kong story appearing in the October 2, 1958, San Francisco *Chronicle*, from a New York *Herald Tribune* service report. The writer rushed headlong to the heart of the matter:

> Aging Mao Tse-tung, chairman of Communist China, has picked young soldier Lin Piao, as his eventual successor, in the opinion of Chinese refugees once closely associated with the Communist hierarchy.

The writer, being a thorough newsman, was not satisfied to rely solely on unnamed refugees. "These and other observers in Hong Kong," who until recently had opted for Liu Shao-chi or Chou En-lai, had learned differently:

> But their reading of recent events is that both Liu and Chou are being sidetracked for "Peoples Marshal" Lin.
> While there is no indication that Mao will abdicate, he is 65 years old and in faltering health.

When in late 1958 it was officially announced that Mao Tse-tung would relinquish his post as Chairman of the People's Republic of China (he retained his position as head of the Communist Party), not to Lin Piao but to Liu Shao-chi, there was a veritable orgy of speculation. While some calm counsel was to be found, generally everything from the "failure of the communes" to a "power struggle" within the Party were cited as the real reason.

MAO FADEOUT—WHAT'S AHEAD IN CHINA? was the lead item on the editorial page of the Detroit *News*, December 18, 1958.

> The official Red Chinese line that President Mao Tse-tung in resigning from the presidency has only been relieved, like President Eisenhower, of nonessential ceremonial duties in order to devote himself to matters of high policy is only credible if one ignores history and the nature of the revolutionary, totalitarian state.

Takashi Oka, in *The Christian Science Monitor* for the same day, took a less didactic view. After paying his respects to "the repressiveness and all-pervasiveness of their totalitarian rule" on the part of the Peking government, Mr. Oka did list several possibilities for Mao's move:

> . . . unrest in the communes, Communist failure to take the offshore islands, or a desire by Mr. Mao to free himself from governmental routine and devote his time to behind-the-scene guidance and expositions of Marxist theory.

But for a precise clarification of the "Mao Mystery," laurels must go to *The Wall Street Journal's* expert on international communism. On December 30, William Henry Chamberlin handled matters in one illuminating sentence: "Yet it is something of a puzzle why the change was made at all whether it means a downgrading, an upgrading or merely a meaningless transfer for the chief architect of Communism in China."

In 1960,* while I was in China, I found Mr. Mao still holding down high responsibilities—his health appeared to be excellent. But for the next year or so the Hong Kong and Washington tea leaf readers on Mao's fortune were heavily engaged in forecasting the results of his battle with Mr. Khrushchev. However, in the New York *Times* of May 27, 1962, Tillman Durdin got back in the swing of things with a report on the condition of the Chinese leader.

> Mao Tse-tung is known to be in failing health with his mental powers faltering. There are surely cleavages in the Chinese Communist leadership as between the moderates and the extremists that could burst into a struggle for control when Mao dies.

But let us return to Robert S. Allen (who in 1950 had wondered where Mao had gone). In his column of January 3, 1959, Mr. Allen thought that Mao had been "forced" to step down from his position as Chief of State and was, in effect, also "deposed" as head of the Communist Party. Mr. Allen gives his ideas of why Mao was made to "appear" still to be keeping his Party position—it was a "face-saving stratagem" but really a "lie." The actuality, Mr. Allen said, was that Mao had already been "shorn of his power" in the Communist Party and would be "ousted" before very long.

In 1950 Mr. Allen had Mao a virtual prisoner of a Russian-controlled government; in 1954 he had Mao possibly dying of cancer; and in 1959 Mao was "shorn of his power" and about to be ousted. Mr. Allen continues to exercise his expertise for the enlightenment of the American public, and Mao Tse-tung, unruffled and apparently in good health, continues to be the unquestioned leader of the Chinese people.

* and again in 1963

Chapter 16

"THIS, TOO, WILL PASS AWAY"

After the revolution in Russia in 1917, the West for a long time cherished the hope that the "oppressed masses of the Soviet Union" would rise up and overthrow their new masters. At first, this hope was supported by action. For two and a half years, U.S., British, French, Japanese, and other allied governments gave large-scale military and other assistance to the White Russians who were attempting to overthrow the Communist regime, and we did so in the hope that we could "strangle Bolshevism in its cradle."

Five major campaigns were launched against the Communist forces, and all failed. The cost in lives, agony, and destruction was appalling. In one retreat alone, a million Russian men, women, and children perished. The brutalities of the White Russian forces have been described by the American historian, Professor D. F. Fleming. "Until the Nazis made wholesale murder a scientific business, the campaign of Admiral Kolchak in Siberia [which the allies were supporting] resulted in the most gigantic tragedy of all recent times."[1]

When the intervention eventually was abandoned, Russia was devastated from Poland to the Pacific. Millions of her people had died of hunger, disease, execution, and torture. The upper classes, for whom the war had been fought, had been killed or were in exile. The regime it had been hoped could be dislodged

[1] *The Cold War and Its Origins* (New York: Doubleday, 1961), Vol. I, p. 20.

had consolidated its position and was firmly committed to a totalitarian policy for survival.

The purpose of mentioning these events is not to discuss the historical consequences of the allied intervention in Russia, but to illustrate a point which has significance for us today. These events in Russia burned themselves deeply and unforgettably into the soul of the Russian people and established an attitude toward the West which still profoundly influences Moscow's political outlook. But Westerners have almost forgotten these tremendous events; many have not even heard of them. And part of the reason why we have so readily dismissed them from our minds is that *American public opinion was very poorly informed about them even while they were occurring.*

The Lippmann-Merz study of the reporting on the Russian Revolution is a deeply disturbing document. They found during this period "passionate argument masquerading as news" in headlines as well as articles.

How far the news of that period was distorted can be seen by the fact that in the two years following November 1917, the New York *Times* stated no less than *ninety-one times* that "the Soviets were nearing their rope's end, or actually had reached it." "Collapse" was reported fourteen times. The "red terror" was constantly reported in the press; the "white terror" was never mentioned.

Nor did the hope of a "collapse" of the Soviet government end with the defeat of military intervention.

The Chicago *Tribune*, for example, published a stream of articles which would lead its readers to conclude that there was a never-ending series of revolts in the Soviet Union, and that there was a constant likelihood of the regime being overthrown. Professor Frederick L. Schuman, in his book *American Policy toward Russia since 1917*, collected the following headlines from the *Tribune* (p. 325):

CLAIM STARVING POOR THREATEN DOOM OF SOVIET (June 15, 1925)
RUSSIANS FREE! TO ROB, STARVE, MURDER AND DIE (Nov. 15, 1925)
SIBERIA TRIES TO SHAKE OFF MOSCOW'S YOKE (Nov. 26, 1925)

RUSSIA UNLOADS JEWELS TO SAVE SOVIET REGIME   (Feb. 10, 1926)
SECRET REPORT SHOWS RUSSIA NEAR COLLAPSE   (Mar. 20, 1926)
UNCOVER SECRET TERRORIST PLOT TO SEIZE RUSSIA   (July 30, 1926)
SOVIET PARTY IN CHAOS AS TRADE, INDUSTRY TOTTER   (Aug. 4, 1926)
RUMANIA HEARS OF WIDESPREAD RUSSIAN REVOLT   (Aug. 7, 1926)
REDS REINFORCE KREMLIN FORT AS MUTINY GROWS   (Aug. 13, 1926)
ECONOMY REGIME IN RUSSIA FAILS: CRISIS IMPENDS   (Aug. 21, 1926)
REPORTS REVOLT AGAINST SOVIET BEGINS IN RUSSIA   (April 9, 1927)
RED ARMY FIGHTS WITH SOUTH RUSSIANS   (April 19, 1927)
RUSSIA CALLS SOLDIERS HOME AS REVOLT RISES   (April 21, 1927)
FAMINE STRIKES RUSSIA: POLAND FEARS INVASION   (July 27, 1927)
INDUSTRY FACES SWIFT DISASTER IN RED RUSSIA   (Oct. 23, 1927)
HUNDREDS DIE IN UKRAINE RIOTS, RUMANIA HEARS   (Nov. 26, 1927)

Professor Schuman's comment was that the reports of revolts were "wholly without foundation," and the other articles "differed only in the degree of their inaccuracy."[2]

There are many who may disregard these criticisms of our press because events to which they refer occurred nearly forty years ago. "Our press would not act this way now," some people have said to me.

They are wrong.

Let us return to today.

Since 1949, continuous efforts have been made by high government officials and by the press to persuade the people of America that China has been on the verge of collapse. Almost from the first, the public was being assured that the regime's days were numbered. What is more, our official foreign policy was based on the assumption that the Communist regime was a "passing phase" and would be replaced, and that we would help to promote its removal.

> . . . there are strong elements within the State Department and the Pentagon who believe that the Communist Chinese regime must be snuffed out sooner or later . . . (Chief of Washington Bureau, *The Christian Science Monitor*, April 5, 1954).

> . . . Senator Knowland recently told me that he based his

[2] New York: International Publishers, 1928, pp. 153–54.

hopes for the future "on the seeds of decay" within the Chinese system and that he regards "an upheaval from within as in the realm of possibility." (George Steiner, *Harper's Magazine*, June 1957.)

. . . The United States holds the view that communism's rule in China is not permanent and that it one day will pass. By withholding diplomatic recognition from Peiping it seeks to hasten that passing. (U. S. Secretary of State John Foster Dulles' memo, August 11, 1958, sent to all eighty-four U.S. missions around the world.)

While we were not prepared, as we were in the case of Russia, to commit our military forces to a direct intervention, there was no question at all that we would contrive by other means to overthrow the Mao Tse-tung government.

In 1951 Dean Rusk, then Assistant Secretary of State for Far Eastern Affairs, did everything but say the U.S. would aid Nationalist China in recapturing the mainland. He did say that as the Chinese people move to assert their freedom they could count on the tremendous support from free peoples in other parts of the world. The Nationalists, Mr. Rusk said, "more authentically represent the views of the great body of the people of China."[3] *U.S. News & World Report* on June 1, 1951, spoke of "Mr. Rusk's determination that the Chinese Communists must be overthrown" and that their government "far from being recognized . . . would be destroyed."

Our national policy was spelled out more precisely by Mr. Walter S. Robertson, then Assistant Secretary of State for Far Eastern Affairs, when he appeared on January 26, 1954, before the House of Representatives Committee on Appropriations.

REPRESENTATIVE FREDERIC R. COUDERT, JR.: "Did I correctly understand you to say that the heart of the present policy towards China and Formosa is that there is to be kept alive a constant threat of military action vis-a-vis Red China in the hope that at some point there will be an internal breakdown?" MR. WALTER ROBERTSON: "Yes, sir, that is my conception."

[3] *Vital Speeches of the Day*, June 15, 1957.

COUDERT: "In other words, a cold war waged under the leadership of the United States, with constant threat of attack against Red China, led by Formosa and other Far Eastern groups, and militarily backed by the United States?"

ROBERTSON: "Yes. . . ."

COUDERT: "Fundamentally, does that not mean that the United States is undertaking to maintain for an indefinite period of years American dominance in the Far East?"

ROBERTSON: "Yes. Exactly."

In 1958, Mr. Dulles's State Department policy statement, distributed to eighty-four U.S. missions around the world, dictated that official policy was designed to hasten the passing of the Communist regime. This policy statement has never been withdrawn.

For years press reports presented an image of China as a country moving irreversibly toward its doom. Almost as soon as the Chinese government had established itself in Peking, its overthrow was predicted. No specific dates were given, but the government's collapse was virtually certain; it was near, its authority was faltering, it was facing its greatest crisis—but the actual moment never came. As in a serial story or a soap opera, the supreme event never quite arrives; it remains forever just about to happen; the denouement, which would end it all, must remain tantalizingly imminent and perpetually unconsummated. Thus, the Peking government, tottering on the brink for more than fourteen years, refuses to collapse. It is still with us.

Four days after the formation of the new government in Peking, Hong Kong correspondents were already speculating on how long it would last. On October 5, AP's Seymour Topping was reporting the possibility that the "regime might go down." But he was somewhat cautious about dates; he preferred to take the long view:

> Don't expect a big upset in Peking soon. If one is to come it probably won't occur for from five to twenty years. Things move slowly in China.[4]

4 New York *Herald Tribune*, October 6, 1949.

On January 1, 1950, the New York *Times* interviewed an official of Nationalist China:

> Lone Liang, former Chinese Ambassador to Czechoslovakia, predicted yesterday that the Chinese . . . Government would be overthrown by the Chinese people.

Conditions on the mainland were being watched for signs of difficulties confronting the regime—any difficulties—which would hasten its end. On March 26, 1950, the AP reported from Tokyo:

> Shanghai . . . is being strangled by the ooze from which it arose . . . mud is choking off the sea approach to what was once the third busiest port in the world . . . within a year Shanghai will be inaccessible to commercial shipping of any importance.

(Ten years later I found Shanghai's docks crowded with foreign shipping and was told by British officials there that the port was handling more ships than ever before in its history.)

China's perpetual collapse was intimately connected with another image—the triumphant return of Chiang Kai-shek. With the masses on the mainland disillusioned, starving, and in revolt, Chiang's assault would give the regime its final push.

In the same week that Shanghai was written off, a small hit-and-run raid by Chiang's forces on Sungmen, an island two hundred miles south of Shanghai, moved the New York *Times* to a stirring editorial:

> Chiang Kai-shek . . . has made himself felt. . . .
> What Nationalist China needed . . . was discipline, a willingness to fight and a faith in the future. . . . Famine stalks the mainland of Communist China. Disillusion must have overtaken the multitudes who have waited in vain for long months for the coming of the Communist heaven.
> The tide may have turned. . . .

From Hong Kong on April 28, 1950, Christopher Rand was reporting to the New York *Herald Tribune*:

> Reports coming to this British colony from various parts of the Chinese mainland indicate that a huge part of that ter-

ritory—perhaps half or more—is now beyond the control of its new Communist-dominated government.

A month later, with perhaps half of China "out of control," further news was brought from Shanghai, the city that was choking in its own mud: 'SHANGHAI DYING' REFUGEES DECLARE was the headline in the New York *Times* on May 23 for an account of the arrival of seven hundred persons evacuated from Shanghai. According to the refugees, most of whom were Westerners, business in Shanghai was going to pot. (But one of them—a director of the American-owned Shanghai Telephone Company—hit a somewhat discordant note. The new government, he said, was "a damned sight more honest than the Kuomintang post-war government.")

On August 10, 1952, the Sunday New York *Times* called in a China expert, Professor Nathaniel Peffer of Columbia University, to give his views:

> . . . the Communist regime, like the ones that preceded it, is proving itself to be a surface, alien thing, artificially imposed on the ancient, authentic Chinese structure. And the history of China testifies that anything that does not rest on Chinese foundations cannot long endure. . . .

A report in *U.S. News & World Report* (August 6, 1952) predicted the worst:

FROM AN EXPERT: "COMMUNISTS HAVE LOST THE CHINESE"

One of the most highly respected authorities on China was discussing the deepening crisis in Communist China. He said:
"The Communists have lost the Chinese.". . . Famine next winter or spring is a real possibility. . . . A million will die. (The *U.S. News* did not name its "expert.")

About a year later, *U.S. News & World Report* (July 24, 1953) was again the bearer of bleak tidings:

COMMUNIST CHINA IN TROUBLE

WAR-FAMINE-CORRUPTION . . . RESISTANCE SPREADS

Communists have a mess on their hands in China. Strain of war beginning to tell. There is trouble on the inside, too. Farmers are getting restive, starting to balk. Nothing is really going as planned.

China looks like one more soft spot in the Soviet satellite empire.

This story from Tokyo included a number of photographs with the following captions:

> FAMINE is spreading over half the provinces of China.
> FARMERS, resisting Communists, are forcing a backdown on "land reform."
> INDUSTRY is in a mess, . . . short of raw materials, equipment, technicians.
> CORRUPTION, despite purges, is sapping the strength of Communist China.

(It is worth recalling that this half-starved, corrupt, "soft spot" in the Soviet empire, in which nothing was going as planned, where farmers were getting restive and where everything was a mess— had fought our armies in Korea to a standstill—and within *three days of this report* we signed an armistice with the Chinese which gave us no victory.)

U.S. News & World Report, nine years later, on November 19, 1962, was still telling a new generation of readers "Realities Will Bring Down Red China." Quoting another unnamed expert, it continued:

> A breakdown of the Communist regime in China in the not-too-distant future is considered inevitable. . . .
> . . . The economy is in a mess, and industrialization is not only at a standstill, it has been moving in reverse. . . .
> The economic and political realities that already have plunged China into grave crisis sooner or later will bring down the regime. . . .

But we are moving ahead of ourselves.

Almost five years after the Peking government had been in power, the New York *Times* (in an editorial, July 8, 1954) was still in doubt as to whether it was here to stay:

. . . the Chinese civil war can scarcely be considered as
ended. . . .
. . . just how effectively and permanently the Peiping regime
can control the mainland in view of the reports of Chinese
unrest . . . is still at least an open question.

Nineteen fifty-seven was another year of gloomy prophecies:

Life Magazine (May 27):
For the first time there are now glimmers of victory in the
struggle for the world: Such a glimmer comes from Red
China now under the greatest strain since the Communists
seized power in 1949. Its own leaders have acknowledged
growing dissension among the masses, economic troubles,
political bungling, unrest among students and discontent
among farmers. . . .

(This report appeared only a few weeks before I arrived in China.
I took it with me, and showed it to Westerners there. I wish that
the editors of *Life* had been present to hear their comments!)

Here are some additional samples of expected revolt and collapse in 1957.

New York *World-Telegram and Sun* (June 26):
WILL RED CHINA FOLLOW HUNGARY?

New York *Herald Tribune* (August 13):
RED CHINA—THIS, TOO, WILL PASS AWAY
Why should this nation founded in freedom, accept the no-
tion that the brutal tyranny of communism is "here to stay"
in mainland China?
. . . there are many ferments in Red China which may yet
overthrow the tyranny, now as repressive as Stalinism ever
was in its bloodiest heyday.

The development of the communes in 1958, which (as our
press so vividly reported) placed the people in barracks, divided
the families, and reduced the population to a condition of "unbelievable" slavery, apparently made a revolt against the regime
less likely. Nevertheless, on December 26, *U.S. News & World
Report* expected "violent reaction to [Mao's] effort to put practically all of China's 650 million people into barracks. . . ." And
the New York *Herald Tribune*, almost a month earlier (November

30) inquired: AS LIFE GETS LESS WORTH LIVING WILL CHINA'S PEASANTS REVOLT?

According to this article by Tribune correspondent Walter Briggs in Taiwan, the hopes of Chiang Kai-shek's return seemed brighter than for a long time. The Generalissimo's eldest son, Chiang Ching-kuo

> recently told this correspondent he expects the Red Army to rise up and lead any peasant revolt. Never in the history he has read, the younger Chiang said, has bitterness among the people not infected the armed forces. . . .

(Four and a half years later, on March 4, 1963, Chiang Ching-kuo was still confident, telling U.S. News & World Report that "development of the anti-Communist situation on the mainland means that 1963 presents the best opportunity for us to return to the mainland.")

The revolt among the peasants and the army not having occurred in 1958 as expected, the press emphasis in 1959 through 1962 shifted largely to the food shortage. If the establishment of the communes had not brought the regime to an end, "starvation" would certainly succeed. For nearly three years the press (see Chapter 6, "The Starving Chinese") kept up a running account of famine conditions inside China. On November 19, 1959, the New York Herald Tribune's columnist Joseph Alsop announced STARVATION RAMPANT IN CHINA COMMUNES; on May 17, 1961, he was asking: CAN CHINA EXPLODE? and by August 1962 apparently all his doubts were gone for he headed a Saturday Evening Post article: THE COMING EXPLOSION IN RED CHINA.

Official U.S. government endorsement of the "collapse" theory has bolstered the press reports.

A year before Mr. Alsop wrote his first "Explosion" article, the New York World-Telegram and Sun (June 6, 1960) reported that:

> A top State Department official (Assistant Secretary of State J. Graham Parsons) has told Congress that discontent among the Chinese peasants poses a "potential threat" to the Communist regime. . . .
> . . . and when one considers that the Red (Chinese) army is derived from the peasantry, the potential threat to the regime becomes evident.

Newspapers throughout the country carried this AP Hong Kong dispatch of May 15, 1961:

> Vice President Lyndon B. Johnson received information indicating the Communist regime in China conceivably could collapse within 18 months due to internal stresses.

(For once an actual date—but a rash prediction!)

And on March 6, 1962, the San Francisco *Chronicle* quoted W. Averell Harriman (then Assistant Secretary of State for Far Eastern Affairs):

> Communist China's staggering food production failures could trigger revolt among the millions of peasants. There is a great deal of unhappiness in China, and there might well be uprisings there.

On April 30, 1962, *U.S. News & World Report* contained yet another of its predictions of disaster:

SIGNS OF A CRACK-UP IN RED CHINA

How long can Red China . . . hold together?
. . . authorities . . . are not yet predicting a blow-up, but are pointing to it as something within the bounds of possibility, despite China's desperate effort to survive as a nation and as a Communist power.
. . . one of the most colossal failures in all human history.
Averell Harriman . . . on April 8th suggested publicly that the situation in Red China could result in an explosion that might wipe out the present Communist leadership. . . .

On August 11, the New York *Times'* Tad Szulc, reporting from Washington, provided a curious example of a report looking both ways at once:

> In the most up-to-date available assessment of the situation on the Chinese mainland [U. S. Government experts] said that the Chinese economy continued to deteriorate. . . .
> The officials stressed that affairs in China might be worse than was realized abroad. . . .
> In the opinion of the American experts, there is probably no starvation in China, . . . that there is "no mood of rebellion."

How China's condition could possibly be "worse" than some of the reports that had appeared in the American press is difficult to imagine.

During the course of 1962 the crisis had apparently deepened. In a long article in the October issue of *Current* Magazine, Albert Ravenholt, another onetime China correspondent, was asking: "Collapse of the Industrial Revolution?" and after reviewing the severe industrial setback that China was undergoing, and referring to the "fateful decision . . . to push the peasants" into the communes, he concluded:

> Now began the passive resistance of the peasants to the regime, a resistance which has grown to such proportions it is threatening the entire structure of Communist authority in China.

Toward the end of 1962 Westerners returning from China were reporting that the food situation there was moving back to normal; they wrote of crowded department stores, the range and variety of the consumer goods that were becoming available, the people in the cities strolling, relaxed, through the parks, the children in ever-larger numbers going off to school. The international trade returns showed that China's commerce was again moving upward. From those who had seen them, we learned that the Chinese leaders, though not complacent, were in a confident mood. Though not many of these reports found their way into the American press, in the newspaper offices and editorial rooms some doubts may have arisen that the end of the Chinese government was not going to take place just yet.

Whatever the reason, there occurred an unusual lull in the flow of predictions of disaster.

Then, in the first issue of 1963, on January 7, *U.S. News & World Report* stated:

> Mao is struggling with an *economic crisis* inside Red China that has all but wrecked Chinese agriculture, industry and transportation. . . .
> Any way Mao turns, 1963 seems sure to be an exceedingly critical year.

March and April will be the months to watch. It is then
that food stocks will be lowest. Unrest among Chinese peasants is expected. Revolts are likely.

On April 11, 1963, the Hong Kong *Far Eastern Economic
Review* devoted many pages to a report of the food situation
in China (see Chapter 6, "The Starving Chinese"). The report,
by Colina MacDougall based on a Hsinhua dispatch, spoke of the
great improvement in the over-all food situation, how "meat, fish,
poultry, eggs, vegetables, etc., are obtainable from the co-operatives
in the cities in unlimited quantities and without restrictions of
any kind."

I searched for any reference by correspondents in Hong Kong
to this report from a distinguished and impeccable businessman's
weekly. I found none.

What I found instead was this in a front-page report from Washington in *The Christian Science Monitor* on April 25:

> Some officials observe that Communist China is engulfed in
> a totally unresolved economic crisis. . . .

For fourteen years a vast number of reports distributed by the
great organs of public opinion—the press, radio, TV—and many of
our political leaders have stressed the weakness and insecurity
of the Chinese government. All the predictions so confidently
expressed have been proven wrong: the Chinese government has
not been "snuffed out"; the Nationalists have not invaded the
mainland; the peasants have not revolted; Shanghai has not
"choked in its own mud"; the Chinese have not starved; there
is no evidence that the government has at any time been "out of
control"; and the regime of Mao Tse-tung is still with us more
secure than ever!

Chapter 17

CHINA HAS NO CASH

... Peking has neither the cash with which to buy nor a surplus of exportable goods with which to barter on a large scale.

—*The Atlantic*, June 1954, p. 4.
(The Atlantic Report on the World Today: Hong Kong)

From the earliest days of the regime the Chinese government has been on record that it wished to trade with the West. But just as regularly as some American businessmen have suggested that it might be to this country's advantage to do business with China— back has come a flood of "proof" from our experts in the press that China has nothing to sell us that we want and no cash to buy what we have.

China almost from the start, it appeared, was on the brink of bankruptcy. As early as 1952, *U.S. News & World Report* (August 29) was telling us that the Chinese "internal situation is almost desperate."

> The Communists have used up their reserves of foreign exchange. Cash, jewels, everything that could be converted into money for trade has been squeezed out of the Chinese people. . . .
> . . . China is out of cash, out of credit. . . .

This continued to be the general story as the years went by; though a look in the international trade journals and the tables of international commerce would have shown that hard-headed European businessmen were apparently finding it profitable to trade with "bankrupt" China.

In 1960 I watched huge lathes rolling off the assembly lines at the vast machine tool plant at Wuhan. (This single plant, at maximum production, was estimated by British industrialists to be turning out more heavy machine tools than the whole of Great Britain.[1]) I saw these machine tools greased and crated for export. Shanghai was full of ships. Captains of foreign vessels were reporting that modern methods of loading and unloading had reduced the turn-around time of ships in Chinese ports to among the lowest in the world.

So I knew, if the press didn't, that China was exporting; and exports mean earning foreign exchange. We might not be in commercial relationship with China. That wasn't true of other Western countries.

Returning to America, I found the old mythologies were still current—the Chinese were "starving" and the economy was about to collapse.

With the serious agricultural shortages (not starvation) of 1961–62 the Chinese economy went into a very sharp recession (not "collapse"). China's foreign trade declined. The prophets of doom appeared at last to be justified.

Then came the "sensation." Bankrupt China began to buy grain, from Canada, Australia, France, Argentina, West Germany, Cambodia, South Africa, and Rhodesia. Not small purchases, but vast; involving, before long, hundreds of millions of dollars.

Newspapers that had predicted collapse took this new information in their stride. On March 1, 1961, *The Christian Science Monitor* reported Chinese Communist purchases of wheat and flour from Australia valued at £A 27,000,000 ($60,750,000) and $60,000,000 worth of wheat and barley from Canada.

Two weeks later Mr. Takashi Oka, the *Monitor's* Hong Kong correspondent, was wondering:

[1] Since 1960 production at the Wuhan plant has been sharply reduced as emphasis has shifted from industrial to agricultural production.

The question Hong Kong observers are now asking themselves is where Peking obtains the foreign exchange needed
to finance grain purchases on the world market.

For those who had been talking so long about the Chinese
reaching the bottom of their barrel, it was impossible to believe
that China had anything like this amount of cash stashed away in
the till. "Is Moscow helping Peking pay for its multimillion-ton
purchases of Canadian and Australian wheat?" asked Mr. Oka.

(As the Soviet Union more than six months earlier had begun
to withdraw its technical experts from China and was putting the
pressure on China by demanding repayment for money advanced
ten years earlier during the Korean War, this surely was a very
unpromising line of speculation.)

By mid-May 1961, the Canadian government had announced
what until then was the largest sale of grain in Canada's history—
$365,700,000 worth—to China. Twenty-five percent cash, the
balance on nine months credit.

On May 15, *U.S. News & World Report* headlined STAR-
VATION IN RED CHINA—DESPERATE REDS TURN WEST. The Canadian
purchase "shows scope of Chinese predicament. Inside China, millions are starving. . . . It's the gravest threat so far to the whole
Communist system."

> *Mortgage on Red China.* In London, experts [unnamed
> as usual] on the Communist bloc describe the deal by Red
> China to buy grain from Canada as "sensational." They
> point out it mortgages a large part of China's surplus earn-
> ings abroad through 1963. And the earlier purchases from
> Canada and Australia have virtually exhausted the Reds'
> foreign-exchange reserves.

So China was back to the bottom of the barrel again.

The state of Peking's foreign reserves was a topic of great con-
cern in *U.S. News & World Report* in the closing months of 1961.
On October 2 they reported "a major disaster in the making; the
Reds may soon be fighting for their lives."

> Foreign-exchange earnings are mortgaged for years ahead
> to the Soviet Union—and now, perhaps, to Canada and
> Australia.

Seven weeks later, on November 20, the magazine had the latest eyewitness news of the China disaster from a Swiss photographer.

> Q. Can China buy enough food from the other countries to meet this crisis? Where can they get it?
>
> A. China already has bought a considerable amount of food from Canada and other countries, but they need much more. The problem for the Chinese Communists is that they haven't the money or the goods to use to buy this food. All they could offer the Canadians, for example, were curios—cheap toys, wood carvings, hand embroidery, copies of old Chinese arts and the like.

One month later, these wily peddlers of curios and cheap toys, having no money or goods, had fooled those silly Canadians again. On December 21, the Vancouver *Sun* of British Columbia printed this headline:

RED CHINA BUYS $71 MILLION GRAIN
NEW CANADIAN SALE
BOOST FOR B.C. PORTS

The general impression left on U.S. readers (but obviously not on Canadian and Australian wheat growers) as 1961 was drawing to an end was that with these staggeringly large purchases, China's foreign reserves must now indeed be exhausted. The purchases were clearly a one-shot, emergency measure to meet an acute food crisis.

But not so.

Nineteen sixty-two purchases from Australia were *greater* even than those of 1961. By midyear a Chinese trade delegation was proposing to the Australian government annual purchases of 100,000,000 bushels of wheat, provided Chinese goods had reasonable access to the Australian market.

Washington from the beginning had looked with great disfavor on these sales of grain by her allies to Communist China. (In March 1962 the U.S. government had quickly blocked a proposal by the International Trading Corporation of Seattle to sell $400,000,000 worth of wheat and barley to China and North Korea.)

But by October the government had second thoughts about these grain sales from Australia and Canada. On October 17 Richard Reston, writing from the capital, reported in the San Francisco *Chronicle:*

> To avoid trouble with our allies, the Kennedy Administration is no longer opposed to other nations, such as Canada, selling agricultural surpluses to China.
>
> As a matter of fact, Washington feels this may be to our advantage. Officials explain that when Red China buys from outside the Communist bloc, it depletes her already shaky foreign exchange reserves, and thereby slows any drive toward industrialization.

(Why, then, one might ask, not sell her some of *our* grain and bring her already shaky reserves down like a pack of cards?)

Australia and Canada and other countries seemed totally unconcerned as to whether Mr. Kennedy approved or disapproved their dealings with China.

> As things stand: *Australia* is to go on sending Red China about a million tons of wheat a year. Canberra officials point out these sales have been a useful windfall at a time when Australia has had balance-of-payment problems. . . .
> —*U.S. News & World Report*,
> December 3, 1962.

> Canada's grain sales to Communist China, which have raised some criticism in the United States, will continue in the largest possible volume. . . .
> —*The Christian Science Monitor*,
> December 18, 1962.

But—the crucial question—is China actually *paying up?* Or are these sales just on-the-cuff, like so many of our "sales" to underdeveloped countries that sooner or later must be written off as a dead loss?

> Communist China guarantees payment in convertible sterling within 273 days from the date of shipment. "There has been no instance of default in payment," the government told Parliament.
> —*The Christian Science Monitor*,
> December 18, 1962.

. . . Red China has paid its bills on time.
> —*U.S. News & World Report*,
> December 3, 1962.

The general manager of the Australian Wheat Board stated recently that: for the past 18 months they [the Chinese] have not been a day late in any of their payments.
> —*Far Eastern Economic Review*,
> January 31, 1963.

China has surprised Canada by paying about $31 million in advance on its Canadian wheat purchases. . . .

Prime Minister John Diefenbaker has told wheat farmers . . . that the Chinese were ahead of schedule in their credit payments.
> —*Far Eastern Economic Review*,
> March 21, 1963.

Red China has come up with another $17,633,000 payment for Canadian wheat, Agriculture Minister Alvin Hamilton said Sunday.

Peking has handed over nearly $50 million in cash for wheat imports since last December.
> —AP report from Regina, Saskatchewan,
> April 1, 1963.

U.S. News & World Report, which had often told its readers that China had no cash (in 1961 it had told them that the "earlier purchases from Canada and Australia had virtually exhausted the Reds' foreign-exchange reserves"), revealed on May 27, 1963, the solution to the "mystery."

> Mystery of how Red China pays for all that grain it buys from Canada and Australia can now be cleared up. . . .
>
> In all, Red China's '62 trade outside the Communist bloc came to 690 million dollars. . . .
>
> . . . Its profits are ample to pay for Western grain. In fact, Peiping is paying its debt to Canada and Australia ahead of time.

The effect of these immense and continuing sales of grain on both Canadian and Australian agriculture has been tremendous.

> Canada's western wheat farmers have never been happier about their Federal government. For them, 1962 was the

best year on record in almost a decade. Canada's farm net income rose nearly 50%. . . .

And, of course, much of last year's increase can be attributed to the sharp rise in grain production in Western Canada where farmers knew they had an assured customer in Peking.[2]

And in Australia:

> . . . In the past two years, China was Australia's number one wheat customer; in 1961/62 China bought nearly one-third of our record wheat export, and during the last six months of 1962, China bought more wheat than during the whole of 1961/62.
> . . . Cessation of trading with China would mean the end of expansion of wheat-growing in Australia. . . .
> China has replaced Britain as number one wheat customer. . . .[3]

It isn't only Australian and Canadian farmers that have benefited from these purchases of wheat by China. Shippers have had a share of the benefits too. The Canadian grain sale of May 1961 alone, it was estimated, at the time, would take 750 ships to move and railway officials believed that it would take over 142,000 railroad cars to transport the grain to the West Coast.[4]

China has had, and will continue to have, serious difficulties in progressing from a backward country; but the facts that I have just cited about her grain purchases should make us pause.

While almost every other underdeveloped country in the world is relying heavily on handouts (aid is the fashionable term) China was going it alone and *paying* for her food—and at a time of special hardship. This should indicate to us, not (as our press would have had us see it) that China was on the verge of collapse, but that in the course of a remarkably few years she has been able to earn and save sufficient foreign exchange to see her through a crisis.

This denotes strength, not weakness.

[2] *Far Eastern Economic Review*, March 21, 1963.
[3] Ibid.
[4] *The Dispatcher*, San Francisco, May 19, 1961.

And it should not be supposed that China's necessity for food purchases has been preventing her from purchasing other things that she required. Her other imports were reduced, they were not eliminated.

In May 1962, Sir William Gunn, head of the Australian Wool Bureau, was quoted as saying that China had "tremendous potential" as a wool customer, and that "China appears certain to buy a record quantity of Australian wool this year."[5]

The New York *Times*, celebrating on October 1, 1962, the thirteenth anniversary of the Peking government, reported: RED CHINA INDUSTRIAL SLUMP; but only six days later, in a dispatch from Australia, its news columns announced: AUSTRALIA LOOKING TO RED CHINA AS VAST WOOL MARKET IN FUTURE. The story reported how China in 1961–62 had taken 44,000,000 pounds of wool, which was double her purchases the previous year, "despite the severe drain on her scarce foreign exchange caused by heavy wheat imports. . . .

> Discussing his forthcoming visit to Peking, Sir William said Communist China, with a population of 650,000,000 was Australia's greatest potential wool market.
> Within 10 or 15 years, he predicted, China would be competing commercially with all the countries of the world.

From countries around the world China today is purchasing planes and tractors, special steels, trucks, autos, oil, tools, ships, electronic apparatus, pipe, complete industrial plants—*and paying for them.* There is no doubt at all in my mind that Sir William Gunn is right—that China will soon take her place among the great trading nations of the world.

Only with us, and the countries on whom we exert our persuasion, is the door still tightly shut.

And our press for years has been telling us that China was "collapsing" and had "no cash."

[5] *Maritime Worker*, Sydney, Australia, May 16, 1962.

Part V

HOW IT WORKS

Chapter 18

I. Preventing People from Seeing for Themselves

When challenged about their reporting about China, there is a standard excuse that newspapers trot out in self-defense—if the reporting about China is poor, it is because "China doesn't allow American reporters in."

In a limited and technical sense this is now true, but like much else that the newspapers say about China, the statement if left without further comment is totally misleading.

The background to a somewhat confused story is this.

In the summer of 1956, the Chinese government formally offered sixty-day visas to eighteen American correspondents, without strings or restrictions. The U.S. government forbade them to go. Three men defied the ban—William Worthy of the Baltimore *Afro-American,* and Edmund Stevens and Philip Harrington of *Look,* who entered China for brief visits in December 1956.

Under pressure from newspaper and magazine publishers, radio and TV networks and the wire services, Secretary of State Dulles in 1957 finally drew up a list of "news media" involving twenty-four correspondents (the Chinese offer was for eighteen) that he considered could safely be permitted to travel to the forbidden land; but he made certain that this "accredited" list would be rejected by the Chinese government by announcing *in advance* that he would refuse reciprocal rights to any Chinese correspondents "bearing passports issued by the Chinese Communist regime," on the transparently phony grounds that American immigration laws "prohibited the issuance of visas to Communists." (Many exceptions, of course, had already been made for Soviet and other Communist correspondents.)[1]

There the matter of the correspondents was stalled until 1960.

Meanwhile, Peking continued to offer visas to Americans who wanted to visit China as ordinary travelers, but they were all forbidden to do so. A number of distinguished citizens, including Mrs. Eleanor Roosevelt and Mr. Averell Harriman, though offered visas by the Chinese, were advised by the State Department that they must not go. By all manner of threats of fines, imprisonment, and the loss of their passports, Secretary Dulles was able to keep Americans cut off from China.

(The ban on travel to China was again breached, however, in September 1957, by forty-one Americans who had been to the Moscow Youth Festival and went on to visit Peking as guests of the Chinese government. Many of these were penalized on their return by having their passports taken away from them.)

I have always felt that Mr. Dulles's refusal in 1956 to allow American correspondents to accept the offer of visas from the Chinese was one of the great diplomatic tragedies of our time. From this decision there flowed a whole host of misunderstandings—but it succeeded in effectively sealing off the American press from direct information about China, which presumably was its purpose. If the newspapers, magazines, wire services, and the radio and TV networks had exerted their enormous power and insisted on their right to send their correspondents anywhere they wished, even Mr. Dulles could not have withstood their combined pressure.

In the great days of American journalism a generation or so ago, when the press was fiercely conscious of its public obligation to secure the news, it would not for a moment have tolerated such an infringement of its freedom. True, for a while some papers

---

[1] Commenting on the text of a State Department announcement that the "U.S. will not accord reciprocity visas to the Chinese," *The Christian Science Monitor*, August 27, 1957, editorially deplored this "insulting note slipped under Peking's door." . . . Since Peking had not applied for such reciprocity, Washington's ban could only be taken as a gratuitous slap in the face. . . .

raised the issue strongly in editorials; protests were made; but never (as it should have done) did the press combine and concert its power sufficiently to have the ban rescinded.

During the summer of 1960, the Peking authorities announced they were abandoning their four-year efforts of reconciliation. They were no longer interested in offering visas to American reporters. Not long after this new policy was made public, I discussed it with Mr. Chou En-lai in Peking. The Chinese government, he explained to me, had made a number of offers in regard to the exchange of correspondents with the United States, all of which had been rejected. The government had reached the conclusion that no basic improvement in Sino-American relations was possible until the primary issue between the two countries had been settled—the question of Taiwan. This does not mean, he added, that the Chinese feel any ill-will to the American people.

This decision of the Chinese government no longer to offer visas to American correspondents made it possible for the Kennedy administration early in 1961 to "consider" applications of some Chinese correspondents for visas to come to the United States (conveniently forgetting the "immigration law" that had prevented this offer in the past), with the certainty that the Peking government would be bound to refuse. It has also enabled the U.S. government and the newspaper publishers to say, with technical truth but with shocking disingenuousness, that "it is the Chinese that are preventing our correspondents from going to China."

Meanwhile, it remains illegal for American citizens other than the "selected list" of correspondents to visit China, and the American people are thus prevented from seeing for themselves what is going on there.

To this story I must add a personal note.

Like many others I have always considered freedom of travel as an inherent right, one of the basic civil liberties that should not be subject (except in time of war) to the caprice or whim of the Executive. One of the reasons why I have retained my British citizenship—though I have lived in the U.S. so long and feel so intimately a part of American life—is that this basic right is recognized by Britain but not yet by America; though I think that day will come. Printed as an integral part of a British passport are words which make the document *valid for every country in the world*. While the United States grants so much freedom in so many other ways, it has never accepted the right to travel as one of the inalienable rights. All my journeys to China—though undertaken with the knowledge of the American government—would not have been possible if I had held a U.S. passport.

NOTE: Since the manuscript of this book was written I went to China for a third visit. See "Postscript from Peking."

II. *Ignoring Information That Is Available*

In the past few years many visitors have traveled in China from almost every country in the world (but not the United States), and among them have been a number of specialists investigating developments in their own branch of knowledge. Highly placed European and Canadian medical authorities have written on advances in medicine and public health in China; Western lawyers have reported about Chinese law; industrialists from a number of countries have inspected factories; leading agronomists from France and elsewhere have voiced opinions on Chinese agriculture; a team of economists from the Sorbonne made a study of the Chinese economy; Quakers from Britain, former Christian missionaries from Canada and Australia, and Buddhists from Ceylon have studied the state of religion in China; scholars from Oxford and Cambridge, Melbourne, and Montreal have visited China and written their impressions on a variety of topics; some of the world's foremost scientists have gone to China and have told us something about Chinese scientific training and research. Among those who have visited China are geologists, artists, writers, poets, architects, archaeologists . . . the list could be continued.

Most of these specialists (discussing, we must remember, their own field of expert knowledge) have had many favorable things to say about advances in China, but we find very little mention of their reports in the American press. Sometimes only the critical part of a report is used.

As an example of this, *Time*, when reporting on China's general economic collapse and industrial inefficiency, quoted a few lines from my book, *Awakened China*, in which I described the inefficiency I found at a certain truck plant—but *Time* did not quote descriptions of other factories which I said "could, as smooth-running operations, compare with any in the Western world."

When comparing the reports of visitors to China which are made use of, with those which are ignored, one can arrive at only one general conclusion—that if a report (or parts of it) can be used to sustain the image of China as a land of unhappy, half-starved peasants, with a collapsing economy and an utterly inefficient industry, and a population in the grip of a mercilessly cruel regime, such reports are used. A report that would shatter such an image is very rarely printed.

One reason sometimes offered for the non-use of favorable comments is that the writers "must obviously be fairly communistic themselves to write such reports"; or that "they have only been shown what the Communists want them to see." Some specialists have even gone so far as to suggest that for someone to be granted a visa to enter China is almost proof that he is "sympathetic" to the regime.

These insinuations are not only an insult to the very able men and women—some of them at the top of their profession—who have been to China; but are demonstrably nonsensical.

No one in his right mind, for example, would suggest that the President of the Royal Bank of Canada is "sympathetic" (in the way that this is meant) or "pretty communistic himself." Yet this is what Mr. James Muir reported to his employees and shareholders after his return from China in 1958:

> The growth in industry, the change in living standards, the modernization of everything and anything, the feats of human effort and colossal impact of human labor are not within our power to describe and still give a worth-

while picture of the scene. All I can say is that it must be seen to be believed. It is truly stupendous. . . . We think the vast majority of the people of China have a government they want, a government that is improving their lot, a government in which they have confidence, a government which stands no chance of being supplanted.[2]

This report was not mentioned in our press so far as I could discover.

Let us take another example of not using available material.

Published weekly in Hong Kong, the *Far Eastern Economic Review* is to my mind one of the best sources of information about developments in mainland China. It is a journal intended primarily for the conservative business and commercial men in the British colony; but its reputation for a high standard of factual reporting has brought it readers throughout the Western world. The information it provides on China, factual and without cold war bias, is often supplemented by reports from its own correspondents in China.

The detached and businesslike presentation of news about China in this journal stands in vivid contrast to the reports we are accustomed to reading in our papers. Though the *Far Eastern Economic Review* is accepted widely as one of the most reliable sources of information about mainland China, in all of the hundreds of dispatches that I have read from the American press correspondents in Hong Kong, I have yet to find one that has quoted from this paper. Correspondents appear more than eager to cable unsubstantiated statements from refugees and unidentified "observers." They seem strangely reluctant to quote from a factual journal.

I was personally involved in another case.

In 1962 the National Broadcasting Company approached me with a request for the use of some movie footage that I had taken while in China for a documentary "White Paper" that they were preparing. I was assured by the NBC producers that they were on this occasion attempting a "really objective report" on

[2] James Muir, "The Challenge of China," souvenir edition of the Royal Bank Magazine (October 1958).

China, "good as well as bad." I consented to send them my footage. When I watched the "White Paper" report on China as it appeared on the television screen, I realized that my idea of appropriate reporting would be very different from that of NBC. With the exception of a short sequence that I had taken in an old people's home, they made no use of any scenes from my footage that would give a viewer any feeling of joy; no scenes of children playing, no holiday-makers at the beach, no crowds at the new swimming pools. The over-all impression was one of gloom and sadness.

In 1961 in Los Angeles, a film on Communist China that was intended for use in schools was withdrawn. It was criticized on the grounds that:

> . . . it showed children smiling in Red China.
> The critics said it was a disservice to imply that anybody could be happy under such conditions.[3]

Another example of what I consider crucial omission:

Professor J. Tuzo Wilson is one of Canada's most eminent scientists. In 1958, as President of the International Union of Geodesy and Geophysics, he spent some time in China visiting scientific institutions. He also went to Taiwan; and before a scientific body in New York he made some comparisons. In the course of reviewing *Awakened China* for the New York *Herald Tribune*, he reveals what happened (my italics):

> . . . Mr. Greene's quotation from one speech of mine brings out the truth of his other theme: that the net effect of American reports of essential questions in China is almost always misleading and slanted. He quotes from a speech I made to the Dallas Council of World Affairs in the course of which I stated that the libraries and equipment in the science departments of the universities in Taiwan were not as good as those on the Chinese mainland. I said this not to annoy the Americans or the Nationalist Chinese, but because I know that thousands of Asians, Africans and South Americans can and do make these comparisons for themselves to the detriment of the Western

[3] San Francisco *Chronicle*, October 11, 1961.

cause. I repeated these remarks in New York, when asked to speak before the American Association for the Advancement of Science, but *all such statements were deleted from the published text*. Such actions, to slant even discussions by scientists, belie our principles and delude no one but ourselves.[4]

III. When Reports Conflict. . . .

On May 1, 1963, the UPI Tokyo "listening post" cabled its version of Peking's May Day celebration. The San Francisco *Examiner* spiced things up with the headline:

STALIN HOLDS HERO SPOT AT RED CHINA MAY DAY

This is part of the UPI Tokyo dispatch, dated May 1, 1963:

> Communist China celebrated May Day with mass parades, giant pictures of Josef Stalin, and verbal attacks on India, the United States and Soviet Premier Khrushchev.
>
> The Communist 'New China News Agency' in a broadcast from Peking indicated that the Russians were absent from the main reception on the eve of the Communist main holiday.
>
> The Chinese reaffirmed their militant friendship with their tiny European ally Albania, an outcast in the East European Communist bloc. . . .

A Western resident in Peking who saw this UPI report wrote to me on its accuracy as follows:

> 1. There were *no* "mass parades." China's May Day for the past three years has gone in for dancing, playing games and seeing shows in parks all over town. Over three million people came out, half the city's population. The nearest thing to a "mass parade" was when sportsmen, dancers, acrobats and children from the central parks poured into Tien An Men Square for an hour at noon to show their floats.
>
> 2. There was *one* giant picture of Stalin. It stands in a row with Marx, Engels, Lenin, all pictures of equal size,

[4] October 1, 1961.

historic revolutionary leaders, looking down on the square at all celebrations. There were no others; China's May Day does not feature individuals, but flags, drums, firecrackers, tissue paper flowers, children.

3. The "main reception" was not held by the state but by "people's organizations," chiefly the Trade Unions. The "New China News Agency" published at length the list of foreign trade-union delegations, with the names of leaders. First on the list, as usual, came the Russians. The Soviet Ambassador also was there.

4. There were *no* "verbal attacks" and no mention of India, Albania or Khrushchev. The only mention of the United States was indirect when Liu Ning-I, chairman of Central Unions, toasted "the Cuban people for frustrating U.S. imperialism's war provocations."

5. The only reference to "militant friendship" was in Chou's brief, eloquent toast "to the liberation of the working class . . . and the oppressed nations and people, to world peace, to the militant friendship of the people of all countries."

On May 12, the London *Observer* ran a full-page feature article: "May Day in Peking." It was written by Mr. Mervyn Jones, a non-Communist journalist in Peking at the time. His account confirms that there were no parades—but dancing, plays and games, at "garden parties" held for two million people in the parks. And, in a full-page feature, no mention of "verbal attacks on India, the United States and Soviet Premier Khrushchev."

> The events of May Day take place in the morning and evening, leaving the afternoon free for food and sleep. This year it was particularly important to end the celebration by noon since a major Buddhist festival (a movable feast) fell on the same day and it had been amicably arranged that the temple services would be held when the garden parties were over.

Mr. Mervyn Jones describes the "flirting girls," the color, the noise, the crowds, the brilliant flags, the fun.

> Young Pioneers in white shirts and red scarves carried big round Chinese lanterns or exquisite artificial flowers. Against the ochre walls and shining yellow tiles of the Imperial Palace, the scene had a gaiety, a vivid freshness and a variety of color that I cannot hope to convey. . . .

Thus, Western eyewitness accounts give us one description, the UPI from its "listening post" in Tokyo gives a very different description, with all kinds of sinister political implications. It must be a tough job "listening" to Peking from so far away!

IV. Reporting Official Pronouncements as Statements of Reality

In my review of the news about China as presented to the American people, one pattern became outstandingly clear—what I regard as the extraordinary *credulity* on the part of the press of official information.

Walter Lippmann and Charles Merz made the same criticism in their review of the press 43 years ago:

In their opinion, (and I share it) statements emanating from governments or political movements should not be taken as factually correct by an independent press. Statements of this kind are used for *special purposes* and are not necessarily trustworthy news. If, for example, a Secretary of State or Prime Minister makes a pronouncement about another nation, the information he gives cannot be taken as news. The only news in the pronouncement is that he made it. The information given in the pronouncement is a challenge to independent investigation.

I have found in my analysis that frequently on matters of transcendent importance, official statements have been accepted as *fact* without independent investigation.

When the Secretary of State in 1950 declared (we now know without any basis of fact) that Russia was incorporating one-third of China into the Soviet Union, this was published and was accepted by the press as true. We can see in retrospect (and a vigilant press should have suspected it at the time) the "special purpose" that Mr. Acheson may have had in mind when he made the statement. We now know that it helped to check effectively a growing movement of opinion in this country in favor of recognizing the new Chinese government. The Secretary of State's enormously important pronouncement was never seen as a "challenge to independent investigation," but was taken at its face value and swallowed hook, line, and sinker.

I could give any number of similar examples: Mr. Dulles's 1958 statement that the Chinese were "imposing mass slavery on 650 million people," and had created a "vast slave state" could have been easily checked with competent Western reporters and travelers who were in China at the time. (Reuters news agency has had a permanent staff in Peking.) Statements about the breaking up of the family; the instability of the Peking regime; that starvation and widespread famine conditions existed; that the border fighting with India was "unprovoked aggression" on the part of China; that India was progressing economically more rapidly than China; and, of course, Chiang Kai-shek's annual prediction of imminent invasion of the mainland—if ever statements required skepticism it was these yearly Chiang pronouncements. It is incredible to me that these last were treated quite solemnly as "news": "There are no boastful empty proclamations now. Instead there are serious preparations," Joseph Alsop reported as late as May 8, 1963.

These are examples of official statements, all proved by time to have been erroneous, but accepted by our independent press as statements of reality.

There is more to this yet.

When Dean Acheson said that Russia was taking over one-third of China's territory, this was not only accepted as a statement of fact, but some of the newspapers published stories that seemed to give support to his statement. For example, following Mr. Acheson's speech, C. L. Sulzberger from Paris and later Tokyo, Christopher Rand from Hong Kong, and others in Washington and New York were sending information about the Russian take-over. These correspondents almost never named names. Sources were wrapped in a blanket of anonymity—"specific indications were received here," "information available in interested capitals," "some circles speculate," "it is believed here"—but nevertheless we are faced with the astonishing fact that correspondents representing responsible journals over a period of months were providing circumstantial support for an official pronouncement that was never grounded on solid fact.

V. Headlines

This is not, I must hasten to admit, an area of great moment. It doesn't concern those of us who like to dawdle over our newspapers or who like to make reading them a vague excuse ("must keep up with the news") for not helping with the dishes or mowing the lawn. Fellow lingerers can skip this section, for it is included not for them but for those who like to take their news quick and pithy—the headline readers.

For them I give two examples to warn them that headlines are not always what they seem.

Appearing in the April 22, 1963, issue of the San Francisco *Chronicle*, a headline announced:

FAMINE AS USUAL IN CHINA

Across three columns. Clear, precise, and certainly pithy. It appears to say everything—why read the story? But an experienced lingerer knows why. Better read on.

> Even through the depths of winter the largest cities, Peking and Shanghai, are reported to have been well supplied with vegetable and fruit grown in communes on the outskirts of the city.
> The price of coffee, cocoa and sugar has come down. . . .
> . . . foodstalls have begun to sell rice cakes, noodles, and other concoctions free of coupons. . . .
> Both milk and butter have reappeared on the market. . . .
> Canned meat and poultry and different kinds of fruit preserves are also back in the shops. . . .

If this is famine as usual, I hope for their sake, that the Chinese have famine all the time.

On May 22, 1963, the New York *Times*' Western Edition stifled its modesty and carried an imposing advertisement for itself. Half a page of it. The *Times'* copy editors, we were told in very large type, are "the men who make sure that the news you read in the Western Edition is the most important and interesting, and that it is presented clearly, accurately, impartially. It's their job to check the facts—to correct English the Queen wouldn't like—to revamp [*sic*] a story if necessary—and to sum up the heart of it in a clear, terse headline."

That's the kind of advertisement that gives the headline readers a real boost. Why read a revamped story if you can get the heart of it in a clear, terse headline?

Six days later the Western Edition carried a headline (clear, terse):

INDIA THREATENED BY PEKING AGAIN

and this was followed by a second headline, somewhat less terse but equally clear:

CHINA SAYS INCURSIONS MAY LEAD TO WARFARE—PRESSES DE-
MAND FOR TALKS.

To compare these headlines with the story that follows is intensely revealing.

It is true that the story begins menacingly enough:

> Communist China warned India today that "further provocation" by New Delhi's forces . . . might lead to renewed warfare.
> Peking's warning included an ultimatum to accept Chinese terms for direct negotiation of the frontier issue.

This lead certainly seems to justify the headlines, and the headlines justify the lead. *But what did the Chinese actually say?*

We are told that the story, filed by Robert Trumbull in Hong Kong, was based on an editorial in the May 27 issue of *Renmin Ribao*, the official newspaper of the Chinese Communist Party. Trumbull quotes from this editorial. Here are the actual words of the "ultimatum" and the manner in which China (according to the headline) "presses demand for talks."

> "If the Indian Government because of domestic or external considerations is not yet ready to negotiate, the Chinese

Government can wait patiently," the Peking statement said.

The statement said that if the Indian Government attempted to regain the territory taken by Chinese forces last year New Delhi would "again pick up a stone to drop on its own feet." . . .

Peking declared that its repatriation of all Indian prisoners of war, which was completed over the weekend "created a favorable atmosphere for a peaceful settlement" of the Chinese-Indian boundary question.

"Whether direct negotiations between India and China can be held quickly or not and whether the Chinese-Indian boundary question can be settled peacefully soon or not depends on the attitude of the Indian Government," the Peking statement asserted.

. . . Communist China's release of all Indian prisoners showed Peking's "reluctance to cross swords" with India.

I have the official translation of the editorial in the Chinese newspaper on which Robert Trumbull based his story. It is a long editorial—over two thousand words; its title is "Another Major Effort by the Chinese Government to Promote Reconciliation Between China and India." The passages quoted by Trumbull give a very fair presentation of the essentially conciliatory tone of the editorial—as can be seen above. But neither the lead nor the headlines can possibly be justified by the contents of the story itself.

Toward the end of the *Times* dispatch it is stated:

> Another call for India to negotiate came from Marshal Chen Yi, Foreign Minister of Communist China. . . .
>
> "We are confident," Marshal Chen said, "that no matter how long the Chinese-Indian boundary question may be dragged out it can only be settled and will certainly be settled peacefully in the end."

INDIA THREATENED BY PEKING AGAIN? Send the headline back to the revamping department.

But—another warning to the headline readers.

Headlines may express the "heart" of a story quite accurately, but not the truth.

I have been twice into Communist China, once for five

months. (Since this was written I have been for a third time.) I found the Chinese to be immensely hard-working, rather excited by the new country they are building, grumbling sometimes about this and that as we all do, but above all *cheerful.* I am not alone. Many travelers to China have reported receiving the same impressions. One visitor to China, Dr. Wilder Penfield (Director Emeritus of the Montreal Neurological Institute, one of the world's leading neurosurgeons, holder of twenty-six honorary degrees, author of numerous books, and known throughout the world for his medical work) said this over station WTIC in Hartford during a Yale University program on March 10, 1963. Asked, shortly after returning, to single out the one most outstanding impression of the Chinese people, Dr. Penfield answered: ". . . It was a feeling of enthusiasm, exhilaration and pleasure that at last they were doing something on their own. They are working, especially the younger people, and they are working with a will. The people in the communes are working hard, but that is the way of the Chinese anyway. I would say in general that there is a feeling of excitement and enthusiasm among the people."

But would you guess it from reading the headlines? Compare these typical headlines about China!

(The following headlines cover a five-year span following my return from my first trip to China.)

1958
HARD YEAR BLIGHTS MAO'S "BLOOMS"—January 17, *The Christian Science Monitor*
PEKING'S HOT POTATO—Feburary 3, New York *Post*
THE ILLS OF RED CHINA—March 22, New York *Herald Tribune*
NEW SERFS IN RED CHINA—April 26, New York *Herald Tribune*
RED CHINA PUSHES WORKERS TO LIMIT—April 27, New York *Times*
POLICE TERROR BANISHES SMILES—July 23, New York *World-Telegram and Sun*
"HELL" IN CHINA—October 22, New York *Times* editorial
ARE THERE SEEDS OF REVOLT IN RED CHINA?—November 2, New York *Times*
CHINA REVOLTS SEEN SPREADING—December 23, Washington *Post and Times Herald*

BEHIND THE SHIFTS IN RED CHINA—TROUBLE—December 26, *U.S. News & World Report*

1959

THE RED CHINA ZOO—February 23, New York *Times*

1959 STEEL DRIVE LAGS IN RED CHINA—February 24, New York *Times*

MAO'S WAR WITH THE CHINESE FAMILY—May 17, New York *Times*

FAMISHED RED CHINA SLAVES STEAL PIGS' SLOP—June 25, New York *World-Telegram and Sun*

U.S. AIDE SAYS REDS IN CHINA ARE FAILING—July 19, New York *Times*

GROWING WOES OF RED CHINA—July 20, *U.S. News & World Report*

1960

NEW CRACKDOWN IN RED CHINA: NOW IT'S THE WORKERS' TURN —May 9, *U.S. News & World Report*

SCARS ON FACE OF RED CHINA—July 8, New York *World-Telegram and Sun*

MESS HALLS OF RED CHINA FAIL TO WIN MANY HEARTS—July 18, New York *Herald Tribune*

MAO'S FARM PROBLEM . . . —August 2, *Wall Street Journal*

CHINA GOADED BY INTERNAL NEEDS—August 28, New York *Times*

EDUCATION FLAW IN RED CHINA SEEN—September 18, New York *Times*

PEIPING COMBATS UNREST IN YOUTH—October 2, New York *Times*

1961

COMMUNIST CHINA IN REAL TROUBLE?—February 20, *U.S. News & World Report*

THE DESCENDING SPIRAL—April 16, New York *Herald Tribune*

JOHNSON TOLD RED CHINA MAY COLLAPSE SOON—May 16, San Francisco *Chronicle*

COMMUNISM'S FAILURES IN CHINA—May 20, *The Christian Science Monitor*

SPREAD OF APATHY IN RED CHINA NOTED—August 7, New York *Times*

SIX HUNDRED CALORIES A DAY—September 13, New York *Herald Tribune*

THE TRUE STORY OF TROUBLE IN RED CHINA—October 2, *U.S. News & World Report*

12 DISMAL YEARS IN CHINA—October 3, San Francisco *News Call-Bulletin*, editorial

CHINA FACES WORST CRISIS OF DECADE—December 3, San Francisco *Examiner*

1962

HARRIMAN SEES REVOLT IN CHINA—March 6, San Francisco *Chronicle*

SIGNS OF A CRACK-UP IN RED CHINA—March 30, *U.S. News & World Report*

A GRIM REPORT ON HUNGER IN CHINA—May 25, San Francisco *Chronicle*, Drew Pearson column

REPORTS OF BLOODY RIOTING IN RED CHINA—June 6, San Francisco *Chronicle*

RED CHINESE EATING BABIES: REV. CURTIS—July 19, Honolulu *Advertiser*

A MOOD OF DEJECTION IN RED CHINA—August 12, San Francisco *Chronicle*, reprint from New York *Times*

STARVING CHINESE—A GRIM FORECAST—August 28, San Francisco *Chronicle*, Drew Pearson column

CHINA ON A MUTED NOTE—October 9, New York *Times* editorial

REALITIES WILL BRING DOWN RED CHINA—November 19, *U.S. News & World Report*

WHY RED CHINA'S RULERS FEAR REVOLT—December 10, *U.S. News & World Report*

1963

PEKING PAPER RAPS FARM INEFFICIENCY—January 14, *The Christian Science Monitor*

CHINA SABOTAGE—March 24, San Francisco *Chronicle*

FERTILIZER LACK BESETS PEKING—April 15, *The Christian Science Monitor*

FAMINE AS USUAL IN CHINA—April 22, San Francisco *Chronicle*

By the spring of 1963 news was at last filtering through that China was not collapsing. Joseph Alsop ceased telling us about downward spirals and coming explosions. Even *U.S. News & World Report* warily admitted that "Communist China cannot be said to be falling apart."[5] With these resolute seers of disaster in a mood of hesitation, things in China must really be looking up!

[5] March 18, 1963.

VI. *Captions and Pictures*

We remember pictures longer than we remember words. There are few more effective ways of creating lasting impressions than by visual images—by photographs or cartoons. And by the same token there is hardly a more effective method of creating erroneous images if one should desire to do so.

In the insert of illustrations we present some examples of what can result from certain uses of pictures. As an example of what can be done to a photograph with scissors and a changed caption, see Figures 1 and 2. Figure 1 is a photograph distributed by UPI which was correctly identified as a picture showing bodies of Viet Cong guerrillas slain in South Vietnam on April 24, 1962. The Bridgeport (Conn.) *Sunday Herald*, in its issue of June 3, 1962, shows only one body (Figure 2) with a new caption saying it was a picture of an exhausted refugee from Communist China.

There have been other cases of misrepresentations of this kind. Edgar Snow, in his book *The Other Side of the River*, refers to a photograph that has been used on several occasions to show Communist brutality, though the picture itself is a photograph of one of the Kuomintang street executions which were a feature of life in Shanghai before the Communists took over the city.

Another way to misrepresent is to give a wrong translation of an otherwise unexceptional picture. In its special issue of December 1959 on Red China, *The Atlantic* devoted a full page to a color reproduction of a Chinese poster, showing a smiling Mao Tse-tung standing before a scene of industrial and agricultural prosperity. This poster as shown in *The Atlantic* is reproduced in black and white as Figure 3. According to *The Atlantic*, Mao is urging his people on to make China "the strongest and richest Socialist nation." The correct translation of the characters is "a strong and rich Socialist nation"—a phrase carrying quite different overtones. My Chinese friends tell me that the characters in question could not easily be mistaken by anyone with even a fairly rudimentary knowledge of written Chinese. But not many Americans have even that much knowledge to guide them.

Cartoons offer a wide field for misrepresentation.

In Figure 5 we present a cartoon printed in *The Christian Science Monitor* on March 23, 1961. It shows a group of newspaper correspondents being kept out of China by a bamboo wall obviously erected by Mao Tse-tung who appears over the top. The implication of this cartoon is that the Chinese are responsible for keeping out American newspaper correspondents. For the full story of who is keeping out whom, see the earlier part of this chapter.

Cartoons can keep alive a story long after the news columns have shown it to be dubious. As an example of this we reproduce a cartoon printed in the San Francisco *Chronicle* entitled "The Great Wall of China" (Figure 6). It shows a crowd of obviously starving Chinese kept back by a wire fence through which they are pitiably stretching out their hands for food. Two weeks before this cartoon appeared, on May 22, 1962, the British government had made a formal announcement in the House of Commons: "There is little evidence that the Chinese refugees attempting to enter Hong Kong were suffering malnutrition." The U. S. Assistant Secretary of State had also announced that the refugees were: "not starving. In fact, they did not show any evidence of malnutrition"; and these reports were confirmed by reporters who interviewed the refugees for the *Far Eastern Economic Review*. Partly because of cartoons of this kind, the American public appears to be still firmly convinced that the refugees *were* starving.

Those who have read Chapter 12 "'Chinese Aggression': The Sino-Indian Border Dispute," will have realized that the reports being presented to the American public about the India-China border dispute were grossly misleading. But the prevailing belief that the fighting was due to Chinese aggressiveness was also presented by cartoons such as Figure 7, also from the San Francisco *Chronicle*. Here we see Mao Tse-tung about to blow up the entire world. It is ironic that on the day that this cartoon appeared, October 23, 1962, the San Francisco *Chronicle's* front-page headlines read: U.S. BLOCKADES CUBA—NAVY IS READY TO FIRE. SHIPS

TO BE TOLD: HALT FOR SEARCHING OR WE'LL SINK YOU. KENNEDY . . .
WARNS RUSS OF WAR.

An erroneous newspaper or magazine caption will be spotted
only by a minute handful of American readers. The Columbia
Record Club once sent me for my advice a series of slides taken in
Communist China which they had bought from and which were
captioned by a Canadian source for possible inclusion in a book on
China they were planning to issue to subscribers to Panorama
Colorslides. One picture described as a "propaganda poster" was
nothing more than the announcement of a football game. Another,
in which a woman was pinning a banner across the top of a door-
way, also described as an example of Communist propaganda, was
an announcement that a tea house would shortly open there.

For an example of this kind of thing, see Figure 4. A picture of
a Chinese poster appearing in *U.S. News & World Report* on
December 10, 1962, was identified in the caption as "Recruiting
poster calls for Army volunteers. A Peasant Army carried Chinese
Communists on to power, but now there are signs of discontent
among the troops. To counter this, China's worried dictators are
offering favored treatment to families of soldiers." In actual fact
the photograph is of a billboard advertising a movie. The small
characters at the bottom give the names of the director, the
cast, and the studio where the film was made.

We often hear that the Chinese conduct "hate America" campaigns; and—worse yet—are teaching their children to "hate" America. We forget that our representation of people we don't happen
to like can just as easily appear to them as being "hate campaigns."
Figure 8 reproduces a cartoon that was printed in *Junior Scholastic*, on October 3, 1962. *Junior Scholastic* is a magazine for
children, and this number was a special issue devoted to "Understanding World News." As part of this "understanding" the young
readers were asked: "Would the Chinese leaders, in an attempt
to make the people forget their hunger, start a war? Even before
these hard times, Chinese Communists were warlike enough . . ."
etc.

To give visual support to the assumption of Chinese (and
Russian) malevolence, we see in this cartoon China and Russia

playing a gruesome game, presumably gambling for the world, while "hunger" looks on. This for children! And this to further the "understanding" of world news!

Looking through past cartoons is probably the best reminder there is of how changeable our national likes and dislikes really are. Our friends of today become our enemies of tomorrow. And who could have believed during World War II that Japan, the country that had stabbed us in the back at Pearl Harbor, would so quickly become our friend and stanch ally in the Far East? The image of the Chinese in American minds has always fluctuated from one extreme to another. On occasions we have thought of them as a great and noble people, deeply cultured, peaceful, humorous, likable. At other times we see them as crafty, devilishly clever, cruel, "inscrutable." Between these extremes our feelings have fluctuated according to political circumstances whether the Chinese happen at the time to be our friends or enemies.

We include two cartoons (Figures 9 and 10) which exemplify these extremes of feeling. One printed at a time when Japan, who was then our potential enemy, was attacking China, who was then our friend, is entitled "When a Fella needs a friend." The other (entitled "Lift babe?") was drawn after the Communists came to power, and shows China as a loathesome tough trying to pick up demure, innocent young Japan. These are good reminders that in the world of international affairs, though our feelings are so real and seem so permanent, nothing ever remains the same for very long.

Two cartoons are included which depict Chiang Kai-shek. It is a remarkable fact that though Chiang's regime has at certain periods been bitterly attacked, though information about the corrupt nature of his government was at these times well known and though millions of innocent people were killed under his regime, the cartoonists have usually dealt kindly with him. He has never, as far as I know, been depicted as a horrible and bloodthirsty brute as some of our other dictator-allies have been shown. The cartoon by Herblock (Figure 11) shows Chiang as a rather likable magician who has cleverly spirited away U.S. aid funds; the other, by Newton Pratt (Figure 12), was drawn during the Quemoy crisis of 1958 at a time when it seemed to many people that Chiang was hoping to embroil the United States in a general war as his one way of returning to the mainland. There is something rather engaging about Chiang sitting cockily in his rickshaw ordering Dulles, the rickshaw boy, to pull him to the mainland.

A SUMMING UP

There is an old Chinese adage which says: Know thyself, know your enemy, fight a hundred battles, win a hundred victories.

It is good advice, but we do not follow it.

Our greatest problem in dealing with China is not China, but our ideas about China. We seem unable to assess China's strength and weakness, her mistakes and achievements, or her political intentions with anything approaching dispassion. Because strong national feelings are involved, there are men in public life who dare not voice publicly what they feel in regard to our China policy. For fourteen years no administration has been able to suggest seriously that our China policy needs re-examination, for even to suggest it might imply a "weakening" of attitude. So our China policy remains non-debatable, which only shows the extent to which we have become prisoners of our own fears.

In 1960, Mr. Adlai Stevenson, then a private citizen, expressed his views on America's foreign policy in a conversation with Theodore H. White. He let his mind range freely. For Stevenson not just strength, but moral leadership was the issue. He said that he had probably talked with more heads of state than any other American. He spoke strongly against our living in Asia "with this mythology of Chiang Kai-shek's return to China," and he called our refusal to recognize, even to talk with, the rulers of modern China "one of the greatest political crimes of our times, for in

1955 we had a chance to talk to them, to begin to resolve some of the problems there."[1]

Here was an able man directing his attention intelligently to the errors in our relationship with China.

Barely one year later, Mr. Stevenson, by then a member of the Kennedy administration, spoke again about China—this time at the United Nations. Speaking against the admittance of China, he said that the United Nations:

> would make a tragic and perhaps irreparable mistake if it yielded to the claims of an aggressive and unregenerate "People's Republic of China" to replace the Republic of China in the United Nations. . . .
>
> The de jure authority of the Government of China extends throughout the territory of China. . . .[2]

The New York *Times'* account of Mr. Stevenson's speech omitted much of his rhetoric, which included these descriptions of China: "warrior state," "modern imperialism," "a massive and brutal threat to man's very survival," "ruthless," "aggressive by nature," "predatory," "far from reformed," "arrogant," "rapacious," "callous." Mr. Stevenson even included that old chestnut pulled out of a speech made by Mao a quarter of a century ago, about "power grows out of the barrel of a gun." (Stevenson's speech, interestingly, was printed in full in the Peking *People's Daily*.)

The contrast in the spirit as well as the content of these two extracts reflects a personal tragedy for Mr. Stevenson. We can neither ignore it nor deride it, for it speaks also of a colossal national tragedy in which we all must share. What happened to Adlai Stevenson happened because the *spirit of negotiation*, in which he could have played such a notable part, and which he knew was necessary if our relations with China were ever to be resolved, had been quite eliminated.

One cause of this stalemate we have reached in regard to China is the picture of that country and its leaders which most Americans have in their minds. When distinguished men cannot voice in

[1] Theodore H. White, *The Making of the President, 1960,* (New York: Atheneum, 1962), pp. 120–21.
[2] New York *Times,* December 2, 1961.

public what they say in private, it is because they judge that American public sentiment would reject the idea of contact with China.

At the Geneva Conference in 1954 Secretary of State Dulles refused Chou En-lai's outstretched hand and deliberately turned his back on him. In 1962 Mr. Averell Harriman considered it prudent to cable Washington for permission to shake hands with Chinese Foreign Minister Chen Yi—though they had been sitting at a conference table together for days.[3] These are indications of how deeply *moral disapproval* of the Chinese has influenced our thinking.

Foreigners stand amazed at these strange goings-on. This does not mean that the British, the French, the Canadians, the Scandinavians are less sensitive to cruelty and malice when they meet it. But it does suggest that their image of the Chinese is different from our own. If our allies do not reject contact with the Chinese perhaps it is because they have not been subjected to the same influences. For fourteen years American newspapers, radio, TV, the weekly newsmagazines, the columnists, with extraordinary consistence and apparent conviction, have presented the Chinese leaders as monsters, so inhumanly callous, so aggressive, so paranoiacally militant, and to top it all such stupid bunglers, that no self-respecting American would want anything to do with them.

The problems involved in lifting a country like China from a state of poverty and backwardness are very great, and no one knows this more clearly than the Chinese leaders. I have talked with some of them, and I have found them not at all as they have been pictured in our press. They seemed to me highly intelligent, historically conscious, and essentially humane men who have the interests of their people at heart. They know China has far to go and that she has much to learn and that they have made many errors. It strikes me as singularly ungenerous of us who were able to develop our nation on a rich and almost virgin continent to speak in tones of contempt at the immense efforts a backward country is making to raise itself up from immemorial poverty. And especially so as we have done nothing at all to help the Chinese

[3] Edgar Snow, *The Other Side of the River*, p. 736.

people, but rather have done everything in our power to hinder them.

The *spirit* of so much that is written about China is all wrong, and this is much more serious than the factual omissions and distortions.

As soon as we begin to think of the people of another country principally in terms of political antagonism, they cease to be people. This is a subtle process and a dangerous one. By small degrees, and almost imperceptibly, our sense of human relatedness with them diminishes until we end up by being indifferent and pitiless. And, what is more, we will not even be conscious that this has happened. What begins as "containing communism" can end with dropping napalm bombs onto defenseless villages and burning everyone in them to a frazzle without experiencing any greater horror than when exterminating a nest of ants.

I do not for a moment suggest that we must approve of what the Chinese are doing or that we shouldn't criticize them as strongly as we wish when we believe that their actions are bringing avoidable suffering. But what I do suggest is that however critical of the Chinese we feel, the human contact, the sense of the Chinese as people, must not be broken. If once we cease to think of them as people, we will be denying the very basis of the democracy we wish to protect.

America was founded and started its life as a nation on a legal document, and it is quite natural that the legal, one might say the formal, aspects of democracy have always played a dominant role in our thinking. But there is another side to democracy that is even more important than the written rules. Democracy in the first instance grew out of the way people felt toward each other—the machinery of representative government came much later. A nation might develop an almost perfect political instrument for democratic government, but if the intuitive, instinctual sympathy that people feel for each other has meanwhile vanished, we are left with nothing. The essential ingredient in a democracy is the identification, the liking, the instinctual trust that flows in thousands of minute and invisible currents through a society. It is this that makes a man feel that he belongs, that allows him to live at ease with his fellows without having to be watchful, competitive, and tough. If this sense of interrelatedness is lost, as individuals we become alienated; we become hard, professionally benevolent, and shrewd. As a nation we become implacable.

The democratic instinct knows that people are people, that differences of skin, of political opinion, of religious belief, are irrelevant differences when set against the vast similarities we all share as human beings.

Now this democratic instinct which recognizes people as people says nothing at all about national frontiers. It is unconcerned with them. It pays no more attention to which side of a national boundary a man happens to be born on than on which side of the railroad tracks or what color skin he is born with or into what economic or political system. For wherever a man is born, into whatever condition, he still shares with us our common humanity.

Today, as a result of our present pathology, we have lost sight of this *universal* aspect of democracy. We look across the oceans and see other people, not in the light of our relatedness with them, but almost wholly in terms of our fears. Are they *with* us or *against* us? Our sense of democracy has shrunk so that it now embraces only those within our own nation and a few special friends, and even some of those are suspect. It is true that as a people we are generous. We have given away so much. But this in a sense only strengthens the point I am making, for in spite of our natural generosity, our aid programs have been less an expression of compassion than an instrument of strategy, which is a very different thing. If this tendency to limit our sense of human relatedness only to those who are "on our side" continues, we may end up one day by becoming like the German Nazi, Hans Frank, who said: "It will be our principle to extend pity to the German people and to none others in the world." I have no doubt that a number of people in our country would feel quite pleased if they opened their newspapers tomorrow morning and read that a hundred million Chinese were starving to death.

It seems obvious to me that the way we feel about another country influences the kind of news we are given about that country. Forty-three years ago Lippmann and Merz concluded after a careful study that the intrusion of bias in the news was so blatant that serious reform would be necessary "before the code that had been violated could be restored."

What was true in regard to our information about Russia forty years ago is true in regard to our information about China today. The code is still violated; the news continues to be distorted.

But is this true too of those in academic circles? The specialists and the China experts—are their writings and judgments also influenced by political prejudice?

I have long noticed that once feelings of animosity and fear come in, objective judgment goes out—regardless of how clever one happens to be. On matters where great national feelings are aroused, scholars and experts are just as likely as the rest of us to allow their judgments to be swayed by the prevailing climate of opinion. Maybe even more so. Einstein perhaps was right when he wrote to Sigmund Freud:

> Experience has shown us that it is the so-called intelligentsia that is more apt to yield to these disastrous collective suggestions, since the intellectual has no direct contact with life but encounters it in its easiest synthetic form upon the printed page.

It is true that a great deal of scholarly research is being done on China today in the United States—probably more than ever before. Its fatal weakness is that it is being done by men who have themselves never been to Communist China. I have noticed that it is not the French or Canadian or British scholars who have been to Communist China who speak about that country in the most bitterly hostile terms—but the American scholars who know about China "only from the printed page."

I do not, I must repeat, want to limit criticism of China—and there is much that she can be criticized for. But the criticism must be based on factual realities. If political animosity (as I believe) makes us humanly indifferent and distorts our understanding—then the quality of most of the reporting about China by the press and experts during the past fourteen years has done us all a disservice. For the quality of the reporting has been such that it was bound to increase our hostility and fear of China and could in no way deepen our understanding of her. Though I think that an exchange of correspondents would be a sensible step I do not believe that this in itself would insure our being better informed about China. A large number of reports by very competent foreign observers have been available but have been used very little by the American press. While political animosity remains, our attitudes will be colored by it—whether it originates by reporters writing from Hong Kong or Peking.

There may, I know, be readers who while agreeing with my general thesis will think I have not made sufficient allowance for the exceptions. I am well aware of these exceptions, occasions when the general press and the China experts have given objective accounts of happenings in China. There is hardly a newspaper that will not be able to pull out of its files some stories and reports which they hope will contradict my charge. Reuters correspondents from Peking have continued to send regular and factual accounts of happenings there, and I am sure that some of these can be produced to show that I have greatly exaggerated my case.

But I do not believe that these occasional exceptions invalidate my argument; for they could do little to counteract in the minds of the readers the overriding impression established by far more numerous reports.

I make no apology for not enlarging more on this theme of the exceptional editor and the exceptional scholar; for the exceptions do not alter my general contention that where it involves the reporting on China the standard in both these professions has been appalling. And I know that the exceptional scholar and exceptional editor will be the first to agree that this is true.

The American people are right in insisting that the press should never fall under the influence of government. As a result, American newspapers enjoy a greater latitude and freedom than the newspapers of any other country in the world. But they have not always excercised their freedom in the public interest.

In return for the freedom from interference that Americans grant their press, they have a right to insist that newspapers and newsmagazines, the radio and TV, provide them with adequate and objective information about the great events of our world. The evidence produced in this book has shown, at least as far as reporting about China is concerned, that the unusual freedom granted the press has not resulted in better news. The sad but irrefutable fact is that the *American people today are less informed and more misinformed about China than the people of any other Western nation.*

How long can this go on? Americans hear of Frenchmen and Englishmen and Germans and Italians traveling to China and they are beginning to resent the State Department regulations that prevent them from traveling there too. They hear of Canada and Australia selling vast quantities of their surplus wheat to China, of the British selling planes and tools, of Germans selling steel, of the Swiss selling precision instruments, of the Japanese selling entire textile plants—and they must wonder why this country is kept in a position of so great a commercial disadvantage, and for what possible compensating benefits. This has gone on so long already that we may find when we wish to change this policy that the damage has already been done—that though the State Department might allow Americans to travel to China, the Chinese will not want them; or that when businessmen are finally permitted to trade with China, they may find that successful business relations have already been set up with others.

The American people, I think, are beginning to sense intuitively that a policy of almost total non-communication with a country comprising a quarter of the human race is a process of *self-isolation* that in the end can harm no one so badly as ourselves.

And this leads me to the most important thing I want to say—and the most hopeful.

I am quite certain that most of the news correspondents and the editorial writers and the producers of the TV and radio news scripts and many of the columnists are profoundly underestimating the capacity of the American people. This goes for the politicians too. The intelligence of the American public has far outstripped the intelligence meted out to them by the press and the political leaders. Americans are ready to listen to the real facts of life. Any newspaper, any TV station, any political leader who begins to treat the public as mature men and women will be overwhelmed by the response. They would find that Americans are far more sophisticated, far more generous in their judgments of other peoples, far less *afraid*, than they ever seem to give them credit for. The American people are never likely to underestimate the dangers of our position in the world or the extent of the threat to our system that the growth of communism presents, but they are sick of being fobbed off with banalities, bored to the limits of their endurance by the mindless repetition of cold-war clichés. They don't want clichés, they want knowledge of the world they are living in and not information of dubious accuracy presented (where China is concerned) nearly always in tones of superiority and contempt.

As a result of this inquiry into America's information on China I have reached the conclusion that the American people have not received the minimum of necessary information on supremely important developments. When—as it will—the truth of this becomes apparent and burns itself into men's consciousness, I believe they will examine the news in regard to other events and will begin to ask themselves what it is that shapes and forms public opinion. Unless the people are assured of news that they can trust, a democratic government cannot successfully be administered.

POSTSCRIPT FROM PEKING

November 1963

In September, after the manuscript of this book was in the hands of the publisher, I came to China for my third visit in six years. I am writing this postscript from Peking.

Certain contrasts between the China I last saw in September 1960 and the China that I found when I arrived nearly two months ago were at once noticeable. In 1960, after the second bad harvest season, anxiety about the winter food supply had led the authorities to urge that every usable patch of ground in the cities should be dug and planted for vegetables. Peking's streets were lined with newly planted cabbage. Today you see no vegetables growing along the streets or in unused lots. There is, instead, a glut of vegetables. Mountains of cabbage, tomatoes, carrots, and Chinese celery are stacked along the sidewalks (and remain quite unguarded at night). At one point a few weeks ago tomatoes were selling at two pounds for three cents. The communes around the city are paid a fixed price for their produce and do not suffer because of the oversupply. Not many evenings ago I watched one store offering customers as much cabbage as they could carry for ten fen (four cents). Fruit, too, is available in almost overwhelming abundance. Fruit trees and grape vines planted in the "Great Leap" days of 1958 are now bearing, and innumerable fruit stalls have sprung up all over the city to cope with the supply. The

1960 problem of scarcity has been replaced today by the problems of refrigeration and storage.

Less perishable foodstuffs seem also available in quantity; the grocery stores and markets are better stocked than I have ever seen them. The two most severely rationed items are cotton cloth (though rayon and other synthetic materials are available without ration) and cooking oil. Meat is still rationed but unlimited amounts can be bought without ration coupons at prices that range from sixteen to twenty-five cents per pound above the ration price. Ducks, chickens, and fish are not on ration and seem plentiful. Grocery stores have available a wide selection of canned goods—meats, fish, fruit, and fruit juices, etc. Though the price of canned goods appears to me to be high in relation to wage levels there was a brisk trade in these items in every store I have visited. Cookies, pastries, chocolates, and candies are in abundant supply and at a cost—judging by the crowds at these counters—well within the means of the general public. Though the food markets always appear filled with people, buying seems to be conducted at a leisurely pace—not feverishly as if customers were afraid that stocks might quickly be exhausted. The relative abundance of food, I was told, began between nine and twelve months ago and the public apparently takes it for granted that these conditions will continue.

Consumer goods also show a very noticeable improvement both in variety and quality. All-wave transistorized radio sets are being sold in a great variety of models—there is no restriction on listening to foreign programs. Victrolas, bicycles, T.V. sets, toys, fishing equipment, sporting guns, household goods, etc., all seem of better quality and finish than when I was here in 1960. Several kinds of cameras are being made in large numbers; their mechanical finish seems to me to be reasonably good, though the Chinese tell me that the lenses are still inferior to those made in Japan and Germany. Packaging and styling of items such as cosmetics, cold creams, soaps, scent, and hair lotions are now excellent, perhaps because they are sold abroad and must compete with others. Bookstores and record shops are doing a big business, and I have yet to go to a concert or ballet that was not packed. There seems without doubt to be more money around. The manager of one of the department stores in Peking told me that more than one hundred thousand people had been in the store the previous Sunday (stores do not close on Sundays in China—the staff rotate their weekly day off), and looking at the crowds in this store I could well believe him.

Another very noticeable change is the increase in the number of small restaurants and eating places—hundreds of them have sprung up all over town. This has happened in other cities also. Shanghai now has more than twenty-six hundred restaurants, pastry shops, and snack bars.

On the national level, a senior government economist told me that the economy was showing a more rapid recovery from the 1960–62 food shortage and recession than the government had expected. Supplies of secondary foods were now so plentiful that the public was not taking up their full grain ration. He thought there might be a significant change taking place in the standard diet of the Chinese people with greater variety and less reliance on grain. Purchases of grain from Canada and Australia are not being used, he told me, for current consumption but to improve national reserves. The government appears determined that the country will not again be caught short in the event of another harvest failure.

With food and consumer items in good supply, a good harvest reported from the countryside this year, and with international trade again moving upward, the mood here today can be described as one of relaxed confidence. China—and of course they know it— is a poor country; but the people seem content. Though their personal possessions may be small, they appear to be extraordinarily *unworried*. The parks and playgrounds are crowded with families enjoying the autumn sunshine, the children's parks are always full of healthy-looking children, and the lake at Pei Hai Park, especially on Sundays, is dotted with rowboats.

There is less fever in the air. The anti-American posters of three years ago have been replaced by posters showing the best way to prepare vegetables or notices urging mothers not to let children under seven run around in the busy streets alone. The standard two-hour lunch break (which will soon be reduced to one-and-a-half hours as the weather gets colder) sets a leisurely tempo to the day and people seem ready to use this period for a siesta or to sit in the sun without feeling they should use it on volunteer labor. I have now been in China almost two months; there have in this time been none of the open-air mass rallies that were held quite frequently in 1960. I have seen no militia training. The fifteen-minute rest periods in midmorning and midafternoon are used by only a few to do exercises—others play badminton, drink tea, sit and smoke, or stay in their offices and workshops.

The dispute with Russia developed gradually and seems to have produced no great shock—and, interestingly, the Russian statements against China have been printed in full in the national press. I asked some school children, teen-agers, what they felt about the dispute. They told me that their teacher had explained from time to time that things were going wrong and why. Their textbooks, which speak of the Russians as their great friends, have not been changed. I asked the children about this and they said at once that the Russian people *are* still their friends—it was Mr. Khrushchev, not the Russian people, who had betrayed the cause of socialism.

Our U.S. newspapers speak of China as being "isolated" from the world. That is not at all the impression that one receives here. China, after all, is now recognized by over fifty countries, trades with over a hundred, and has cultural relations with 163 countries. Peking is crowded with visitors—tourists and business-men—from almost every quarter of the world. There were more foreign visitors at the National Day celebration on October 1 this year than ever before. Last month there were one thousand visitors (the majority were businessmen) from Japan alone. In my hotel I have talked with businessmen or technical experts from Britain, Australia, New Zealand, France, Scandinavia, Canada, West Germany, and Ceylon. Many were negotiating very sizable contracts. The Western world appears only too ready to pick up the trade that before the rift went to the Soviet Union.

To turn to the American papers and magazines to see what they are saying about China is for me a disheartening experience. In *Time* Magazine, dated September 13, it was reported that Mao, sixty-nine, now needs help in walking. I saw him not many days later walking briskly enough, unaided and seemingly in good health. In the New York *Times* of October 1 (international edition) I read Robert Trumbull's report from Hong Kong. Under the heading Peking's Problems, he writes of "the deepening economic and political challenge" in China and that there "are reports that Peking's domestic problems have been intensified by another disappointing harvest." (The AP in Tokyo, on the other hand, in a dispatch on October 11, reports on China's "recovery of confidence in the wake of a good 1962 harvest and prospects for a better one this year." The account goes on to mention an economy that is moving upward and the almost daily reports of new gains on many economic fronts.)

On September 20 *Time* quoted some remarks by Raymond Scheyven, Belgium's former Economic Affairs Minister and a highly respected European economist. Mr. Scheyven had spent a month traveling in China. *Time* (under the headings RED CHINA, A VERY BACKWARD COUNTRY) summarized Mr. Scheyven's report of what he had seen as follows:

> He was told that cloth rationing would continue for at least five years. Scheyvan added that optimists gave China 20 years to catch up with the industrial nations of the West, and pessimists 40 to 50 years. Said Scheyven, "I gave it approximately 60 years."

But the Agence France-Presse gives quite another impression in reporting what Mr. Scheyven said by giving some of his further comments, not quoted by *Time:*

> . . . he said the population of China seemed to him to be in excellent health, well-fed, and well-clothed.[1]

And a few days later he said:

[1] A.F.P. dispatch from Hong Kong, September 9, 1963.

. . . We are committing the same mistake regarding China that we once committed regarding the Soviet Union. There is no "nightmare" China, and there is no China "failure."[2]

I notice from a variety of papers that have reached me here from the United States that the communes are still being blamed for the food shortages of 1960–62 and (for example in *Time* of September 13) that they "exist no longer except on paper." However, I can assure the editors of *Time* from firsthand observation that the communes, though considerably modified since I was here before, most certainly still exist. As for their having failed and having been the cause of the agricultural setback, this is what one of Britain's leading economists, Mrs. Joan Robinson of Cambridge University, had to say after a recent six-week study tour of the communes. In the course of a detailed report printed in the October issue of the *China Trade and Economic News-Letter* of London, Mrs. Robinson said:

A curious legend in the foreign press is that the commune system broke down and failed during the difficult years of natural disasters.

But just the opposite is true. It was precisely the [commune] organisation that made it possible to keep people fed, to help people work and to repair the damage. . . .

The commune with its three levels of organisation—team, brigade, commune—is a brilliant scheme for combining the small-scale with the large-scale organisation. . . .

There are statements in the Western press, now being repeated in the U.S.S.R., saying that the commune has destroyed family life. The family is defended and protected by the commune, and I saw that generally three generations of people lived together, with grandmothers looking after the house and the babies and young men and women

[2] A.F.P. dispatch from Brussels, September 18, 1963. Six weeks later, according to a report in the New York *Times* of October 22 (international edition), Mr. Scheyven said he was convinced "that most people in the West have grave misconceptions about the Chinese mainland." One of the misconceptions that he listed was that "The Chinese are worse off than they were before" and that most "Chinese yearning for freedom eventually will rise in revolt. . . ." Another misconception was that "as a result of the Chinese-Soviet ideological struggle . . . China will be isolated from the rest of the world."

in the field. The horror-comic stories of men and women living in separate dormitories would be believed only by half-wits. . . .

Summing up her conclusions on her third visit to China, Mrs. Robinson said:

> The most striking feature of China today for those who know life in Asia is that people have enough to eat and no one goes to bed worrying if he will have a meal tomorrow.

But the New York *Times*, from its vantage point in Times Square in an editorial on October 2 (international edition), paints a much gloomier picture of China:

> Domestically the Chinese economy continues in deep difficulties. Agricultural production is still not sufficient to feed China's masses at even minimally satisfactory levels. . . .

Not long before I reached China, Mao Tse-tung, asked by a Negro to express his views on the current Negro movement in the United States, issued a statement supporting the Negroes' struggle for equality. The key sentence of his statement was:

> I call upon the workers, peasants, revolutionary intellectuals, enlightened elements of the Bourgeoisie, and other enlightened persons of all colours, white, black, yellow, brown, etc. to unite to oppose racial discrimination practised by U.S. imperialism and to support the American Negroes in their struggle against racial discrimination.

He added that only the reactionary ruling class oppresses the Negroes and the white people generally do not.

We may not like the terminology of this statement, we may bridle at being called an "imperialist" nation, but how is it possible that this appeal against discrimination be interpreted as itself being racist? The New York *Times* in an editorial on September 14, under the heading PEKING'S GRAND DESIGN, concludes that "China has made no secret recently of its resolve to enter upon a Napoleonic phase of expansion." The *Times* lists four major objectives, the second of which is "an increasing antiwhite cam-

paign to enlist the world's nonwhite majority on China's side."
And the *Christian Century*, in an editorial on September 11 writes
(my italics):

> A summons to colored peoples *to unite in war against
> the white race* was issued from Peking in the name of Mao
> Tse-tung. His call for *worldwide racial war* reflects a degree
> of hate and desperation which can only be described as
> psychotic. . . .

Thus does the *Christian Century* interpret Mao's call to end
racial discrimination!

I have said enough, I think, to show why I find reading the U.S.
press on China while in China a very disheartening experience.
The reports seem to me to bear so little relationship to this country
that I happen to be in. The real gems of misreporting are sometimes passed around at Western dinner parties or among the Western diplomats here for the laughs, but the rest are usually passed
off with a shrug. I have yet to speak to any Westerner here,
whatever his political views, however strongly he opposes this
communist regime, who has said a good word about American
press reporting about what is going on here. It is, for someone who
is fond of America, somewhat humiliating.

Some days ago I went to visit a friend who lives on the other
side of Peking and not finding him in I walked back to my
hotel—first through the narrow *hutungs*, then across the wide Tien
An Men Square toward Chung Wen Men. It was late afternoon.
There were still crowds of shoppers in the streets. Children, of
course, were everywhere, endlessly good-natured. Crossing a neighborhood park I stopped to watch the last few minutes of a basket-
ball game. Nearby, under the trees, some old men were playing
chess. These, I reminded myself, were the people who had resolved
"to enter upon a Napoleonic phase of expansion." Militaristic? I
saw Nazi Germany and Italy before the war with their incessant
glorification of war, their military parades and strutting soldiers.
There is certainly nothing like that here. It struck me as I was walking home how few soldiers one actually sees, how little the military

are in evidence. They do not even take part in the National Day parade on October 1. It was just conceivable, I thought, that great preparations for "Napoleonic" adventures were going on behind the scenes—but would there not be some reflection of this in the press, some indication that the public was being prepared for great events and great sacrifices?

Tired after the long walk, I lay on my bed and turned on the Voice of America. Mr. Joseph Alsop was reporting from Hong Kong. The tone and substance were unmistakable, and he ended his talk by saying:

> But Mao has not only frustrated the extraordinary genius of the people he leads. He has brought China to a worse pass than China ever experienced from floods and droughts and wicked rulers and foreign invasions and all the other harsh chances of Chinese history. This is now the central political fact in Asia.[3]

They seemed words from a very distant country.

Does that sad and negative appraisal of China, I wonder, really represent the voice of the American people? And if it does, how much longer can we as a nation afford to remain behind our self-made curtain of ignorance?

Peking,
November 1963.

[3] This report which I heard on the Voice of America appeared as one of Mr. Alsop's "Matter of Fact" columns in the Hong Kong *Tiger Standard* of October 9, 1963. It presumably also appeared in the New York *Herald Tribune* and the many other papers that carry Mr. Alsop's column.

INDEX